ECLECTIC EDUCATIONAL SERIES

RAY'S™

NEW PRACTICAL

ARITHMETIC

BY

JOSEPH RAY, M.D.

Originally published by
Van Antwerp, Bragg & Co.

This edition published by

MOTT
MEDIA

1130 Fenway Circle, Fenton, Michigan 48430
www.mottmedia.com

ISBN-10: 0-88062-061-7
ISBN-13: 978-0-88062-061-1
Printed by Color House Graphics, Grand Rapids, Michigan, USA.

PRESENT PUBLISHER'S PREFACE

We are honored and happy to bring to you the classic Arithmetics by Joseph Ray. In the 1800s these popular books sold more than any other arithmetics in America, in fact over 120,000,000 copies. Now with this reprinting, they are once again available for America's students.

Ray's Arithmetics are organized in an orderly manner around the discipline of arithmetic itself. They present principles and follow up each one with examples which include difficult problems to challenge the best students. Students who do not master a concept the first time can return to it later, work the more difficult problems, and master the concept. Thus in these compact volumes is a complete arithmetic course to study in school, to help in preparing for ACT and SAT tests, and to use for reference throughout a lifetime.

In order to capture the spirit of the original Ray's, we have refrained from revising the problems and prices. Only a few words have been changed, as we felt it wise. Thus students will have to rely on their arithmetic ability to solve the problems. Also the charm of a former era lives on in this reprinting. Flour and salt are sold by the barrel, kegs may contain tar, and postage stamps cost 3¢ each. Through this content, students learn social history of the 1800s in a unique, hands-on manner at the same time they are mastering arithmetic.

The series consists of four books ranging from Primary Arithmetic to Higher Arithmetic, as well as answer keys to accompany them. We have added a teacher's guide to help today's busy teachers and parents.

We wish to express our appreciation to the staff of the Special Collections Library at Miami University, Oxford, Ohio, for its cooperation in allowing us to use copies of their original Ray's Arithmetics.

George M. Mott, President
MOTT MEDIA, INC.

PREFACE

Changes in the methods of instruction in our schools and in the modes of transacting business have made it necessary to revise Ray's Practical Arithmetic.

No other work on Arithmetic ever had so extensive use or widespread popularity. Teachers everywhere, throughout the length and breadth of the land, are familiar with its pages, and millions of pupils have gained their arithmetical knowledge from the study of its principles. More than ten thousand editions of it have gone forth from the press.

In view of these facts, it has been the constant aim in making this revision to preserve carefully those distinctive features of the former editions, which constituted the peculiar philosophical method of its learned author, viz.:

1st. Every principle is clearly explained by an *analysis* or *solution* of simple examples, from which a Rule is derived. This is followed by graduated exercises designed to render the pupil familiar with its application.

2d. The arrangement is strictly philosophical; no principle is anticipated; the pupil is never required to perform any operation until the principle on which it is founded has first been explained.

The publishers desire to express their thanks to the many teachers whose suggestions and corrections are embodied in the present edition. Especial mention is due Prof. M. W. Smith and Mr. A. P. Morgan for many valuable features of this revision.

In conclusion, the publishers wish to reiterate that the object throughout has been to combine *practical utility* with *scientific accuracy*; to present a work embracing the best methods, with all real improvements. How far this object has been secured is again submitted to those engaged in the laborious and responsible work of education.

Cincinnati, August, 1877.

TABLE OF CONTENTS.

RAY'S NEW PRACTICAL ARITHMETIC

DEFINITIONS.

Article 1. 1. A **Unit** is a single thing of any kind; as, one, one apple, one dollar, one pound.

2. A **Number** consists of one or more units; as, one, five, seven cents, nine men.

3. **Arithmetic** treats of numbers, and is the art of computing by them.

4. Numbers are expressed in two ways; first, by *words;* second, by *characters.*

5. A **System of Notation** is a method of expressing numbers by characters.

6. Two systems of Notation are in use, the *Arabic* and the *Roman.* The Arabic system is used in all our arithmetical calculations.

THE ARABIC SYSTEM OF NOTATION.

2. 1. To express numbers, the Arabic Notation employs ten characters, called *figures*; namely, 1, 2, 3, 4, 5, 6, 7, 8, 9, 0.

REMARK 1.—The Arabic System of Notation is so called because its characters appear to have been introduced into Europe by the

Arabians; but it is now generally acknowledged that they originated in India.

REM. 2.—The Arabic Notation is also called the *Decimal System* and the *Common System.*

2. The **Order** of a figure is the place it occupies in a number.

UNITS OF THE FIRST ORDER, OR UNITS.

3. 1. A unit or single thing is *one*, written 1.
One unit and one more are *two*, " 2.
Two units and one more are *three*, " 3.
Three units and one more are *four*, " 4.
Four units and one more are *five*, " 5.
Five units and one more are *six*, " 6.
Six units and one more are *seven*, " 7.
Seven units and one more are *eight*, " 8.
Eight units and one more are *nine*, " 9.

2. These nine characters are called *significant* figures, because they denote something.

3. The character 0, called *naught*, stands for *nothing;* its use is to fill vacant orders. The 0 is also called *cipher* and *zero.*

4. When a figure stands alone or in the first place at the right of a number, it represents one or more *units of the first order.*

5. Units of the first order are called simply *units*, and the place they occupy is called the *units' place.*

UNITS OF THE SECOND ORDER, OR TENS.

4. 1. Nine units and one more are called *ten;* it also is represented by the figure 1; but the one is made to occupy the second place from the right by writing a 0 in the units' place.

2. One ten is written thus . . . . . . 10.
Two tens are *twenty*, written . . . . 20.
Three tens are *thirty*, " . . . . 30.
Four tens are *forty*, " . . . . 40.
Five tens are *fifty*, " . . . . 50.
Six tens are *sixty*, " . . . . 60.
Seven tens are *seventy*, " . . . . 70.
Eight tens are *eighty*, " . . . . 80.
Nine tens are *ninety*, " . . . . 90.

3. When a figure in a number stands in the second place from the right, it represents one or more *units of the second order.*

4. Units of the second order are called *tens;* and the place they occupy is called the *tens' place.*

TENS AND UNITS.

5. 1. The numbers between 10 and 20, 20 and 30, etc., are expressed by representing the tens and units of which they are composed.

2. One ten and one unit are *eleven*, written 11.
One ten and two units are *twelve*, " 12.
One ten and three units are *thirteen*, " 13.
One ten and four units are *fourteen*, " 14.
One ten and five units are *fifteen*, " 15.
One ten and six units are *sixteen*, " 16.
One ten and seven units are *seventeen*, " 17.
One ten and eight units are *eighteen*, " 18.
One ten and nine units are *nineteen*, " 19.
Two tens and one unit are *twenty-one*, " 21.
Two tens and two units are *twenty-two*, " 22.

NUMBERS TO BE WRITTEN.

1. Twenty-three; twenty-four; twenty-five; twenty-six; twenty-seven; twenty-eight; twenty-nine.
2. Thirty-seven; forty-two; fifty-six; sixty-nine; seventy-three; eighty-seven; ninety-four.
3. Eighty-three; forty-five; ninety-nine; fifty-one; thirty-six: seventy-eight; sixty-two.
4. Fifty-five; ninety-three; eighty-one; sixty-seven; forty-nine; seventy-four; thirty-eight.
5. Seventy-six; forty-four; eighty-two; fifty-seven; thirty-five; ninety-one; sixty-three.

NUMBERS TO BE READ.

1.	71;	32;	53;	84;	65;	46;	97.
2.	58;	34;	79;	66;	41;	85;	92.
3.	75;	43;	88;	61;	59;	33;	95.
4.	39;	72;	54;	86;	47;	98;	64.
5.	68;	77;	31;	89;	52;	96;	48.

UNITS OF THE THIRD ORDER, OR HUNDREDS.

6. 1. Ten tens are *one hundred;* it is represented by the figure 1 written in the third order, the orders of tens and units being each filled with a cipher.

One	hundred	is	written	thus,	100.
Two	hundred	"	"	"	200.
Three	hundred	"	"	"	300.
Four	hundred	"	"	"	400.
Five	hundred	"	"	"	500.
Six	hundred	"	"	"	600.
Seven	hundred	"	"	"	700.
Eight	hundred	"	"	"	800.
Nine	hundred	"	"	"	900.

2. Units of the third order are called *hundreds;* and the place they occupy is called the *hundreds' place.*

HUNDREDS, TENS, AND UNITS.

7. 1. The numbers between 100 and 200, 200 and 300, etc., are expressed by representing the hundreds, tens, and units of which they are composed.

2. One hundred and one unit are *one hundred and one,* written 101.

One hundred and one ten are *one hundred and ten,* written 110.

One hundred and one ten and one unit are *one hundred and eleven,* written 111.

One hundred and two tens are *one hundred and twenty,* written 120.

One hundred, two tens, and five units are *one hundred and twenty-five,* written 125.

NUMBERS TO BE WRITTEN.

1. One hundred and thirty; one hundred and forty; one hundred and fifty; one hundred and sixty; one hundred and seventy; one hundred and eighty.

2. One hundred and twenty-three; four hundred and fifty-six; seven hundred and eighty-nine; one hundred and forty-seven; two hundred and fifty-eight; three hundred and sixty-nine.

3. One hundred and two; three hundred and forty-five; six hundred and seventy-eight: two hundred and thirty-four; five hundred and sixty-seven; eight hundred and ninety.

4. Four hundred and fifty-three; seven hundred and eighty-six; nine hundred and twelve; two hundred and thirty; four hundred and fifty; six hundred and seventy.

5. One hundred and fifty-three; four hundred and eighty-six; seven hundred and twenty-nine; one hundred and three; four hundred and six; seven hundred and nine.

NUMBERS TO BE READ.

1. 210; 320; 430; 540; 650; 760.
2. 213; 546; 879; 417; 528; 639.
3. 201; 435; 768; 324; 657; 980.
4. 543; 876; 192; 329; 548; 765.
5. 513; 846; 279; 301; 604; 907.

UNITS OF HIGHER ORDERS.

8. 1. Ten hundreds are *one thousand;* it is represented by 1 in the fourth order; thus, 1000.

2. Ten thousands form a unit of the fifth order; thus, 10000; one hundred thousands, a unit of the sixth order; thus, 100000, etc.

3. Invariably, *ten units of any order make a unit of the next higher order.*

4. The names of the first nine orders may be learned from the following

TABLE OF ORDERS.

9th.	8th.	7th.	6th.	5th.	4th.	3d.	2d.	1st.
Hundred millions	Ten millions	Millions	Hundred thousands	Ten thousands	Thousands	Hundreds	Tens	Units

DEFINITIONS AND PRINCIPLES.

9. 1. The first nine numbers are represented by the nine figures,—1, 2, 3, 4, 5, 6, 7, 8, 9.

2. All other numbers are represented by combinations of two or more of the ten figures,—1, 2, 3, 4, 5, 6, 7, 8, 9, 0.

3. The numbers that end with 2, 4, 6, 8, or 0 are called *even* numbers.

4. The numbers that end with 1, 3, 5, 7, or 9 are called *odd* numbers.

5. The *value* of a figure is the number of units it expresses.

6. The value of a figure is always *local;* that is, it depends upon the place it occupies in a number.

REM.—The principle of *local value* is what peculiarly distinguishes the Arabic System of Notation from all other systems that have existed.

7. The number a figure expresses when it stands in units' place is called its *simple* value.

8. The value of a figure is increased *tenfold* by removing it one place to the left.

9. The value of a figure is decreased *tenfold* by removing it one place to the right.

GROUPING OF ORDERS INTO PERIODS.

10. 1. For convenience in writing and reading numbers, the different orders are grouped into *periods* of three orders each.

REM.—A number is *pointed off* into periods of three figures each by commas.

2. The first three orders—units, tens, hundreds—constitute the first, or *unit* period.

3. The second group of three orders—thousands, ten thousands, hundred thousands—constitutes the second, or *thousand* period.

4. The third group of three orders constitutes the third, or *million* period.

5. The periods from the first to the twelfth inclusive may be learned from the following

Table of Periods.

No.	Name.	No.	Name.
First	Unit.	Seventh	Quintillion.
Second	Thousand.	Eighth	Sextillion.
Third	Million.	Ninth	Septillion.
Fourth	Billion.	Tenth	Octillion.
Fifth	Trillion.	Eleventh	Nonillion
Sixth	Quadrillion.	Twelfth	Decillion.

6. The grouping of the orders into periods is shown in the following

Table.

5. Trillion.			4. Billion.			3. Million.			2. Thousand.			1. Unit.		
Hundred trillions . . .	Ten trillions	Trillions	Hundred billions . . .	Ten billions	Billions	Hundred millions . . .	Ten millions	Millions	Hundred thousands . .	Ten thousands . . .	Thousands	Hundreds	Tens	Units . . . . .

7. It is plain that *each period is composed of units, tens, and hundreds of that period.*

To Write Numbers in the Arabic System.

11. 1. Write six hundred and fifty-four *trillion* three hundred and twenty-one *billion* nine hundred and eighty-seven *million* six hundred and fifty-four *thousand* three hundred and twenty-one.

Trillion.			Billion.			Million.			Thousand.			Unit.		
6	5	4,	3	2	1,	9	8	7,	6	5	4,	3	2	1.
Hundreds	Tens	Units	Hundreds	Tens	Units	Hundreds	Tens	Units	Hundreds	Tens	Units	Hundreds	Tens	Units

Rule.—*Begin at the left, and write each period as a number composed of hundreds, tens, and units—filling the vacant orders with ciphers.*

REM.—In the left hand period, however, when the hundreds or the hundreds and tens are wanting, the vacant orders are not filled with ciphers.

NUMBERS TO BE WRITTEN.

2. Two thousand; thirty thousand; four hundred thousand.

3. Five million; sixty million; seven hundred million.

4. Eight billion; ninety billion; one hundred billion.

5. One thousand two hundred; two thousand one hundred.

6. Three thousand four hundred and fifty; six thousand seven hundred and eighty-nine.

7. Twelve thousand three hundred and forty-five.

8. Six hundred and seventy-eight thousand nine hundred and twelve.

9. One million three hundred and fifty-seven thousand nine hundred and twenty-four.

10. Sixty-eight million one hundred and forty-three thousand seven hundred and ninety-two.

11. One thousand and one; one thousand and ten; one thousand one hundred.

12. One thousand one hundred and one; one thousand one hundred and ten; one thousand one hundred and eleven.

13. Two thousand and three; four thousand and fifty.

14. Forty-five thousand and twenty-six.

15. Eighty thousand two hundred and one.

16. Ninety thousand and one.

17. Four hundred and ten thousand two hundred and five.

18. One hundred thousand and ten.

19. Three million seventy thousand five hundred and nine.

20. Forty-five million eighty-three thousand and twenty-six.

21. Nine hundred and nine million ninety thousand.

22. Seven hundred million ten thousand and two.

23. Forty billion two hundred thousand and five.

24. Seven hundred and twenty-six billion fifty million one thousand two hundred and forty-three.

25. Eighty billion seven hundred and three million five hundred and four.

12. Numeration is the reading of numbers when expressed according to a system of notation.

To Read Numbers in the Arabic System.

1. Read 654321987654321.

Trillion.			Billion.			Million.			Thousand.			Unit.		
6	5	4,	3	2	1,	9	8	7,	6	5	4,	3	2	1.
Hundreds	Tens	Units	Hundreds	Tens	Units	Hundreds	Tens	Units	Hundreds	Tens	Units	Hundreds	Tens	Units

Rule.—1. *Begin at the right, and point off the number into periods of three figures each.*

2. *Begin at the left, and read each period as a number composed of hundreds, tens, and units, giving the name of the period.*

Rem. 1.—The left hand period will sometimes contain but one or two figures.

Rem. 2.—It is customary to omit the name of the unit period.

NUMBERS TO BE READ.

2. 41582; 763491; 2519834; 375486921; 4923176358.
3. 37584216974; 432685729145; 6253971438267.
4. 1300; 2540; 6070; 8009; 13200; 1005.
5. 682300; 8600050; 3040; 50004; 704208.
6. 7085; 62001; 400009; 2102102; 9001003.

7. 130670921; 6900702003; 23004090701; 9420163070.
8. 570000010326049; 2001034785119924850.
9. 4576300002010800050 7.
10. 800820020802008.

THE ROMAN SYSTEM OF NOTATION.

DEFINITIONS.

13. 1. To express numbers, the Roman Notation employs seven *letters;* namely, I, V, X, L, C, D, M.

REM.—The Roman System of Notation is so called because it was the method of expressing numbers used by the ancient Romans. It is now used to mark the chapters of books, the dial plates of clocks, etc.

2. In the Roman Notation, numbers are expressed in four ways.

1st. *Each of the seven letters expresses a number,* as follows: I, *one;* V, *five;* X, *ten;* L, *fifty;* C, *one hundred;* D, *five hundred;* M, *one thousand.*

2d. *Seven numbers are expressed by repetitions of the letters I, X, and C.* Thus, II represent *two;* III, *three;* XX, *twenty;* XXX, *thirty;* CC, *two hundred;* CCC, *three hundred;* CCCC, *four hundred.*

3d. *Four numbers are expressed by a subtractive combination,* as follows: IV, *four;* IX, *nine;* XL, *forty;* XC, *ninety.*

4th. *All other numbers are formed by additive combinations of two or more of the preceding eighteen numbers, the smaller being always situated on the right of the larger number.*

For example, VI is *six;* XVII, *seventeen;* LXXVIII, *seventy-eight;* CLXXXIX, *one hundred and eighty-nine;* MDCCCLXXVII, *eighteen hundred and seventy-seven.*

Write in the Roman Notation.

1. The numbers from one to twenty.
2. The numbers from twenty to thirty.

3.	30;	40;	50;	60;	70;	80;	90.
4.	57;	29;	61;	38;	46;	72;	93.
5.	100;	101;	106;	117;	129;	168.	
6.	199;	246;	309;	482;	527;	693.	
7.	734;	859;	975;	1001;	1010.		
8.	1048;	1119;	1285;	1326.			
9.	1492;	1776;	1861;	1900.			

THE FUNDAMENTAL RULES.

DEFINITIONS.

14. 1. An **integer** is a whole number.

2. Numbers are either *abstract* or *concrete.*

3. An **abstract** number is a number simply, as 5, 12, 20.

4. A **concrete** number is a number applied to one or more objects; as 1 apple, 5 pounds, 12 men.

5. The name of the object of a concrete number is its *denomination.* Thus, in 5 pounds, the denomination is *pounds.*

6. Numbers are either *simple* or *compound.*

7. A **simple** number is a single number, either abstract or concrete; as 3, 7 dollars, 1 pint.

8. A **compound** number is made up of two or more concrete numbers of different denominations; as 3 pecks 7 quarts 1 pint.

9. There are four primary operations of Arithmetic; namely, *Addition*, *Subtraction*, *Multiplication*, and *Division*; —these are called the *Fundamental Rules.*

ADDITION

15. 1. If you have 2 cents and find 3 cents, how many will you then have? *Ans.* 5 cents.

Why? Because 2 cents and 3 cents are 5 cents.

2. I spent 12 cents for a slate, and 5 cents for a copy-book: how many cents did I spend?

Ans. 17 cents. Why?

3. John gave 6 cents for an orange, 7 cents for pencils, and 9 cents for a ball: how many cents did all cost? *Ans.* 22 cents. Why?

4. Joseph gave 5 cents for a daily paper, 10 cents for a weekly paper, 25 cents for a monthly magazine, 30 cents for a book of poems, and 40 cents for a novel: how much did he spend? *Ans.* 110 cents.

16. 1. The operation in these examples is termed *Addition;* hence, **Addition** is the process of uniting two or more numbers into one number.

2. The number obtained by addition is the *Sum* or *Amount.*

3. When the numbers to be added are simple, the operation is called *Addition of Simple Numbers.*

4. The sign of Addition (+), called *plus*, means *more;* when placed between two numbers, it shows that they are to be added; thus, 4 + 2 means that 4 and 2 are to be added together.

5. The sign of *equality* (=) denotes that the quantities between which it stands are equal; thus, the expression $4+2=6$ means that the sum of 4 and 2 is 6: it is read, 4 *plus* 2 *equals* 6.

ADDITION TABLE.

2 + 0 = 2	3 + 0 = 3	4 + 0 = 4	5 + 0 = 5
2 + 1 = 3	3 + 1 = 4	4 + 1 = 5	5 + 1 = 6
2 + 2 = 4	3 + 2 = 5	4 + 2 = 6	5 + 2 = 7
2 + 3 = 5	3 + 3 = 6	4 + 3 = 7	5 + 3 = 8
2 + 4 = 6	3 + 4 = 7	4 + 4 = 8	5 + 4 = 9
2 + 5 = 7	3 + 5 = 8	4 + 5 = 9	5 + 5 = 10
2 + 6 = 8	3 + 6 = 9	4 + 6 = 10	5 + 6 = 11
2 + 7 = 9	3 + 7 = 10	4 + 7 = 11	5 + 7 = 12
2 + 8 = 10	3 + 8 = 11	4 + 8 = 12	5 + 8 = 13
2 + 9 = 11	3 + 9 = 12	4 + 9 = 13	5 + 9 = 14
6 + 0 = 6	7 + 0 = 7	8 + 0 = 8	9 + 0 = 9
6 + 1 = 7	7 + 1 = 8	8 + 1 = 9	9 + 1 = 10
6 + 2 = 8	7 + 2 = 9	8 + 2 = 10	9 + 2 = 11
6 + 3 = 9	7 + 3 = 10	8 + 3 = 11	9 + 3 = 12
6 + 4 = 10	7 + 4 = 11	8 + 4 = 12	9 + 4 = 13
6 + 5 = 11	7 + 5 = 12	8 + 5 = 13	9 + 5 = 14
6 + 6 = 12	7 + 6 = 13	8 + 6 = 14	9 + 6 = 15
6 + 7 = 13	7 + 7 = 14	8 + 7 = 15	9 + 7 = 16
6 + 8 = 14	7 + 8 = 15	8 + 8 = 16	9 + 8 = 17
6 + 9 = 15	7 + 9 = 16	8 + 9 = 17	9 + 9 = 18

17. When the sum of the figures in a column does not exceed 9, it is written under the column added.

Examples.

1. I own 3 tracts of land: the first contains 240 acres; the second, 132 acres; the third, 25 acres: how many acres in all?

Solution.—Since units of *different* orders can not be added together, write units of the same order in the same column, so that the figures to be added may be in the most *convenient position*.

Begin at the right, and say 5 and 2 are 7 units, which write in units' place; 2 and 3 are 5, and 4 are 9 tens, which write in tens' place; 1 and 2 are 3 hundreds, which write in hundreds' place.

```
240 acres.
132 acres.
 25 acres.
---
397 acres.
```

2. I owe one man $210, another $142, and another $35: what is the sum of my debts?

3. Find the sum of 4321, 1254, 3120.

4. Find the sum of 50230, 3105, 423.

18. When the sum of the figures in a column exceeds 9, *two* or *more* figures are required to express it.

Example.

1. Add the numbers 3415, 503, 1870, and 922.

```
3415
 503
1870
 922
----
6710
```

Solution.—Write units of the same order in the same column. Then say 2 and 3 are 5, and 5 are 10 *units*, which are no (0) units, written in the units' place, and 1 ten, carried to the tens; 1 and 2 are 3, and 7 are 10, and 1 are 11 *tens*, which are 1 ten, written in the tens' place, and 1 hundred, carried to the hundreds; 1 and 9 are 10, and 8 are 18, and 5 are 23, and 4 are 27 *hundreds*, which are 7 hundreds, written in the hundreds' place, and 2 thousands, carried to the thousands; 2 and 1 are 3, and 3 are 6 *thousands*, written in the thousands' place.

Carrying the tens is simply adding *tens* to *tens*, ***hundreds*** to *hundreds*, etc., on the principle that only units of the same order can be added.

For convenience, the addition begins at the right hand column, with the units of the lowest order, so that, if the sum of the figures in any column exceeds 9, the tens can be carried to the sum of the next higher order.

REM.—To illustrate the greater convenience of adding the units' column first, take the above example.

SOLUTION.—Commencing the addition with the thousands' column, the sum is 4; next adding the hundreds, the sum is 26 hundreds, which equal 2 thousands and 6 hundreds; next adding the tens, the sum is 10 tens, equal to 1 hundred; and finally adding the units, the sum is 10 units, equal to 1 ten. As these sums have also to be added, this much extra work must be done in order to complete the solution.

```
3415
 503
1870
 922
----
4
26
 10
  10
----
6710
```

19. Rule.—1. *Write the numbers to be added, so that figures of the same order may stand in the same column.*

2. *Begin at the right hand, and add each column separately. Place the units obtained by adding each column under it, and carry the tens to the next higher order. Write down the entire sum of the last column.*

PROOF.—Add the columns downward, commencing with the column of units.

1. Find the sum of 3745, 2831, 5983, and 7665.

In adding long columns of figures, it is necessary to retain the numbers carried. This may be done by placing them in smaller figures under their proper columns, as 3, 2, 1, in the margin.

```
 3745
 2831
 5983
 7665
-----
20224
 321
```

EXAMPLES.

(2)	(3)	(4)	(5)	(6)	(7)
184	204	103	495	384	1065
216	302	405	207	438	6317
135	401	764	185	348	5183
320	311	573	825	843	7102
413	109	127	403	483	3251
101	43	205	325	834	6044
1369	1370	2177	2440	3330	28962

(8)	(9)	(10)	(11)	(12)
3725	5943	82703	987462	6840325
5834	6427	102	478345	7314268
4261	8204	6005	610628	3751954
7203	7336	759	423158	6287539

13. 11 + 22 + 33 + 44 + 55 = how many?
14. 23 + 41 + 74 + 83 + 16 = how many?
15. 45 + 19 + 32 + 74 + 55 = how many?
16. 51 + 48 + 76 + 85 + 4 = how many?
17. 263 + 104 + 321 + 155 = how many?
18. 94753 + 2847 + 93688 + 9386 + 258 + 3456 are how many?

19. January has 31 days; February, 28; March, 31; April, 30; and May, 31: how many days are there in these five months?

20. June has 30 days; July, 31; August, 31; September, 30; October, 31: how many days in all?

21. The first 5 months have 151 days, the next 5 have 153 days, November has 30, and December, 31: how many days in the whole year?

22. I bought 4 pieces of muslin: the first contained 50 yards, the second, 65, the third, 42, the fourth, 89: how many yards in all?

23. I owe one man $245, another $325, a third $187, a fourth $96: how much do I owe?

24. General Washington was born A. D. 1732, and lived 67 years: in what year did he die?

25. Alfred the Great died A. D. 901; thence to the signing of Magna Charta was 314 years; thence to the American Revolution, 560 years: in what year did the American Revolution begin?

26. A has 4 flocks of sheep; in the first are 65 sheep and 43 lambs; in the second, 187 sheep and 105 lambs; in the third, 370 sheep and 243 lambs; in the fourth, 416 sheep and 95 lambs: how many sheep and lambs has he?

27. A man bought 30 barrels of pork for $285, 18 barrels for $144, 23 barrels for $235, and 34 barrels for $408: how many barrels did he buy, and how many dollars did he pay?

28. The first of four numbers is 287; the second, 596; the third, 841; and the fourth, as much as the first three: what is their sum?

29. The Pyramids of Egypt were built 1700 years before the founding of Carthage; Carthage was founded 47 years before and was destroyed 607 years after the founding of Rome, or 146 years before the Christian era. How many years before Christ were the Pyramids built?

30. Add three thousand and five; forty-two thousand six hundred and twenty-seven; 105; three hundred and seven thousand and four; 80079; three hundred and twenty thousand six hundred.

31. Add 275432; four hundred and two thousand and

thirty; three hundred thousand and five; 872026; four million two thousand three hundred and forty-seven.

32. Add eight hundred and eighty million eight hundred and eighty-nine; 2002002; seventy-seven million four hundred and thirty-six thousand; two hundred and six million five thousand two hundred and seven; 49003; nine hundred and ninety million nineteen thousand nine hundred and nineteen.

33. North America has an area of 8955752 square miles; South America, 6917246 square miles; and the West Indies, 94523 square miles: what is the area of the entire continent?

34. A man pays $600 for a lot, $1325 for building materials, $30 for digging the cellar, $120 for stone-work, $250 for brick-work, $140 for carpenter-work, $120 for plastering, and $115 for painting: how much did his house and lot cost him?

35. A man bequeaths $7850 to his wife, $3275 to each of his two sons, and $2650 to each of his three daughters: what is the amount of his bequest?

36. A merchant spent $8785 for dress goods, and $12789 for sheetings. He sold the dress goods at a profit of $878, and the sheetings at a profit of $1250: for how much did he sell the whole?

37. A merchant began business with $7000 cash, goods worth $12875, bank stock worth $5600, and other stocks worth $4785. In one year he gained $3500: what was he worth at its close?

38. A house has two parlors, each requiring 30 yards of carpet; four bed-rooms, each requiring 25 yards; a dining-room and sitting-room, each requiring 20 yards: how many yards are required to carpet the entire house?

20. An excellent practice, in order to secure readiness and accuracy, is to add two columns at once. The following example illustrates the method:

	(1)
Beginning with 47, add the 3 tens above, which equal 77; then the 4 units, making 81; then the 6 tens above, 141; and the 5 units, 146; then the 7 tens above, 216; and the 9 units, 225; then the 9 tens above, 315, and finally the 2 units, 317. Put down the 17, and carry the 3 hundreds to the hundreds' column. Then 93 and 3 to carry are 96, and 60 are 156, and 2 are 158, and 40 are 198, and 8 are 206, and 60 are 266, and 7 are 273, and 70 are 343, and 8 are 351, which write in its proper place.	7892 6779 4865 6234 9347 35117

EXAMPLES.

(2)	(3)	(4)	(5)	(6)
3686	9898	4356	893742	234567
4724	8989	6342	743698	765432
6583	4545	7989	437821	987654
5798	5454	4878	643567	456789
6953	6363	6749	892742	778899

(7)	(8)	(9)	(10)
5493275	4819	18356	849627
6182463	9263	49276	532472
9538719	2752	94678	293784
2645834	8275	36525	468135
8256386	6498	42983	926547

(11)	(12)	(13)	(14)	(15)
7421	6873	4729	237285	884261
6322	2196	6234	64371	724353
798	583	5781	2143	416213
4352	79	3143	842	598624
547	684	7182	55	784344
674	4348	6989	789	627517
2315	7896	7222	4621	843641
7218	233	6643	15115	47821
1847	594	7859	647890	52348
5721	6483	6742	77442	2932
6843	7542	8982	84931	4751
4722	3967	3451	894623	896
5976	29	8692	446217	722
6843	478	7341	134162	823344
1234	1717	6822	192317	874132

SUBTRACTION.

21. 1. If you have 9 apples, and give 4 away, how many will you have left? *Ans.* 5 apples.

Why? Because 4 apples from 9 apples are 5 apples.

2. Frank had 15 cents; after spending 7, how many were left? *Ans.* 8 cents. Why?

3. If you take 8 from 13, how many are left? *Ans.* 5.

4. If I have 25 cents, and spend 10 of them for a lead-pencil, how much will I have left? *Ans.* 15 cents.

5. Twelve from twenty leaves how many? *Ans.* 8.

22. 1. The operation in the preceding examples is termed *Subtraction;* hence, **Subtraction** is the process of finding the difference between two numbers.

2. The larger number is called the *Minuend;* the less, the *Subtrahend;* and the number left after subtraction, the *Difference* or *Remainder.*

3. When the given numbers are simple, the operation is called *Subtraction of Simple Numbers.*

23. The sign of Subtraction (—) is called *minus,* meaning *less;* when placed between two numbers, it denotes that the number on the right is to be taken from the one on the left; thus, $8 - 5 = 3$ means that 5 is to be taken from 8, and is read, 8 *minus* 5 *equals* 3.

SUBTRACTION TABLE.

2 — 2 = 0	3 — 3 = 0	4 — 4 = 0	5 — 5 = 0
3 — 2 = 1	4 — 3 = 1	5 — 4 = 1	6 — 5 = 1
4 — 2 = 2	5 — 3 = 2	6 — 4 = 2	7 — 5 = 2
5 — 2 = 3	6 — 3 = 3	7 — 4 = 3	8 — 5 = 3
6 — 2 = 4	7 — 3 = 4	8 — 4 = 4	9 — 5 = 4
7 — 2 = 5	8 — 3 = 5	9 — 4 = 5	10 — 5 = 5
8 — 2 = 6	9 — 3 = 6	10 — 4 = 6	11 — 5 = 6
9 — 2 = 7	10 — 3 = 7	11 — 4 = 7	12 — 5 = 7
10 — 2 = 8	11 — 3 = 8	12 — 4 = 8	13 — 5 = 8
11 — 2 = 9	12 — 3 = 9	13 — 4 = 9	14 — 5 = 9
6 — 6 = 0	7 — 7 = 0	8 — 8 = 0	9 — 9 = 0
7 — 6 = 1	8 — 7 = 1	9 — 8 = 1	10 — 9 = 1
8 — 6 = 2	9 — 7 = 2	10 — 8 = 2	11 — 9 = 2
9 — 6 = 3	10 — 7 = 3	11 — 8 = 3	12 — 9 = 3
10 — 6 = 4	11 — 7 = 4	12 — 8 = 4	13 — 9 = 4
11 — 6 = 5	12 — 7 = 5	13 — 8 = 5	14 — 9 = 5
12 — 6 = 6	13 — 7 = 6	14 — 8 = 6	15 — 9 = 6
13 — 6 = 7	14 — 7 = 7	15 — 8 = 7	16 — 9 = 7
14 — 6 = 8	15 — 7 = 8	16 — 8 = 8	17 — 9 = 8
15 — 6 = 9	16 — 7 = 9	17 — 8 = 9	18 — 9 = 9

24. When each figure of the subtrahend is *not greater* than the corresponding figure of the minuend.

EXAMPLES.

1. A man having $135, spent $112: how much had he left?

Solution.—Since the difference between units of the *same order* only can be found, write units of the same order in the same column, so that the figures between which the subtraction is to be made may be in the most *convenient position.*

Begin at the right, and say 2 from 5 leaves 3, which put in units' place; 1 from 3 leaves 2, which put in tens' place; 1 from 1 leaves 0, and, there being no figures on the left of this, the place is vacant.

135	minuend.
112	subtrahend.
23	remainder.

2. A farmer having 245 sheep, sold 123: how many sheep had he left?

3. A man bought a farm for $751, and sold it for $875: how much did he gain?

What is the difference

4. Between 734 and 531?
5. Between 8752 and 3421?
6. Between 79484 and 25163?
7. Between 49528 and 16415?

25. When the lower figure in any order is *greater* than the upper, a difficulty arises, which we will now explain.

Examples.

1. James had 13 cents; after spending 5, how many cents had he left?

5 can not be subtracted from 3, but it can be from 13; 5 from 13 leaves 8.

$$\begin{array}{r} 13 \\ 5 \\ \hline 8 \end{array}$$

2. From 73 subtract 45.

SOLUTION.—5 units can not be taken from 3 units. Take 1 (ten) from the 7 (tens), and add this 1 (ten) or 10 units to the 3 units, which makes 13 units; then, subtract the 5 units, and there will remain 8 units, to be put in units' place. Since 1 ten is taken from the 7 tens, there remain but 6 tens. Subtract 4 tens from 6 tens and put the remainder, 2 tens, in tens' place. The difference is 28.

$$\begin{array}{r} 73 \\ 45 \\ \hline 28 \end{array}$$

REM. 1.—Instead of actually taking 1 ten from the 7 tens, and adding it to the 3 units, the operation is performed *mentally;* thus,

5 from 13 leaves 8, and 4 from 6 leaves 2.

REM. 2.—In such cases, the value of the upper number is not changed, since the 1 ten which is taken from the order of tens is added to the number in the order of units.

REM. 3.—Taking a unit of a higher order and adding it to the units of the next lower, so that the figure beneath may be subtracted from the sum, is called *borrowing ten.*

REM. 4.—After increasing the units by 10, instead of considering the next figure of the upper number as *diminished* by 1, the result will be the same, if the next figure of the lower number be *increased* by 1; thus, in the previous example, instead of diminishing the 7 tens by 1, add 1 to the 4 tens, which makes 5; thus, 5 from 13 leaves 8, and 5 from 7 leaves 2.

REM. 5.—This process depends upon the fact that having *borrowed* 1 from the 7 tens, we have to subtract from it both 1 ten and 4 tens, or their sum, 5 tens.

3. Find the difference between 805 and 637.

SOLUTION—1st Method.—Writing the less number under the greater, with units of the same order in the same column, it is required to subtract the 7 units from 5 units.

$$\begin{array}{r} 805 \\ 637 \\ \hline 168 \end{array}$$

The five can not be increased by borrowing from the next figure, because it is 0; therefore, borrow 1 hundred from the 8 hundreds, which leaves 7 hundreds in hundreds' place; this 1 hundred makes 10 tens; then, borrowing 1 ten from the 10 tens, and adding it to the 5 units, 9 tens will be in the tens' place, and 15 units in the units' place.

Subtracting 7 from 15, 8 units are left, to be written in units' place; next, subtracting 3 tens from 9 tens, there are left 6 tens, to be written in tens' place; lastly, subtracting 6 hundreds from 7 hundreds, there remains 1 hundred, to be written in hundreds' place.

2d Method.—If the 5 units be increased by 10, say 7 from 15 leaves 8; then, increasing the 3 by 1, say 4 from 0 can not be taken, but 4 from 10 leaves 6; then, increasing 6 by 1, say 7 from 8 leaves 1.

REM. 1.—The second method is generally used; it is more convenient, and less liable to error, especially when the upper number contains ciphers.

REM. 2.—Begin at the right to subtract, so that if any lower figure is greater than the upper, 1 may be borrowed from a higher order.

REM. 3.—If the difference of two numbers be added to the less number, the sum will be equal to the greater. Thus, if 5 subtracted from 8 leave 3, then 3 added to 5 will equal 8.

26. Rule.—1. *Write the less number under the greater, placing figures of the same order in the same column.*

2. *Beginning at the right hand, subtract each figure from the one directly over it, and write the remainder beneath.*

3. *If the lower figure exceeds the upper, add ten to the upper figure, subtract the lower from it, and carry one to the next lower figure, or take one from the next upper figure.*

PROOF.—Add the remainder to the subtrahend; if the sum is equal to the minuend, the work is correct.

EXAMPLES.

	(1)	(2)	(3)	(4)
Minuends,	7640	860012	4500120	3860000
Subtrahends,	1234	430021	2910221	120901
Remainders	6406	429991	1589899	3739099
Proof,	7640	860012	4500120	3860000

5. Take 1234567 from 4444444.

6. Take 15161718 from 91516171.

7. Take 34992884 from 63046571.

8. 153425178 — 53845248 = ?

9. 100000000 — 10001001 = ?

10. Take 17 cents from 63 cents.

11. A carriage cost $137, and a horse $65: how much more than the horse did the carriage cost?

12. A tree 75 feet high was broken; the part that fell was 37 feet long: how high was the stump?

13. America was discovered by Columbus in 1492: how many years had elapsed in 1837?

14. I deposited in the bank $1840, and drew out $475: how many dollars had I left?

15. A man has property worth $10104, and owes debts to the amount of $7426: when his debts are paid, how much will be left?

16. A man having $100000, gave away $11: how many had he left?

17. Subtract 19019 from 20010.

18. Required the excess of nine hundred and twelve thousand and ten, above 50082.

19. Take 4004 from four million.

20. Subtract 1009006 from two million twenty thousand nine hundred and thirty.

21. Subtract four hundred and five thousand and twenty-two from 2000687.

22. What is the difference between thirteen million two hundred and one and 17102102?

23. A man invested in business $30,000; at the end of the first year he found that all his assets amounted to only $26,967; how much had he lost?

24. Take 9238715 from 18126402.

25. Take 9909090009 from 19900900900.

Examples in Addition and Subtraction.

1. $275 + 381 + 625 - 1098 = ?$

2. $6723 - 479 - 347 - 228 = ?$

3. In January, 1876, a merchant bought goods to the amount of $2675; in February, $4375; and in March, $1897; after making one payment of $3000, and another of $4947, how much did he still owe?

4. I owe three notes, whose sum is $1300—one note being for $250, and another for $650: what is the amount of the third note?

5. Mr. Jones deposited $450 in bank on Monday; on Tuesday, $725; on Wednesday, $1235; on Thursday, $4675; and on Friday, $1727. On Saturday morning he drew out $5935, and Saturday afternoon, $877: how much money had he left in bank?

6. At the end of one year I found I had spent $2300. Of this amount, $350 were paid for board, $125 for clothing, $375 for books, $150 for incidentals, and the remainder for two acres of ground: how much did the two acres cost?

7. A speculator bought three houses. For the first he gave $4875; for the second, $2250 more than for the first; and for the third he gave $3725. He afterward sold them all for $20838: how much did he gain?

8. A man owns property valued at $49570, of which $16785 are in personal property, and $24937 in real estate; the remainder was deposited in bank: how much has he in bank?

9. A merchant bought a bill of goods for $7895, and paid $175 for freight, and $3 for drayage. He sold the goods for $10093: how much did he gain?

10. A farmer invested $10000, as follows: in land, $5750; in horses, $925; in cattle, $1575; in hogs, $675;

and the remainder in implements and tools: how much did he invest in implements and tools?

11. A speculator on Monday gained $4625; on Tuesday, $3785; on Wednesday he lost $6955; on Thursday he lost $895; on Friday he gained $985, and on Saturday he lost $1375: how much did he gain during the entire week?

12. The following is Mr. Brown's private account for two weeks: First week, received $50 for salary, and spent $25 for clothing, $7 for board, $2 for washing, and $5 for sundries. Second week, received $50 for salary, loaned $35 to Tom Jones, paid $7 for board, $2 for washing, and $8 for sundries. How much did Mr. Brown have at the end of the two weeks?

Multiplication.

27. 1. If 1 orange cost 2 cents, what will 3 oranges cost?

Solution.—Three oranges will cost 3 times as much as one orange; that is, 2 cents taken 3 times: $2+2+2=6$.

2. If 1 lemon cost 3 cents, how many cents will 4 lemons cost? $3+3+3+3=12$.

3. In an orchard there are 4 rows of trees, and in each row, 21 trees: how many trees in the orchard?

Solution.—1. By writing 21 four times, as in the margin, and adding, the whole number of trees is 84.

2. Instead of writing 21 four times, write it once, place the number 4 underneath, it being the number of times 21 is to be taken, and say, 4 times 1 are 4, which put in units' place; then, 4 times 2 are 8, which put in tens' place; the result is 84, the same as found by addition.

1st row,	21	trees.
2d row,	21	trees.
3d row,	21	trees.
4th row,	21	trees.
	84	

$$\begin{array}{r} 21 \\ 4 \\ \hline 84 \end{array}$$

The latter method of obtaining the result is called Multiplication; therefore, *Multiplication is a short method of performing many additions of the same number.*

DEFINITIONS.

28. 1. **Multiplication** is taking one number as many times as there are units in another.

2. The **multiplicand** is the number to be taken; the **multiplier** is the number denoting how many times the multiplicand is taken; the result is termed the **product.**

Thus, 4 times 5 are 20; 5 is the *multiplicand*, 4 the *multiplier*, and 20 the *product.*

3. The multiplicand and multiplier are together called **factors,** because they make or produce the product.

4. When the multiplicand is a simple number, the operation is called *Multiplication of Simple Numbers.*

29. The sign of Multiplication ($\times$), read *multiplied by*, when placed between two numbers, shows that the first is to be multiplied by the second; thus, $4 \times 3 = 12$ shows that 4 *multiplied by* 3 *equals* 12.

In the table, the sign ($\times$) may be read *times;* thus, 2 times 2 are 4; 2 times 3 are 6.

Multiplication Table.

$1 \times 1 = 1$	$1 \times 2 = 2$	$1 \times 3 = 3$	$1 \times 4 = 4$
$2 \times 1 = 2$	$2 \times 2 = 4$	$2 \times 3 = 6$	$2 \times 4 = 8$
$3 \times 1 = 3$	$3 \times 2 = 6$	$3 \times 3 = 9$	$3 \times 4 = 12$
$4 \times 1 = 4$	$4 \times 2 = 8$	$4 \times 3 = 12$	$4 \times 4 = 16$
$5 \times 1 = 5$	$5 \times 2 = 10$	$5 \times 3 = 15$	$5 \times 4 = 20$
$6 \times 1 = 6$	$6 \times 2 = 12$	$6 \times 3 = 18$	$6 \times 4 = 24$
$7 \times 1 = 7$	$7 \times 2 = 14$	$7 \times 3 = 21$	$7 \times 4 = 28$
$8 \times 1 = 8$	$8 \times 2 = 16$	$8 \times 3 = 24$	$8 \times 4 = 32$
$9 \times 1 = 9$	$9 \times 2 = 18$	$9 \times 3 = 27$	$9 \times 4 = 36$
$10 \times 1 = 10$	$10 \times 2 = 20$	$10 \times 3 = 30$	$10 \times 4 = 40$
$11 \times 1 = 11$	$11 \times 2 = 22$	$11 \times 3 = 33$	$11 \times 4 = 44$
$12 \times 1 = 12$	$12 \times 2 = 24$	$12 \times 3 = 36$	$12 \times 4 = 48$

1 × 5 = 5	1 × 6 = 6	1 × 7 = 7	1 × 8 = 8
2 × 5 = 10	2 × 6 = 12	2 × 7 = 14	2 × 8 = 16
3 × 5 = 15	3 × 6 = 18	3 × 7 = 21	3 × 8 = 24
4 × 5 = 20	4 × 6 = 24	4 × 7 = 28	4 × 8 = 32
5 × 5 = 25	5 × 6 = 30	5 × 7 = 35	5 × 8 = 40
6 × 5 = 30	6 × 6 = 36	6 × 7 = 42	6 × 8 = 48
7 × 5 = 35	7 × 6 = 42	7 × 7 = 49	7 × 8 = 56
8 × 5 = 40	8 × 6 = 48	8 × 7 = 56	8 × 8 = 64
9 × 5 = 45	9 × 6 = 54	9 × 7 = 63	9 × 8 = 72
10 × 5 = 50	10 × 6 = 60	10 × 7 = 70	10 × 8 = 80
11 × 5 = 55	11 × 6 = 66	11 × 7 = 77	11 × 8 = 88
12 × 5 = 60	12 × 6 = 72	12 × 7 = 84	12 × 8 = 96

1 × 9 = 9	1 × 10 = 10	1 × 11 = 11	1 × 12 = 12
2 × 9 = 18	2 × 10 = 20	2 × 11 = 22	2 × 12 = 24
3 × 9 = 27	3 × 10 = 30	3 × 11 = 33	3 × 12 = 36
4 × 9 = 36	4 × 10 = 40	4 × 11 = 44	4 × 12 = 48
5 × 9 = 45	5 × 10 = 50	5 × 11 = 55	5 × 12 = 60
6 × 9 = 54	6 × 10 = 60	6 × 11 = 66	6 × 12 = 72
7 × 9 = 63	7 × 10 = 70	7 × 11 = 77	7 × 12 = 84
8 × 9 = 72	8 × 10 = 80	8 × 11 = 88	8 × 12 = 96
9 × 9 = 81	9 × 10 = 90	9 × 11 = 99	9 × 12 = 108
10 × 9 = 90	10 × 10 = 100	10 × 11 = 110	10 × 12 = 120
11 × 9 = 99	11 × 10 = 110	11 × 11 = 121	11 × 12 = 132
12 × 9 = 108	12 × 10 = 120	12 × 11 = 132	12 × 12 = 144

30. 1. The product of two numbers is not altered by changing the order of the factors. Thus, $6 \times 4 = 24$, and $4 \times 6 = 24$.

2. The multiplier is always an *abstract* number, and the product is always of the *same denomination as the multiplicand;* thus, in the example $5 \times 3 = 15$, the multiplicand is an *abstract* number; in the example 5 cents × 3 = 15 cents, the multiplicand is a *concrete* number.

When the Multiplier does not Exceed 12.

Examples.

31. 1. How many yards of cloth are there in 3 pieces, each containing 123 yards?

Solution.—Having placed the multiplier under the multiplicand, say, 3 times 3 are 9 (units), which write in units' place; 3 times 2 are 6 (tens), which write in tens' place; 3 times 1 are 3 (hundreds), which write in hundreds' place.

OPERATION.

123	multiplicand.
3	multiplier.
369	product.

2. What will 2 houses cost at $231 each?
3. What will 3 horses cost at $132 each?
4. What is the product of 201×4?
5. What is the product of 2301×3?
6. At $43 an acre, what will 5 acres of land cost?

Solution.—Say, 5 times 3 are 15 (units); write the 5 in units' place, and carry the 1 (ten); then, 5 times 4 are 20, and 1 carried make 21 (tens), which write.

OPERATION.

$$\begin{array}{r} \$43 \\ 5 \\ \hline \$215 \end{array}$$

Rule.—1. *Write the multiplicand, with the multiplier under it, and draw a line beneath.*

2. *Begin with units; multiply each figure of the multiplicand by the multiplier, and carry as in addition.*

Rem.—Begin at the right hand to multiply, for convenience, so that the excess of tens in any lower order may be carried to the order next higher.

EXAMPLES.

	(7)	(8)	(9)	(10)
Multiplicand,	5142	4184	3172	41834
Multiplier,	5	6	5	7
Product,				

11. Multiply 49 by 3.
12. Multiply 57 by 4.
13. Multiply 128 by 5.
14. Multiply 367 by 6.
15. Multiply 1427 by 7.
16. Multiply 19645 by 8.
17. Multiply 44386 by 9.
18. Multiply 708324 by 7.
19. Multiply 96432 by 10.
20. Multiply 46782 by 11.
21. Multiply 86458 by 12.

When the Multiplier Exceeds 12.

22. What is the product of 43×25?

ANALYSIS.—Since 25 is equal to 2 tens and 5 units—that is, $20 + 5$,—multiply by 5 and write the product, 215; then multiply by the 2 tens, and set the product, 8 hundreds and 6 tens, under the 2 hundreds and 1 ten.

$$
\begin{array}{rl}
43 & \\
25 & \\
\hline
215 & = 43 \times 5 \\
86 & = 43 \times 20 \\
\hline
1075 & = 43 \times 25
\end{array}
$$

Multiplying by 5 units gives 5 times 43, and multiplying by 2 tens gives 20 times 43; add them, because 5 times 43 and 20 times 43 equal 25 times 43.

Hence, multiply by the units' figure of the multiplier, and write the product so that the right-hand figure will fall in units' place; then multiply by the tens' figure, and write the right-hand figure of the product in the tens' place.

Therefore, in multiplying by a figure of any order, write the last figure of the product in the same order as the multiplier.

NOTE.—The products of the multiplicand by the separate figures of the multiplier are called *partial products.*

General Rule.—1. *Write the multiplier under the multiplicand, placing figures of the same order in a column.*

2. *Multiply the multiplicand by each figure of the multiplier in succession, beginning with units, always setting the right hand figure of each product under that figure of the multiplier which produces it.*

3. *Add the partial products together: their sum will be the product sought.*

PROOF.—Multiply the multiplier by the multiplicand: the product thus obtained should be the same as the first product.

23. Multiply 2345 by 123.

SOLUTION.

2345	multiplicand.
123	multiplier.
7035	=2345× 3
469	=2345× 20
2345	=2345×100
288435	=2345×123

PROOF.

123	multiplier.
2345	multiplicand.
615	=123× 5
492	=123× 40
369	=123× 300
246	=123×2000
288435	=123×2345

24. Multiply 327 by 203.

REMARK.—When there is a cipher in the multiplier, leave it, and multiply by the other figures, being careful to place the right-hand figure of each partial product under the multiplying figure.

327
203
981
654
66381

EXAMPLES.

25. 235 × 13 =	34. 624 × 85 =
26. 346 × 19 =	35. 976 × 97 =
27. 425 × 29 =	36. 342 × 364 =
28. 518 × 34 =	37. 376 × 526 =
29. 279 × 37 =	38. 476 × 536 =
30. 869 × 49 =	39. 2187 × 215 =
31. 294 × 57 =	40. 3489 × 276 =
32. 429 × 62 =	41. 1646 × 365 =
33. 485 × 76 =	42. 8432 × 635 =

43. Multiply 6874 by 829.
44. Multiply 2873 by 1823.
45. Multiply 4786 by 3497.
46. Multiply 87603 by 9865.
47. Multiply 83457 by 6835.
48. Multiply 31624 by 7138.

49. What will 126 barrels of flour cost, at $6 a barrel?

50. What will 823 barrels of pork cost, at $12 a barrel?

51. What will 675 pounds of cheese cost, at 13 cents a pound?

52. What will 496 bushels of oats cost, at 24 cents a bushel?

53. If a man travel 28 miles a day, how many miles will he travel in 152 days?

54. There are 1760 yards in one mile: how many yards are there in 209 miles?

55. There are 24 hours in a day, and 365 days in a year: if a ship sail 8 miles an hour, how far will she sail in a year?

56. Multiply two thousand and twenty-nine by one thousand and seven.

57. Multiply eighty thousand four hundred and one by sixty thousand and seven.

58. Multiply one hundred and one thousand and thirty-two by 20001.

59. A grocer bought 2 barrels of sugar, each weighing 215 pounds, for 8 cents a pound: how much did he pay for the sugar?

60. A grocer bought a barrel of molasses, containing 36 gallons, for 45 cents a gallon; and sold it for 55 cents a gallon: how much did he gain?

61. A commission merchant sold 2650 bushels of wheat for a farmer, at 95 cents a bushel, and charged him 2 cents a bushel for selling: how much money was due the farmer?

62. A farmer bought 6 horses of one man for 75 dollars each, and 5 horses of another for 125 dollars each, and sold them all for 150 dollars each: how many dollars did he gain?

63. A merchant bought one box of goods for 250 dollars, two more for 325 dollars each, and three more for 175 dollars each; he sold them all so as to gain 356 dollars: for how much did he sell them?

64. A farmer bought 24 sheep, at 5 dollars a head; 36 hogs, at 14 dollars a head; and 9 cows, at 45 dollars a head: when he sold them all, he lost 275 dollars: for how much did he sell them?

65. To 75×37 add 85×54, and subtract 5284.

66. To 69×53 add 48×27, and subtract 4279.

67. I bought 50 bags of coffee, averaging 63 pounds in a bag, paying 34 cents a pound: how much did it cost?

CONTRACTIONS IN MULTIPLICATION.

CASE I.

32. When the multiplier can be separated into factors.

1. What will 15 oranges cost, at 8 cents each?

Cost of	1 orange,	8 ct.
		5
Cost of	5 oranges,	40 ct.
		3
Cost of	15 oranges,	120 ct.

ANALYSIS.—Since 15 is 3 times 5, 15 oranges will cost 3 times as much as 5 oranges.

Therefore, instead of multiplying 8 by 15, first find the cost of 5 oranges, by multiplying 8 cents by 5; then take 3 times that product for the cost of 15 oranges.

Rule.—1. *Separate the multiplier into two or more factors.*

2. *Multiply the multiplicand by one of the factors, and this product by another factor, till every factor is used; the last product will be the one required.*

REM.—Do not confound the *factors* of a number with the *parts* into which it may be separated. Thus, the factors of 15 are 5 and 3, while the parts into which 15 may be separated are any numbers whose *sum* equals 15: as, 7 and 8; or, 2, 9, and 4.

EXAMPLES.

2. What will 24 acres of land cost, at $124 an acre?

3. How far will a ship sail in 56 weeks, at the rate of 1512 miles per week?

4. How many pounds of iron are there in 54 loads, each weighing 2873 pounds?

5. Multiply 2874 by 72.

6. Multiply 8074 by 108.

CASE II.

33. When the multiplier is 1 with ciphers annexed; as 10, 100, 1000, etc.

1. Placing *one* cipher on the right of a number (8, 3) changes the units into tens, the tens into hundreds, and so on, and, therefore, *multiplies the number by ten;* thus, annex one cipher to 25, and it becomes 250.

2. Annexing *two* ciphers changes units into hundreds, tens into thousands, etc., and *multiplies the number by one hundred;* thus, annex two ciphers to 25, and it becomes 2500.

Rule.—*Annex as many ciphers to the multiplicand as there are ciphers in the multiplier, and the number thus formed will be the product required.*

1. Multiply 245 by 100.
2. Multiply 138 by 1000.
3. Multiply 428 by 10000.
4. Multiply 872 by 100000.
5. Multiply 9642 by 1000000.
6. Multiply 10045 by 1000000.

CASE III.

34. When there are ciphers at the right of one or both of the factors.

1. Find the product of 625 by 500.

ANALYSIS.—The multiplier may be considered as composed of two factors: 5 and 100. Multiplying by 5, the product is 3125; and the product of this number by 100 is 312500, which is the same as annexing two ciphers to the first product.

```
   625
   500
312500
```

2. Find the product of 2300×170.

ANALYSIS.—The number 2300 may be regarded as composed of the two factors 23 and 100; and 170, of the two factors 17 and 10.

$$\begin{array}{r} 2300 \\ 170 \\ \hline 161 \\ 23 \\ \hline 391000 \end{array}$$

The product of 2300 by 170 will be found by multiplying 23 by 17, and this product by 100, and the resulting product by 10 (**33**); that is, by finding the product of 23 by 17, and then annexing 3 ciphers to the product, as there are 3 ciphers at the right of both factors.

Rule.—*Multiply without regarding the ciphers on the right of the factors; then annex to the product as many ciphers as are at the right of both factors.*

3. Multiply 2350 by 60.
4. Multiply 80300 by 450.
5. Multiply 10240 by 3200.
6. Multiply 9600 by 2400.
7. Multiply 18001 by 26000.
8. Multiply 8602 by 1030.
9. Multiply 3007 by 9100.
10. Multiply 80600 by 7002.
11. Multiply 70302 by 80300.
12. Multiply 904000 by 10200.

DIVISION.

35. 1. If you divide 6 apples equally between 2 boys, how many will each boy have?

ANALYSIS.—It will require 2 apples to give each boy 1. Hence, each boy will have as many apples as 2 is contained times in 6, which are 3.

How many times 2 in 6? *Ans.* 3.
Why? Because 3 times 2 are 6.

2. If you divide 8 peaches equally between 2 boys, how many will each have? *Ans.* 4 peaches. Why?

3. How many times 2 in 10? *Ans.* 5. Why?

The process by which the preceding examples are solved is called *Division.*

DEFINITIONS.

36. 1. **Division** is the process of finding how many times one number is contained in another.

2. The **divisor** is the number by which to divide; the **dividend** is the number to be divided; the **quotient** is the number denoting how many times the divisor is contained in the dividend.

Thus, 3 is contained in 12, 4 times; here, 3 is the ***divisor***, **12 the** ***dividend***, and 4 the *quotient*.

3. Since 3 is contained in 12 four times, 4 times 3 are 12; that is, the divisor and quotient multiplied produce the dividend.

4. Since 3 and 4 are factors of the product 12, the divisor and quotient correspond to the factors in multiplication; the dividend, to the product. Therefore, *Division is the process of finding one of the factors of a product, when the other factor is known.*

37. A boy has 8 cents: how many lemons can he buy, at 2 cents each?

ANALYSIS.—He can buy 4, because 4 lemons, at 2 cents each, will cost 8 cents.

The boy would give 2 cents for 1 lemon, and then have 6 cents left.

After giving 2 cents for the 2d lemon, he would have 4 cents left.

Then, giving 2 cents for the 3d, he would have 2 cents left.

Lastly, after giving 2 cents for the 4th, he would have nothing left.

	8 cents.
1st lemon,	2 cents.
Left,	6 cents.
2d lemon,	2 cents.
Left,	4 cents.
3d lemon,	2 cents.
Left,	2 cents.
4th lemon,	2 cents.
Left	0 cents.

The natural method of performing this operation is by subtraction; but, when it is known *how many times* 2 can be subtracted from 8, instead of subtracting 2 four times, say 2 in 8 four times, and 4 times 2 are 8.

Therefore, Division may be termed *a short method of making many subtractions of the same number.*

The divisor is the number subtracted; the dividend, the number from which the subtraction has been made; the quotient shows how many subtractions have been made.

38. 1. Division is indicated in three ways:

1st. 3)12, which means that 12 is to be divided by 3.

2d. $\frac{12}{3}$ which means that 12 is to be divided by 3.

3d. 12÷3, which means that 12 is to be divided by 3.

2. In using the first sign when the divisor does not exceed 12, draw a line under the dividend, and write the quotient beneath; if the divisor exceeds 12, draw a curved line on the right of the dividend, and place the quotient on the right of this.

3. The sign (÷) is read *divided by.*

Examples.

$$2\overline{)8} \atop \quad 4 \qquad \Big| \qquad 15)45(3 \atop \underline{45} \qquad \Big| \qquad \frac{15}{5}=3 \qquad \Big| \qquad 21 \div 3 = 7.$$

Division Table.

1 ÷ 1 = 1	2 ÷ 2 = 1	3 ÷ 3 = 1	4 ÷ 4 = 1
2 ÷ 1 = 2	4 ÷ 2 = 2	6 ÷ 3 = 2	8 ÷ 4 = 2
3 ÷ 1 = 3	6 ÷ 2 = 3	9 ÷ 3 = 3	12 ÷ 4 = 3
4 ÷ 1 = 4	8 ÷ 2 = 4	12 ÷ 3 = 4	16 ÷ 4 = 4
5 ÷ 1 = 5	10 ÷ 2 = 5	15 ÷ 3 = 5	20 ÷ 4 = 5
6 ÷ 1 = 6	12 ÷ 2 = 6	18 ÷ 3 = 6	24 ÷ 4 = 6
7 ÷ 1 = 7	14 ÷ 2 = 7	21 ÷ 3 = 7	28 ÷ 4 = 7
8 ÷ 1 = 8	16 ÷ 2 = 8	24 ÷ 3 = 8	32 ÷ 4 = 8
9 ÷ 1 = 9	18 ÷ 2 = 9	27 ÷ 3 = 9	36 ÷ 4 = 9
10 ÷ 1 = 10	20 ÷ 2 = 10	30 ÷ 3 = 10	40 ÷ 4 = 10
11 ÷ 1 = 11	22 ÷ 2 = 11	33 ÷ 3 = 11	44 ÷ 4 = 11
12 ÷ 1 = 12	24 ÷ 2 = 12	36 ÷ 3 = 12	48 ÷ 4 = 12

5 ÷ 5 = 1	6 ÷ 6 = 1	7 ÷ 7 = 1	8 ÷ 8 = 1
10 ÷ 5 = 2	12 ÷ 6 = 2	14 ÷ 7 = 2	16 ÷ 8 = 2
15 ÷ 5 = 3	18 ÷ 6 = 3	21 ÷ 7 = 3	24 ÷ 8 = 3
20 ÷ 5 = 4	24 ÷ 6 = 4	28 ÷ 7 = 4	32 ÷ 8 = 4
25 ÷ 5 = 5	30 ÷ 6 = 5	35 ÷ 7 = 5	40 ÷ 8 = 5
30 ÷ 5 = 6	36 ÷ 6 = 6	42 ÷ 7 = 6	48 ÷ 8 = 6
35 ÷ 5 = 7	42 ÷ 6 = 7	49 ÷ 7 = 7	56 ÷ 8 = 7
40 ÷ 5 = 8	48 ÷ 6 = 8	56 ÷ 7 = 8	64 ÷ 8 = 8
45 ÷ 5 = 9	54 ÷ 6 = 9	63 ÷ 7 = 9	72 ÷ 8 = 9
50 ÷ 5 = 10	60 ÷ 6 = 10	70 ÷ 7 = 10	80 ÷ 8 = 10
55 ÷ 5 = 11	66 ÷ 6 = 11	77 ÷ 7 = 11	88 ÷ 8 = 11
60 ÷ 5 = 12	72 ÷ 6 = 12	84 ÷ 7 = 12	96 ÷ 8 = 12
9 ÷ 9 = 1	10 ÷ 10 = 1	11 ÷ 11 = 1	12 ÷ 12 = 1
18 ÷ 9 = 2	20 ÷ 10 = 2	22 ÷ 11 = 2	24 ÷ 12 = 2
27 ÷ 9 = 3	30 ÷ 10 = 3	33 ÷ 11 = 3	36 ÷ 12 = 3
36 ÷ 9 = 4	40 ÷ 10 = 4	44 ÷ 11 = 4	48 ÷ 12 = 4
45 ÷ 9 = 5	50 ÷ 10 = 5	55 ÷ 11 = 5	60 ÷ 12 = 5
54 ÷ 9 = 6	60 ÷ 10 = 6	66 ÷ 11 = 6	72 ÷ 12 = 6
63 ÷ 9 = 7	70 ÷ 10 = 7	77 ÷ 11 = 7	84 ÷ 12 = 7
72 ÷ 9 = 8	80 ÷ 10 = 8	88 ÷ 11 = 8	96 ÷ 12 = 8
81 ÷ 9 = 9	90 ÷ 10 = 9	99 ÷ 11 = 9	108 ÷ 12 = 9
90 ÷ 9 = 10	100 ÷ 10 = 10	110 ÷ 11 = 10	120 ÷ 12 = 10
99 ÷ 9 = 11	110 ÷ 10 = 11	121 ÷ 11 = 11	132 ÷ 12 = 11
108 ÷ 9 = 12	120 ÷ 10 = 12	132 ÷ 11 = 12	144 ÷ 12 = 12

39. If 7 cents be divided as equally as possible among 3 boys, each boy would receive 2 cents, and there would be 1 cent left, or *remaining* undivided.

The number left after dividing, is called the **remainder.**

REM.—1. Since the remainder is a part of the dividend, it must be of the same denomination. If the dividend be dollars, the remainder will be dollars; if pounds, the remainder will be pounds.

REM. 2.—The remainder is always *less* than the divisor; for, if it were equal to it, or greater, the divisor would be contained at least once more in the dividend.

REM. 3.—If the dividend and divisor are simple numbers, the operation is called *Division of Simple Numbers.*

SHORT DIVISION.

40. When the division is performed mentally, and merely the result written, it is termed *Short Division.* Short Division is used when the divisor does not exceed 12.

1. How many times is 2 contained in 468?

Here, the dividend is composed of three numbers: 4 hundreds, 6 tens, and 8 units; that is, of 400, 60, and 8.

	Divisor.		Dividend.		Quotient.	
Now,	2	in	400	is contained	200	times.
	2	in	60	" "	30	times.
	2	in	8	" "	4	times.
Hence,	2	in	468	is contained	234	times.

The same result can be obtained without actually separating the dividend into parts:

Thus, 2 in 4 (hundreds), 2 times, which write in hundreds' place; then, 2 in 6 (tens), 3 times, which write in tens' place; then, 2 in 8 (units), 4 times, which write in units' place.

	Dividend.
Divisor, 2)	4 6 8
Quotient,	2 3 4

2. How many times 3 in 693?
3. How many times 4 in 848?
4. How many times 2 in 4682?
5. How many times 4 in 8408?

6. How many times 3 in 36936?
7. How many times 2 in 88468?

41. 1. How many times is 3 contained in 129?

SOLUTION.—Here, 3 is not contained in 1; but 3 is contained in 12 (tens), 4 times, which write in tens' place; 3 in 9 (units), 3 times, which write in units' place.

```
3)129
   43
```

2. How many times is 3 contained in 735?

SOLUTION.—Here, 3 is contained in seven (hundreds), 2 times, and 1 hundred over; the 1 hundred, united with the 3 tens, makes 13 tens, in which 3 is contained 4 times and 1 ten left; this 1 ten, united with the 5 units, makes 15 units, in which 3 is contained 5 times.

```
3)735
  245
```

3. How many times is 3 contained in 618?

SOLUTION.—Here, 3 is contained in 6 (hundreds), 2 times; as the 1 in ten's place will not contain 3, a cipher is placed in ten's place; the 1 ten is then added to the 8 units, making 18 units, and the quotient figure 6 is placed in units' place.

```
3)618
  206
```

4. How many times is 3 contained in 609?

Here, the solution is the same as in the above example; there being no tens, their order is indicated by 0.

```
3)609
  203
```

5. How many times is 3 contained in 743?

After dividing, there is 2 left, the division of which is merely indicated by placing the divisor under the remainder; thus, $\frac{2}{3}$. The quotient is written thus, 247$\frac{2}{3}$; read, 247, and *two divided by three;* or, 247, with a *remainder, two.*

```
3)743
  247⅔
```

6. How many times 3 in 462?
7. How many times 5 in 1170?
8. How many times 4 in 948?

Rule.—1. *Write the divisor at the left of the dividend, with a curved line between them, and draw a line beneath the dividend. Begin at the left hand, divide successively each figure of the dividend by the divisor, and write the result in the same order in the quotient.*

2. *If there is a remainder after dividing any figure, prefix it to the figure in the next lower order, and divide as before.*

3. *If the number in any order does not contain the divisor, place a cipher in the same order in the quotient, prefix the number to the figure in the next lower order, and divide as before.*

4. *If there is a remainder after dividing the last figure, place the divisor under it, and annex it to the quotient.*

Proof.—Multiply the quotient by the divisor, and add the remainder, if any, to the product: if the work is correct, the sum will be equal to the dividend.

Rem.—This method of proof depends on the principle (**36**, 4) that a dividend is a product, of which the divisor and quotient are factors.

9. Divide 653 cents by 3.

SOLUTION.		PROOF.
		217
	Dividend.	3
Divisor,	3)653	651 = cents divided.
Quotient,	$217\frac{2}{3}$	2 = remainder.
		653 = dividend.

	(10)	(11)	(12)
	6)454212	7)874293	8)3756031
Ans.			
	6	7	8
Proof,	454212	874293	3756031

PARTS OF NUMBERS.

NOTE.—When any number is divided into two equal parts, one of the parts is called *one-half* of that number.

If divided into three equal parts, one of the parts is called *one-third;* if into four equal parts, *one-fourth;* if into five equal parts, *one-fifth;* and so on.

Hence, to find *one-half* of a number, divide by 2; to find *one-third,* divide by 3; *one-fourth,* divide by 4; *one-fifth,* by 5, etc.

13. Divide 8652 by 2.
14. Divide 406235 by 3.
15. Divide 675043 by 4.
16. Divide 984275 by 5.
17. Divide 258703 by 6.
18. Divide 8643275 by 7.
19. Divide 6032520 by 8.
20. Divide 9032706 by 9.
21. Divide 1830024 by 10.
22. Divide 603251 by 11.
23. Divide 41674008 by 12.

24. If oranges cost 3 cents each, how many can be bought for 894 cents?

25. If 4 bushels of apples cost 140 cents, how much is that a bushel?

26. If flour cost $4 a barrel, how many barrels can be bought for $812?

27. A carpenter receives $423 for 9 months' work: how much is that a month?

28. There are 12 months in 1 year: how many years are there in 540 months?

29. There are 4 quarts in 1 gallon: how many gallons are there in 321276 quarts?

30. At $8 a barrel, how many barrels of flour can be bought for $1736?

31. There are 7 days in one week: how many weeks are there in 734566 days? 104938.

32. A number has been multiplied by 11, and the product is 495: what is the number?

33. The product of two numbers is 3582: one of the numbers is 9: what is the other?

34. Find one-half of 56.

35. Find one-half of 3725.

36. Find one-third of 147.

37. Find one-fourth of 500.

38. Find one-fifth of 1945.

39. Find one-sixth of 4476.

40. Find one-seventh of 2513.

41. Find one-eighth of 5992.

42. Find one-ninth of 8793.

43. Find one-tenth of 1090.

44. Find one-eleventh of 4125.

45. Find one-twelfth of 5556.

46. I divided 144 apples equally among 4 boys; the eldest boy gave one-third of his share to his sister: what number did the sister receive?

47. James found 195 cents, and gave to Daniel one-fifth of them: Daniel gave one-third of his share to his sister: how many cents did she receive?

48. One-eleventh of 275 is how much greater than one-eighth of 192?

Long Division.

42. When the entire work of the division is written down, it is termed *Long Division.* Long Division is commonly used when the divisor exceeds 12.

1. Divide 3465 dollars equally among 15 men.

```
15)3465(231
   30 hund.
    46 tens.
    45
     15 units.
     15
```

Solution.—Fifteen is not contained in 3 (thousands); therefore, there will be no thousands in the quotient. Take 34 (hundreds) as a *partial* dividend; 15 is contained in 34, 2 times; that is, 15 men have 200 dollars each, which requires in all $15 \times 2 = 30$ hundreds of dollars.

Subtract 30 hundreds from 34 hundreds, and 4 hundreds remain; to which bring down the 6 tens, and you have 46 (tens) for a second partial dividend.

46 contains 15, 3 times; that is, each man has 30 dollars more, and all require $15 \times 3 = 45$ tens of dollars.

Subtract 45, and bring down the 5 units, which gives 15 (units) for a third partial dividend; in this the divisor is contained once, giving to each man 1 dollar more.

Hence, each man receives 2 hundred dollars, 3 ten dollars, and 1 dollar; that is, 231 dollars.

Divisor.	Parts.	Quotients.
15	3000	200
	450	30
	15	1
	3465	231

By this process, the dividend is separated into parts, each part containing the divisor a certain number of times.

The first part, 30 hundreds, contains the divisor 2 times; the second part, 45 tens, contains it 3 times; the third part, 15 units, contains it 1 time.

The several parts together equal the given dividend, and the several partial quotients make up the entire quotient.

2. In 147095 days, how many years, each of 365 days?

```
365)147095(403 years.
    1460
    ----
      1095
      1095
      ----
```

SOLUTION.—Taking 147 (thousands) for the first partial dividend, we find it will not contain the divisor; hence use four figures.

Again, after multiplying and subtracting, as in the preceding example, and bringing down the 9 tens, the partial dividend, 109 (tens), will not contain the divisor; hence, write a cipher (no tens) in the quotient, and bring down the 5 units; the last partial dividend is 1095 (units), which contains the divisor three times.

3. Divide 4056 by 13.

Rule.—1. *Place the divisor on the left of the dividend, draw a curved line between them, and another on the right of the dividend.*

2. *Find how many times the divisor is contained in the fewest left hand figures of the dividend that will contain the divisor, and place this number in the quotient at the right.*

3. *Multiply the divisor by this quotient figure; place the product under that part of the dividend from which it was obtained.*

4. *Subtract this product from the figures above it; to the remainder bring down the next figure of the dividend, and divide as before, until all the figures of the dividend are brought down.*

5. *If, at any time, after bringing down a figure, the number thus formed is too small to contain the divisor, place a cipher in the quotient, and bring down another figure, after which divide as before.*

PROOF.—Same as in Short Division.

REM.—1. The product must never be *greater* than the partial dividend from which it is to be subtracted; when so, the quotient figure is *too large*, and must be diminished.

REM.—2. After subtracting, the remainder must always be *less* than the divisor; when the remainder is not less than the divisor, the last quotient figure is *too small*, and must be increased.

REM.—3. The order of each quotient figure is the same as the lowest order in the partial dividend from which it was obtained.

4. Divide 78994 by 319.

SOLUTION.

$319)78994(247\frac{201}{319}$

```
319)78994(247 201/319
    638
    ----
    1519
    1276
    -----
     2434
     2233
     ----
      201 Rem.
```

PROOF.

```
          247 Quotient.
          319 Divisor.
         ----
         2223
         247
        741
        -----
        78793
Add       201 Remainder.
        -----
        78994 = the Dividend.
```

5. Divide 11577 by 14.
6. Divide 48690 by 15.
7. Divide 1110960 by 23.
8. Divide 122878 by 67.
9. Divide 12412 by 53.
10. Divide 146304 by 72.
11. Divide 47100 by 54.
12. Divide 71104 by 88.
13. Divide 43956 by 66.
14. Divide 121900 by 99.
15. Divide 25312 by 112.
16. Divide 381600 by 123.
17. Divide 105672 by 204.
18. Divide 600000 by 1234.
19. Divide 1234567 by 4321.
20. Divide 50964242 by 7819.

21. Divide 48905952 by 9876.
22. Divide 4049160 by 12345.
23. Divide 552160000 by 973.

24. At $15 an acre, how many acres of land can be bought for $3465?

25. If a man travel 26 miles a day, in how many days will he travel 364 miles?

26. If $1083 be divided equally among 19 men, how many dollars will each have?

27. A man raised 9523 bushels of corn on 107 acres: how much was that on one acre?

28. In 1 hogshead there are 63 gallons: how many hogsheads in 14868 gallons?

29. The President receives $50000 a year (365 days): how much is that a day?

30. The yearly income from a railroad is $379600: how much is that a day? (365 da. = 1 yr.).

31. The product of two numbers is 6571435; one of the factors is 1235: what is the other?

32. Divide one million two hundred and forty-seven thousand four hundred by 405.

33. Divide 10 million four hundred and one thousand by one thousand and six.

34. A colony of 684 men bought a tract of land, containing 109440 acres: if equally divided, to how many acres was each man entitled?

35. A farmer raised 8288 bushels of corn, averaging 56 bushels to the acre: how many acres did he plant?

36. The capital of a joint-stock company is $262275, and is divided into 269 shares: what is the value of each share?

37. The earth, at the equator, is about 24899 miles in

circumference, and turns on its axis once in 24 hours: how many miles an hour does it turn?

38. A railroad 238 miles long, cost \$3731840: what was the cost per mile?

39. A fort is 27048 feet distant from a city; the flash of a cannon was seen 24 seconds before the sound was heard: how many feet a second did the sound travel?

40. Light travels at the rate of 11520000 miles a minute: how many minutes does it require for the light of the sun to reach the earth, the sun being 92160000 miles distant?

Examples for Review.

41. Subtract 86247 from 94231 and divide the remainder by 16.

42. Divide the sum of 46712 and 6848 by 104.

43. Divide the product of 497×583 by 71.

44. To the difference between 2832 and 987 add 678, and divide the sum by 87.

45. Multiply the difference between 4896 and 2384 by 49, and divide the product by 112.

46. Multiply the sum of $228 + 786$ by 95, and divide the product by 114.

47. Multiply the sum of 478 and 296 by their difference, and divide the product by 387.

48. A horse-dealer received \$7560 for horses; he sold a part of them for \$3885; if he sold the rest for \$175 apiece, how many horses did he sell the second time?

49. A farmer expended at one time \$7350 for land, and at another, \$4655, paying \$49 an acre each time: how many acres did he buy in both purchases?

50. A refiner bought 58 hogsheads of sugar, at $77 a hogshead, and afterward sold them for $5742: how much did he gain on each hogshead?

51. A man bought 240 acres of land, at $26 an acre, giving in payment a house valued at $2820, and horses valued at $180 apiece: how many horses did he give?

52. A speculator bought 25 acres of land for $10625, and after dividing it into 125 village lots, sold each lot for $250: how much did he gain on the whole? On each acre? On each lot?

CONTRACTIONS IN DIVISION.

CASE I.

43. When the divisor can be separated into factors.

1. A man paid $255 for 15 acres of land: how much was that per acre?

SOLUTION.—15 acres are 3 times 5 acres; dividing $255 by 3 gives $85, the value of 5 acres; dividing $85 by 5 gives $17, the value of 1 acre.

```
      Dollars.
  3 ) 255 = the value of 15 acres.
  5 ) 85  = the value of  5 acres.
      17  = the value of  1 acre.
```

The solution shows that instead of dividing by the number 15, whose factors are 3 and 5, we may first divide by one factor, then divide the quotient thus obtained by the other factor.

2 Find the quotient of 37, divided by 14.

SOLUTION.—Dividing by 2, the quotient is 18 *twos* and 1 unit remaining. Dividing by 7, the quotient is 2, with a remainder of 4 *twos;* the whole remainder then is 4 *twos* plus 1, or 9.

```
2 ) 37
7 ) 18 and 1 over.
     2 and 4 twos left.
```

Rule.—1. *Divide the dividend by one of the factors of the divisor; then divide the quotient thus obtained by the other factor.*

2. *Multiply the last remainder by the first divisor; to the product add the first remainder; the amount will be the true remainder.*

REM.—When the divisor can be resolved into more than two factors, you may divide by them successively. The true remainder will be found by multiplying each remainder by all the preceding divisors, except that which produced it. To their sum add the remainder from first divisor.

3. Divide 2583 by 63. ($63 = 7 \times 9$)
4. Divide 6976 by 32. ($32 = 4 \times 8$)
5. Divide 2744 by 28. ($28 = 7 \times 4$)
6. Divide 6145 by 42. ($42 = 6 \times 7$)
7. Divide 19008 by 132.
8. Divide 7840 by 64.
9. Divide 14771 by 72.
10. Divide 10206 by 81.
11. Divide 81344 by 121.
12. Divide 98272 by 108.

CASE II.

44. To divide by 1 with ciphers annexed; as 10, 100, 1000, etc.

To multiply 6 by 10, annex one cipher, thus, 60. On the principle that division is the reverse of multiplication, to divide 60 by 10, *cut off* a cipher.

Had the dividend been 65, the 5 might have been separated in like manner as the cipher; 6 being the quotient, 5 the remainder. The same will apply when the divisor is 100, 1000, etc.

Rule.—*Cut off as many figures from the right of the dividend as there are ciphers in the divisor; the figures cut off will be the remainder, the other figures, the quotient.*

1. Divide 34872 by 100.

OPERATION.

```
1|00)348|72
     348 Quo.  72 Rem.
```

2. Divide 2682 by 10.
3. Divide 4700 by 100.
4. Divide 37201 by 100.
5. Divide 46250 by 100.
6. Divide 18003 by 1000.

CASE III.

45. To divide when there are ciphers on the right of the divisor, or on the right of the divisor and dividend.

1. Divide 4072 by 800.

OPERATION.

```
1|00)40|72
   8)40
      5 Quo...72 Rem.

8|00)40|72
      5 Quo...72 Rem.
```

SOLUTION.—Regard 800 as composed of the factors 100 and 8, and divide as in the margin.

In dividing by 800, separate the two right hand figures for the remainder, then divide by 8.

2. Divide 77939 by 2400.

OPERATION.

```
24|00)779|39(32 1139/2400
      72
      59
      48
      11
```

SOLUTION.—Since 2400 equals 24×100, cut off the two right hand figures, the same as dividing by 100; then divide by 24.

Dividing by 100, the remainder is 39; dividing by 24, the remainder is 11. To find the true remainder, multiply 11 by 100, and add 39 to the product (Art. **43**, Rule); this is the same as annexing the figures cut off, to the last remainder.

3. Divide 62700 by 2500.

SOLUTION.—The same as for the example above.

OPERATION.

$$
\begin{array}{r}
25|00)\,627|00\,(25\tfrac{200}{2500} \\
\underline{50}\phantom{|00\,(25\tfrac{200}{2500}} \\
127\phantom{|00\,(25\tfrac{200}{2500}} \\
\underline{125}\phantom{|00\,(25\tfrac{200}{2500}} \\
2\phantom{|00\,(25\tfrac{200}{2500}}
\end{array}
$$

Rule.—1. *Cut off the ciphers at the right of the divisor, and as many figures from the right of the dividend.*

2. *Divide the remaining figures in the dividend by the remaining figures in the divisor.*

3. *Annex the figures cut off to the remainder, which gives the true remainder.*

4. Divide 73005 by 4000.
5. Divide 36001 by 9000.
6. Divide 1078000 by 11000.
7. Divide 40167 by 180.
8. Divide 907237 by 2100.
9. Divide 364006 by 6400.
10. Divide 76546037 by 250000.
11. Divide 43563754 by 63400.

GENERAL PRINCIPLES OF DIVISION.

46. The value of the quotient depends on the relative values of divisor and dividend. These may be changed by Multiplication and by Division, thus:

1st. The dividend may be multiplied, or the divisor divided.

2d. The dividend may be divided, or the divisor multiplied.

3d. Both dividend and divisor may be multiplied, or both divided, at the same time.

ILLUSTRATIONS.

Let 24 be a dividend, and 6 the divisor; the quotient is 4. $24 \div 6 = 4$.

If the dividend, 24, be *multiplied* by 2, the quotient will be multiplied by 2; for, $24 \times 2 = 48$; and $48 \div 6 = 8$, which is the former quotient, 4, *multiplied* by 2.

Now, if the divisor, 6, be *divided* by 2, the quotient will be multiplied by 2; for, $6 \div 2 = 3$; and $24 \div 3 = 8$, which is the former quotient, 4, *multiplied* by 2.

PRINCIPLE I.—*If the dividend be multiplied, or the divisor be divided, the quotient will be multiplied.*

47. Take the same example, $24 \div 6 = 4$.

If the dividend, 24, be *divided* by 2, the quotient will be divided by 2; for, $24 \div 2 = 12$; and $12 \div 6 = 2$, which is the former quotient, 4, *divided* by 2.

And, if the divisor, 6, be *multiplied* by 2, the quotient will be divided by 2; for, $6 \times 2 = 12$; and $24 \div 12 = 2$, which is the former quotient, 4, *divided* by 2.

PRIN. II.—*If the dividend be divided, or the divisor be multiplied, the quotient will be divided.*

48. Take the same example, $24 \div 6 = 4$.

If the dividend, 24, and divisor, 6, be *multiplied* by 2, the quotient will not be changed; for, $24 \times 2 = 48$; and $6 \times 2 = 12$; $48 \div 12 = 4$; the former quotient, 4, *unchanged.*

And if the dividend, 24, and divisor, 6, be *divided* by 2, the quotient will not be changed; for, $24 \div 2 = 12$; and $6 \div 2 = 3$; $12 \div 3 = 4$; the former quotient, 4, *unchanged.*

PRIN. III.—*If both dividend and divisor be multiplied or divided by the same number, the quotient will not be changed.*

PROMISCUOUS EXAMPLES.

49. 1. In 4 bags are $500; in the first, $96; in the second, $120; in the third, $55: what sum in the 4th bag?

2. Four men paid $1265 for land: the first paid $243; the second $61 more than the first; the third $79 less than the second: how much did the fourth man pay?

3. I have five apple trees: the first bears 157 apples; the second, 264; the third, 305; the fourth, 97; the fifth, 123: I sell 428, and 186 are stolen: how many apples are left?

4. In an army of 57068 men, 9503 are killed; 586 join the enemy; 4794 are prisoners; 1234 die of wounds; 850 are drowned: how many return?

5. On the first of the year a speculator is worth $12307: during the year he gains $8706; in January he spends $237; in February, $301; in each of the remaining ten months he spends $538: how much had he at the end of the year?

6. The Bible has 31173 verses: in how many days can I read it, by reading 86 verses a day?

7. I bought 28 horses for $1400: 3 died; for how much each must I sell the rest to incur no loss?

8. How many times can I fill a 15 gallon cask, from 5 hogsheads of 63 gallons each?

9. A certain dividend is 73900; the quotient 214; the remainder, 70: what is the divisor?

10. Multiply the sum of 148 and 56 by their difference; divide the product by 23.

11. How much woolen cloth, at $6 a yard, will it take to pay for 8 horses at $60 each, and 14 cows at $45 each?

12. Two men paid \$6000 for a farm: one man took 70 acres at \$30 an acre, the other the remainder at \$25 an acre: how many acres in all?

13. My income is \$1800 a year. If I spend \$360 a year for provisions, \$300 for rent, \$150 for clothing, \$100 for books, and \$90 for incidentals, in how many years can I save \$10400?

14. A man bought 40 acres of ground at \$15 an acre, and 80 acres at \$25 an acre. He sold 90 acres for \$4500, and the remainder at \$60 an acre: for how much did he sell the whole land? How much did he gain?

15. A merchant bought 275 yards of cloth at \$4 a yard; he sold 250 yards at \$5 a yard, and the remainder at \$6 a yard: how much did he gain?

16. A broker buys 125 shares of stock for \$85 a share, and 75 shares at \$115 a share. He invests it all in other stock at \$175 a share: how many shares does he get by the last purchase?

17. A farmer sends to a dealer 20 horses and 15 mules to be sold. The dealer sells the horses for \$125 each, and the mules for \$150 each, charging \$95 for selling. The farmer then buys 50 head of cattle at \$45 each, with part of the money, and deposits the remainder in bank: how much does he deposit in bank?

COMPOUND NUMBERS.

To TEACHERS.—While placing Fractions immediately after Simple Whole Numbers is philosophical, and appropriate in a higher arithmetic for *advanced* pupils, the experience of the author convinces him that, in a book for *young* learners, Compound Numbers should be introduced before, instead of after, Fractions—for the following reasons:

1st. The operations of Addition, Subtraction, Multiplication, and Division of *compound numbers* are analogous to the same operations in *simple numbers*, and serve to illustrate the principles of the Fundamental Rules.

2d. The subject of Fractions is important and difficult. Before studying it, most pupils require more mental discipline than is furnished by the elementary rules; this is acquired by the study of Compound Numbers.

3d. The *general principles* involved in their study, do not require a knowledge of Fractions. The examples involving fractions are few, and are introduced, as they should be, with other exercises in that subject.

Teachers, who prefer it, can direct their pupils to defer Compound Numbers until they have studied Fractions as far as page 159.

DEFINITIONS.

50. A **compound number** is made up of two or more *concrete numbers* of different denominations; as, 3 pecks 7 quarts 1 pint.

REM. 1.—The different denominations of a compound number must belong to the same *table;* thus, in the example given, the pecks may be *reduced* to quarts or pints, and the pints and quarts are *parts* of a peck. 3 pecks 7 dollars would not be a compound number.

REM. 2.—Compound numbers resemble simple numbers in the following particulars: the *denominations* of compound numbers correspond to the *orders* of simple numbers, and a certain number of units of a lower denomination make one unit of the next higher denomination.

REM. 3.—Most compound numbers differ from simple numbers in this; ten units of each lower denomination do not uniformly make one unit of the next higher denomination.

REM. 4.—In United States Money and the Metric System of Weights and Measures, however, ten units of a lower denomination do make one unit of the next higher denomination.

51. 1. The operations with compound numbers are *Reduction*, *Addition*, *Subtraction*, *Multiplication*, and *Division*.

2. **Reduction** is the process of changing the denomination of a number without altering its value.

Thus, 5 yards may be changed to feet; for, in 1 yard there are 3 feet; then, in 5 yards there are 5 times 3 feet, which are 15 feet.

3. Reduction takes place in two ways: 1st. From a higher denomination to a lower. 2d. From a lower denomination to a higher.

UNITED STATES MONEY.

52. United States money is the money of the United States of America.

TABLE.

10 mills, m.,	make	1 cent,	marked	ct.
10 cents	"	1 dime,	"	d.
10 dimes	"	1 dollar,	"	$.
10 dollars	"	1 eagle,	"	E.

REM. 1.—United States money was established, by act of Congress, in 1786. The first money coined, by the authority of the United States, was in 1793. The coins first made were copper cents. In 1794 silver dollars were made. Gold eagles were made in 1795; gold dollars, in 1849. Gold and silver are now both legally standard. The trade dollar was minted for Asiatic commerce.

REM. 2.—The coins of the United States are classed as *bronze, nickel, silver,* and *gold.* The name, value, composition, and weight of each coin are shown in the following

TABLE.

COIN.	VALUE.	COMPOSITION.	WEIGHT.
BRONZE.			
One cent.	1 cent.	95 parts copper, 5 parts tin & zinc.	48 grains Troy.
NICKEL.			
3-cent piece.	3 cents.	75 parts copper, 25 parts nickel.	30 grains Troy.
5-cent piece.	5 cents.	75 " " 25 " "	77.16 " "
SILVER.			
Dime.	10 cents.	90 parts silver, 10 parts copper.	2.5 grams.
Quarter dollar.	25 cents.	90 " " 10 " "	6.25 "
Half dollar.	50 cents.	90 " " 10 " "	12.5 "
Dollar.	100 cents.	90 " " 10 " "	412½ grains Troy.
GOLD.			
Dollar.	100 cents.	90 parts gold, 10 parts copper.	25.8 grains Troy.
Quarter eagle.	2½ dollars.	90 " " 10 " "	64.5 " "
Three dollar.	3 dollars.	90 " " 10 " "	77.4 " "
Half eagle.	5 dollars.	90 " " 10 " "	129 " "
Eagle.	10 dollars.	90 " " 10 " "	258 " "
Double eagle.	20 dollars.	90 " " 10 " "	516 " "

REM. 3.—A deviation in weight of ½ a grain to each piece, is allowed by law in the coinage of Double Eagles and Eagles; of ¼ of a grain in Half Eagles and the other gold pieces; of 1½ grains in all

silver pieces; of 3 grains in the five-cent piece; and of 2 grains in the three-cent piece and one cent.

REM. 4.—The mill is not coined. It is used only in calculations.

53. 1. A sum of money is expressed as *dollars and cents*, and, when written in figures, is always preceded by the *dollar sign* ($).

REM.—Calculations are sometimes carried out to mills, but, in business transactions, the final result is always taken to the nearest cent.

2. A period (.), called the *decimal point*, is used to separate the dollars and cents.

3. Eagles are read as tens of dollars, and dimes are read as tens of cents.

Thus, $24.56 is read 24 dollars 56 cents; *not* 2 eagles 4 dollars 5 dimes 6 cents. $16.375 is read 16 dollars 37 cents 5 mills.

4. Hence, *the figures to the left of the decimal point express a number of dollars; the two figures to the right of the decimal point, a number of cents; and the third figure to the right, mills.*

REM.—If the number of cents is less than 10, a cipher must be put in the tens' place.

EXAMPLES TO BE WRITTEN.

1. Twelve dollars seventeen cents eight mills.
2. Six dollars six cents six mills.
3. Seven dollars seven mills.
4. Forty dollars fifty-three cents five mills.
5. Two dollars three cents.
6. Twenty dollars two cents two mills.
7. One hundred dollars ten cents.
8. Two hundred dollars two cents.
9. Four hundred dollars one cent eight mills.

EXAMPLES TO BE READ.

$18.625	$ 70.015	$6.12	$ 29.00
$20.324	$100.28	$3.06	$100.03
$79.05	$150.05	$4.31	$ 20.05
$46.00	$100.00	$5.43	$ 40.125

REDUCTION OF U. S. MONEY.

54. 1. As there are 10 mills in 1 cent, in any number of cents there are 10 times as many mills as cents. Therefore to reduce cents to mills—

Rule.—*Multiply the number of cents by ten; that is, annex one cipher.*

2. Conversely, to reduce mills to cents—

Rule.—*Divide the number of mills by ten; that is, cut off one figure from the right.*

3. As there are 10 cents in 1 dime and 10 dimes in 1 dollar, there are $10 \times 10 = 100$ cents in 1 dollar; then, in any number of dollars there are 100 times as many cents as dollars. Therefore, to reduce dollars to cents—

Rule.—*Multiply the number of dollars by one hundred; that is, annex two ciphers.*

4. Conversely, to reduce cents to dollars—

Rule.—*Divide the number of cents by one hundred; that is, cut off two figures from the right.*

5. As there are 10 mills in 1 cent and 100 cents in 1 dollar, there are $100 \times 10 = 1000$ mills in 1 dollar; then, in any number of dollars there are 1000 times as many mills as dollars. Therefore, to reduce dollars to mills—

Rule.—*Multiply the number of dollars by one thousand: that is, annex three ciphers.*

6. Conversely to reduce mills to dollars.

Rule.—*Divide the number of mills by one thousand; that is, cut off three figures from the right.*

55. The reduction of mills or cents to dollars may be made simply with the decimal point. Thus,

1st. If the sum is mills. **Rule.**—*Put the decimal point between the third and fourth figures from the right.*

2d. If the sum is cents. **Rule.**—*Put the decimal point between the second and third figures from the right.*

1. Reduce 17 ct. to mills.
2. Reduce 28 ct. to mills.
3. Reduce 43 ct. and 6 m. to mills.
4. Reduce 70 ct. and 6 m. to mills.
5. Reduce 106 m. to cents.
6. Reduce 490 mills to cents.
7. Reduce 9 dollars to cents.
8. Reduce 14 dollars to cents.
9. Reduce 104 dollars to cents.
10. Reduce $60 and 13 ct. to cents.
11. Reduce $40 and 5 ct. to cents.
12. Reduce 375 ct. to dollars.
13. Reduce 9004 ct. to dollars.
14. Reduce 4 dollars to mills.
15. Reduce $14 and 2 ct. to mills.
16. Reduce 2465 mills to dollars.
17. Reduce 3007 mills to dollars.
18. Reduce 3187 cents to dollars.
19. Reduce 10375 mills to dollars.

ADDITION OF U. S. MONEY.

56. 1. Add together 4 dollars 12 cents 5 mills; 7 dollars 6 cents 2 mills; 20 dollars 43 cents; 10 dollars 5 mills; 16 dollars 87 cents 5 mills.

Rule.—1. *Write the numbers and add as in simple numbers.*

2. *Place the decimal point in the sum under the decimal points above.*

Proof.—The same as in Addition of Simple Numbers.

OPERATION.

$. ct. m.
4.125
7.062
20.430
10.005
16.875
$58.497

2. What is the sum of 17 dollars 15 cents; 23 dollars 43 cents; 7 dollars 19 cents; 8 dollars 37 cents; and 12 dollars 31 cents?

3. Add 18 dollars 4 cents 1 mill; 16 dollars 31 cents 7 mills; 100 dollars 50 cents 3 mills; and 87 dollars 33 cents 8 mills.

4. William had the following bills for collection: $43.75; $29.18; $17.63; $268.95; and $718.07: how much was to be collected?

5. Bought a gig for $200; a watch for $43.87; a suit of clothes for $56.93; a hat for $8.50; and a whip for $2.31: what was the amount?

6. A person has due him, five hundred and four dollars six cents; $420.19; one hundred and five dollars fifty cents; $304; $888.47: what is the whole amount due him?

7. Add five dollars seven cents; thirty dollars twenty cents three mills; one hundred dollars five mills; sixty dollars two cents; seven hundred dollars one cent one mill; $1000.10; forty dollars four mills; and $64.58 7.

SUBTRACTION OF U. S. MONEY.

57. 1. From one hundred dollars five cents three mills, take eighty dollars twenty cents and seven mills.

Rule.—1. *Write the numbers and subtract as in Simple Numbers.*

2. *Place the decimal point in the remainder under the decimal points above.*

OPERATION.

$.	ct.	m.
100.	05	3
80.	20	7
$19.	84	6

PROOF.—The same as in Subtraction of Simple Numbers.

2. From $29.342 take $17.265.
3. From $46.28 take $17.75.
4. From $20.05 take $5.50.
5. From $3, take 3 ct.
6. From $10, take 1 mill.
7. From $50, take 50 ct. 5 mills.
8. From one thousand dollars, take one dollar one cent and one mill.
9. B owes 1000 dollars 43 cents; if he pay nine hundred dollars sixty-eight cents, how much will he still owe?

MULTIPLICATION OF U. S. MONEY.

58. 1. What will 13 cows cost, at 47 dollars 12 cents 5 mills each

Rule.—1. *Multiply as in Simple Numbers.*

2. *Put the decimal point in the same place in the product, as it is in the multiplicand.*

OPERATION.

```
 $47.125
      13
  141375
  47125
$612.625
```

PROOF.—The same as in Multiplication of Simple Numbers.

2. Multiply $7.835 by 8.
3. Multiply $12, 9 ct. 3 m. by 9.
4. Multiply $23, 1 ct. 8 m. by 16.
5. Multiply $35, 14 ct. by 53.
6. Multiply $125, 2 ct. by 62.
7. Multiply $40, 4 ct. by 102.
8. Multiply 12 ct. 5 m. by 17.
9. Multiply $3.28 by 38.

10. What cost 338 barrels of cider, at 1 dollar 6 cents a barrel?

11. Sold 38 cords of wood, at 5 dollars 75 cents a cord: to what did it amount?

12. At 7 ct. a pound, what cost 465 pounds of sugar?

NOTE.—Instead of multiplying 7 cents by 465, multiply 465 by 7, which gives the same product, Art. 30. But, to place the decimal point, remember that 7 cents is the true multiplicand.

OPERATION.

465
.07
$32.55

13. What cost 89 yards of sheeting, at 34 ct. a yard?

14. What will 24 yards of cloth cost, at $5.67 a yard?

15. I have 169 sheep, valued at $2.69 each: what is the value of the whole?

16. If I sell 691 bushels of wheat, at $1.25 a bushel, what will it amount to?

17. I sold 73 hogsheads of molasses, of 63 gallons each, at 55 ct. a gallon: what is the sum?

18. What cost 4 barrels of sugar, of 281 pounds each, at 6 cents 5 mills a pound?

19. Bought 35 bolts of tape, of 10 yards each, at 1 cent a yard: what did it cost?

20. If I earn 13 ct. an hour, and work 11 hours a day, how much will I earn in 312 days?

21. I sold 18 bags of wheat, of 3 bushels each, at $1.25 a bushel: what is the amount?

22. What cost 150 acres of land, at 10 dollars 1 mill per acre?

23. What cost 17 bags of coffee, of 51 pounds each, at 24 cents 7 mills per pound?

DIVISION OF U. S. MONEY.

59. Case I.—To find how many times one sum of money is contained in another.

1. How much cloth, at 7 cents a yard, will $1.75 buy?

Solution.—As many yards as 7 cents is contained times in 175 cents, which are 25.

OPERATION.

$$7\overline{)175}$$
$$25$$

Rule.—1. *Reduce both sums of money to the same denomination.*

2. *Divide as in Simple Numbers.*

2. How much rice, at 9 cents a pound, can be bought for 72 cents?

3. How many towels, at 37 cents and 5 mills apiece, can be bought for $6?

4. How many yards of calico, at 8 cents a yard, can be bought for $2.80?

5. How many yards of ribbon, at 25 cents a yard, can be purchased for $3?

6. At $8.05 a barrel, how many barrels of flour will $161 purchase?

7. At 7 cents 5 mills each, how many oranges can be bought for $1.20?

8. At $1.125 per bushel, how many bushels of wheat can be purchased for $234?

Case II.—To divide a sum of money into a given number of equal parts.

1. A man worked 3 days for $3.75, what were his daily wages?

OPERATION.

Solution.—His daily wages were $3.75 ÷ 3 = $1.25.

$$\begin{array}{r} 3\,)\,\underline{3.75} \\ \$1.25 \end{array}$$

2. A farmer sold 6 bushels of wheat for $9: how much a bushel did he get?

Solution.—He got for each bushel $9÷6. $9 divided by 6 gives a quotient $1, with a remainder $3 = 300 cents. 300 cents divided by 6 gives a quotient 50 cents.

OPERATION.

$$\begin{array}{r} 6\,)\,\underline{9.00} \\ \$1.50 \end{array}$$

Rule.—1. *Divide as in Simple Number*

2. *Put the decimal point in the same place in the quotient as it is in the dividend.*

Rem. 1.—If the dividend is dollars, and the division not exact, annex two ciphers after the decimal point for cents; and, if necessary, a third cipher for mills.

Rem. 2.—Should there be a remainder after obtaining the mills, it may be indicated by the sign + placed after the quotient.

3. Divide 65 dollars equally among 8 persons.

4. A farmer received $29.61 for 23 bushels of wheat: how much was that per bushel?

5. If 4 acres of land cost $92.25, how much is that an acre?

6. Make an equal division of $57.50 among 8 persons.

7. A man received $25.76 for 16 days' work: how much was that a day?

8. I bought 755 bushels of apples for $328.425: what did they cost a bushel?

9. My salary is $800 a year: how much is that a day, there being 313 working days in the year?

10. Divide ten thousand dollars equally among 133 men: what is each man's share?

11. A man purchased a farm of 154 acres, for two thousand seven hundred and five dollars and 1 cent: what did it cost per acre?

12. I sold 15 kegs of butter, of 25 pounds each, for $60: how much was that a pound?

13. I bought 8 barrels of sugar, of 235 pounds each, for $122.20: what did 1 pound cost?

Promiscuous Examples.

60. 1. I owe A $47.50; B, $38.45; C, $15.47; D, $19.43: what sum do I owe?

2. A owes $35.25; B, $23.75; C, as much as A and B, and $1 more: what is the amount?

3. A paid me $18.38; B, $81.62; C, twice as much as A and B: how much did I receive?

4. I went to market with $5; I spent for butter 75 cents, for eggs 35 cents, for vegetables 50 cents, for flour $1.50: how much money was left?

5. A lady had $20; she bought a dress for $8.10, shoes for $5.65, eight yards of delaine at 25 cents a yard, and a shawl for $4: what sum was left?

6. I get $50 a month, and spend $30.50 of it: how much will I have left in 6 months?

7. A farmer sold his marketing for $21.75: he paid for sugar $3.85, for tea $1.25, for coffee $2.50, for spices $1.50: how much had he left?

8. I owe A $37.06; B, $200.85; C, $400; D, $236.75, and E $124.34; my property is worth $889.25: how much do I owe more than I am worth?

9. Bought 143 pounds of coffee, at 23 cents a pound: after paying $12.60, what was due?

10. A owed me $400: he paid me 435 bushels of corn, at 45 cents a bushel: what sum is due?

11. If B spend 65 cents a day, how much will he save in 365 days, his income being $400?

12. Bought 21 barrels of apples, of 3 bushels each, at 35 cents a bushel: what did they cost?

13. What cost four pieces of cambric, each containing 19 yards, at 23 cents a yard?

14. If 25 men perform a piece of work for $2000, and spend, while doing it, $163.75, what will be each man's share of the profits?

15. If 16 men receive $516 for 43 days' work, how much does each man earn a day?

16. C earned $90 in 40 days, working 10 hours a day: how much did he earn an hour?

17. A merchant failing, has goods worth $1000, and $500 in cash, to be equally divided among 22 creditors: how much will each receive?

MERCHANTS' BILLS.

A **Bill or Account**, is a written statement of articles bought or sold, with their prices, and entire cost.

18. Bought	9 pounds Coffee,	at	$0.32	per lb.	$
	4 pounds Tea,	"	1.25	do.	
	45 pounds Sugar	"	.09	do.	
	17 pounds Cheese	"	.20	do.	
What is the amount of my bill?					$15.33

19. Bought

22 yards Silk,	at	$1.75	per yd.	$
18 yards Muslin,	"	.15	do.	
25 yards Linen,	"	.65	do.	
6 yards Gingham,	"	.18	do.	

What is the whole amount?

20. Bought—

4 pounds Prunes,	at	$0.18	per lb.	$
8 pounds Peaches,	"	.23	do.	
7 pounds Rice,	"	.11	do.	
6 pounds Oat-meal,	"	.09	do.	
13 pounds Java Coffee,	"	.35	do.	
26 pounds Sugar,	"	.12	do.	

What is the whole amount?

21. Bought

43 yards Muslin,	at	$0.13	per yd.	$
28 yards Calico,	"	.09	do.	
23 yards Alpaca,	"	.23	do.	

What is the whole amount?

REDUCTION OF COMPOUND NUMBERS.

DRY MEASURE.

61. Dry Measure is used in measuring grain, vegetables, fruit, coal, etc.

TABLE.

2 pints (pt.)	make	1 quart,	marked	qt.
8 quarts	"	1 peck,	"	pk.
4 pecks	"	1 bushel,	"	bu.

REM. 1.—The *standard unit* of Dry Measure is the bushel; it is a cylindrical measure $18\frac{1}{2}$ inches in diameter, 8 inches deep, and contains $2150\frac{2}{5}$ cubic inches.

REM. 2.—When articles usually measured by the above table are sold by weight, the *bushel* is taken as the unit. The following table gives the legal weight of a bushel of various articles in avoirdupois pounds:

ARTICLES.	LB.	EXCEPTIONS.
Beans.	60	N. Y., 62; Me., 64.
Blue Grass Seed.	14	
Clover Seed.	60	Pa., 62; N. J., 64.
Coal (mineral).	80	Ind., 70 and 80; Ky., 76.
Corn (shelled).	56	Cal., 52; Ariz., 54; N. Y., 58.
Flax Seed.	56	Kan., 54; N. J., N. Y., 55.
Hemp Seed	44	
Oats.	32	Md., 26; Me., N. H., N. J., Pa., 30; Nebr., 34; Oregon, Wash., 36.
Potatoes.	60	Wash., 50; Ohio, 58.
Rye.	56	La., 32; Cal., 54. [N. and S. Dak., 80.
Salt.	50	Ky., Ill., 55; Mich., 56; Mass., 70; Col., 80;
Timothy Seed.	45	Wash., 40; N. and S. Dak., 42; N. Y., 44.
Wheat.	60	

TO TEACHERS.—Numerous questions should be asked on each table similar to the following:

1. How many pints in 2 quarts? In 4? In 6? In 8? In 10?
2. How many quarts in 3 pk.? In 5? In 7? In 9?
3. How many pecks in 9 bu.? In 11? In 13? In 15? In 17? In 19?
4. How many quarts in 10 bu.? In 12? In 14? In 18? In 25? In 56?
5. How many pecks in 16 qt.? In 24? In 32? In 40? In 48? In 64?
6. How many bushels in 32 qt.? In 64? In 96?
7. How many pints in 1 bu.? In 2? In 5?

62. The preceding examples show that—

To reduce quarts to pints, multiply the number of quarts by the number of pints in a quart.

To reduce pecks to quarts, or bushels to pecks, multiply in the same manner.

Hence, to reduce from a higher to a lower denomination, ***multiply*** **by the number of units of the lower denomination that make one unit of the higher denomination.**

They also show that—

To reduce pints to quarts, divide the number of pints by the number of pints in a quart.

To reduce quarts to pecks, or pecks to bushels, divide in the same manner.

Hence, to reduce from a lower to a higher denomination, ***divide*** **by the number of units of the lower denomination that make one unit of the higher denomination.**

1. Reduce 3 bushels to pints.

OPERATION.

3	bu.
4	
12	pk.
8	
96	qt.
2	
192	pt.

SOLUTION.—To reduce bu. to pk. multiply by 4, because there are 4 pk. in 1 bu., or 4 times as many pk. as bu. To reduce pk. to qt. multiply by 8, because there are 8 qt. in 1 pk. To reduce qt. to pt. multiply by 2, because there are 2 pt. in 1 qt.

2. Reduce 192 pints to bushels.

OPERATION.

2)	192	pt.
8)	96	qt.
4)	12	pk.
	3	bu.

SOLUTION.—To reduce pt. to qt. divide by 2, because there are 2 pt. in 1 qt. To reduce qt. to pk. divide by 8, because there are 8 qt. in 1 pk. To reduce pk. to bu. divide by 4, because there are 4 pk. in 1 bu.

The two preceding examples show that *reduction from a higher to a lower denomination, and from a lower to a higher denomination, prove each other.*

3. Reduce 7 bu. 3 pk. 6 qt. 1 pt. to pints.

SOLUTION.—Multiply the bu. by 4, making 28 pk., and add the 3 pk. Then multiply the 31 pk. by 8 and add the 6 qt.; multiply the 254 qt. by 2 and add the 1 pt.; the result is 509 pt.

OPERATION.

```
bu. pk. qt. pt.
 7   3   6   1
 4
 31 pk. in 7 bu. 3 pk.
  8
254 qt. in 31 pk. 6 qt.
  2
509 pt. in the whole
```

4. Reduce 509 pt. to bushels.

SOLUTION.—To reduce pt. to qt. divide by 2, and there is 1 left; as the dividend is pt. the remainder must be pt. To reduce qt. to pk. divide by 8, and 6 qt. are left. To reduce pk. to bu. divide by 4, and 3 pk. are left. The answer is, therefore, 7 bu. 3 pk. 6 qt. 1 pt.

OPERATION.

```
2)509
8)254 qt. 1 pt.
 4)31 pk. 6 qt.
    7 bu. 3 pk.
```

63. RULES FOR REDUCTION.

I. FROM A HIGHER TO A LOWER DENOMINATION.

1. *Multiply the highest denomination given, by that number of the next lower which makes a unit of the higher.*

2. *Add to the product the number, if any, of the lower denomination.*

3. *Proceed in like manner with the result thus obtained, till the whole is reduced to the required denomination.*

II. FROM A LOWER TO A HIGHER DENOMINATION.

1. *Divide the given quantity by that number of its own denomination which makes a unit of the next higher.*

2. *Proceed in like manner with the quotient thus obtained, till the whole is reduced to the required denomination.*

3. *The last quotient, with the several remainders, if any, annexed, will be the answer.*

PROOF.—Reverse the operation: that is, reduce the answer to the denomination from which it was derived. If this result is the same as the quantity given, the work is correct.

5. Reduce 4 bu. 2 pk. 1 qt. to pints.
6. Reduce 7 bu. 3 pk. 7 qt. 1 pint to pints.
7. Reduce 3 bu. 1 pt. to pints.
8. Reduce 384 pt. to bushels.
9. Reduce 47 pt. to pecks.
10. Reduce 95 pt. to bushels.
11. Reduce 508 pt. to bushels.

LIQUID MEASURE.

64. Liquid Measure is used for measuring all liquids.

TABLE.

4 gills (gi.)	make	1 pint,	marked	pt.
2 pints	"	1 quart,	"	qt.
4 quarts	"	1 gallon,	"	gal.

REM.—The *standard unit* of liquid measure is the *gallon*, which contains 231 cubic inches.

1. Reduce 17 gal. to pints.
2. Reduce 13 gal. to gills.
3. Reduce 126 gal. to pints.
4. Reduce 1260 gal. to gills.
5. Reduce 1120 gi. to gallons.
6. How many gallons in 1848 cubic inches?
7. How many gallons in a vessel containing 138138 cubic inches?

AVOIRDUPOIS WEIGHT.

65. Avoirdupois Weight is used for weighing all ordinary articles.

TABLE.

16 ounces (oz.)	make	1 pound,	"	lb.
100 pounds	"	1 hundred-weight,	"	cwt.
20 cwt., or 2000 lb.,	"	1 ton,	"	T.

REM. 1.—The standard avoirdupois pound of the United States is determined from the Troy pound, and contains 7000 grains Troy.

REM. 2.—At the Custom House (and in some trades) 2240 pounds are considered a ton.

1. Reduce 2 cwt. to pounds.
2. Reduce 3 cwt. 75 lb. to pounds.
3. Reduce 1 T. 2 cwt. to pounds.
4. Reduce 3 T. 75 lb. to pounds.
5. Reduce 4 cwt. 44 lb. to pounds.
6. Reduce 5 T. 90 lb. to pounds.
7. Reduce 2 cwt. 77 lb. 12 oz. to ounces.
8. Reduce 2 cwt. 17 lb. 3 oz. to ounces.
9. Reduce 1 T. 6 cwt. 4 lb. 2 oz. to ounces.
10. Reduce 4803 lb. to cwt.
11. Reduce 22400 lb. to tons.
12. Reduce 2048000 oz. to tons.
13. Reduce 64546 oz. to cwt.
14. Reduce 97203 oz. to tons.
15. Reduce 544272 oz. to tons.
16. What is the total weight of 52 parcels, each containing 18 lb.?
17. What is the weight of 180 iron castings, each weighing 75 lb.?

LONG MEASURE.

66. Long Measure is used in measuring distances, or length, in any direction.

TABLE.

12 inches (in.)	make	1 foot,	marked	ft.
3 feet	"	1 yard,	"	yd.
$5\frac{1}{2}$ yards, or $16\frac{1}{2}$ feet,	"	1 rod,	"	rd.
320 rods	"	1 mile,	"	mi.

REM.—The standard unit of length is the *yard*. The standard yard for the United States is preserved at Washington. A copy of this standard is kept at each state capital.

1. Reduce 2 yd. 2 ft. 7 in. to inches.
2. Reduce 7 yd. 11 in. to inches.
3. Reduce 12 mi. to rods.
4. Reduce 7 mi. 240 rd. to rods.
5. Reduce 9 mi. 31 rd. to rods.
6. Reduce 133 in. to yards.
7. Reduce 181 in. to yards.
8. Reduce 2240 rd. to miles.
9. Reduce 2200 rd. to miles.
10. Reduce 1 mi. to yards.
11. Reduce 1 mi. to feet.

SQUARE MEASURE.

67. Square Measure is used in measuring any thing which has both length and breadth; that is, *two* dimensions.

A figure having 4 equal sides and 4 right angles is a *square*.

A *square inch* is a square, each side of which is 1 inch in length.

A *square foot* is a square, each side of which is 1 foot.

A *square yard* is a square, each side of which is 1 yard (3 feet).

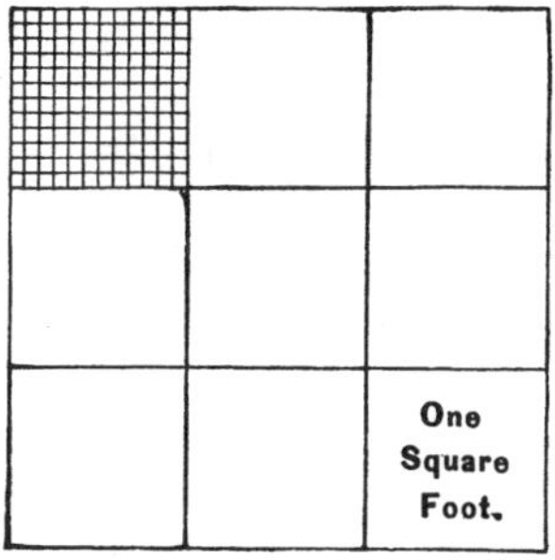

Suppose the figure to represent a square yard. It will then be 3 feet each way, and contain 9 square feet. Each foot will be 12 inches each way, and contain 144 square inches.

The number of small squares in any large square is, therefore, equal to the number of units in one side multiplied by itself.

REM.—By 3 *feet square* is meant a square figure, each side of which is 3 feet, or 9 *square feet;* but by 3 *square feet* is meant 3 squares each one foot long and one foot wide; therefore, the difference in area between a figure 3 *feet square* and one containing 3 *square feet,* is 6 square feet.

TABLE.

144	square inches	make	1 square foot,	marked	sq. ft.
9	square feet	"	1 square yard,	"	sq. yd.
$30\frac{1}{4}$	square yards	"	1 square rod,	"	sq. rd.
160	square rods	"	1 acre,	"	A.
640	acres	"	1 square mile,	"	sq. mi.

1. Reduce 8 sq. yd. to square inches.
2. Reduce 4 A. to square rods.
3. Reduce 1 sq. mi. to square rods.
4. Reduce 2 sq. yd. 3 sq. ft. to sq. in.
5. Reduce 5 A. 100 sq. rd. to sq. rd.
6. Reduce 960 sq. rd. to acres.

7. Reduce 3888 sq. in. to square yards.
8. Reduce 20000 sq. rd. to acres.
9. Reduce 515280 sq. rd. to square miles.

10. Reduce 4176 sq. in. to sq. yd.

68. A **Rectangle** is a figure having four sides and four right angles. See the figure below.

The **unit of measure** for surfaces, is a *square* whose side is a linear unit; as a square inch, a square foot, etc.

The **Area** or Superficial contents of a figure, is the number of times it contains its *unit of measure.*

1. How many square inches in a board 4 inches long and 3 inches wide?

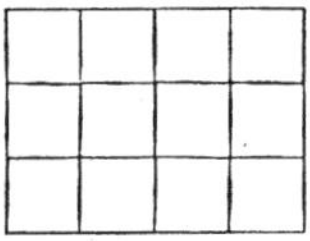

EXPLANATION.—Dividing each of the longer sides into 4 equal parts, the shorter sides into 3 equal parts, and joining the opposite divisions by straight lines, the surface is divided into squares.

In each of the longer rows there are 4 squares, that is, as many as there are inches in the longer side; and there are as many such rows as there are inches in the shorter side. Hence,

The whole number of squares in the board is equal to the product obtained by multiplying together the numbers representing the length and breadth; that is, $4 \times 3 = 12$.

Rule for Finding the Area of a Rectangle.—*Multiply the length by the breadth; the product will be the area.*

REM.—Both the length and breadth, if not in units of the same denomination, should, be made so before multiplying.

2. In a floor 16 feet long and 12 feet wide, how many square feet?

3. How many square yards of carpeting will cover a room 5 yards long and 4 yards wide?

4. How many square yards of carpeting will cover two rooms, one 18 feet long and 12 feet wide, the other 21 feet long and 15 feet wide?

5. How many square yards in a ceiling 18 feet long and 14 feet wide?

6. In a field 35 rods long and 32 rods wide, how many acres?

7. How much will it cost to carpet two rooms, each 18 feet long and 15 feet wide, if the carpet costs $1.25 per square yard?

8. What will it cost to plaster a ceiling 21 feet long and 18 feet wide, at 17 cents per square yard?

69. The Area of a Rectangle being equal to the product of the length by the breadth, and as the product of two numbers, divided by either of them, gives the other (**36**, 4); therefore,

Rule.—*If the area of a rectangle be divided by either side, the quotient will be the other side.*

Illustration.

In Example 1, **68**, if the area 12 be divided by 4, the quotient 3 is the width; or, divide 12 by 3, the quotient 4 is the length.

Rem.—Dividing the area of a rectangle by one of its sides, is really dividing the number of squares in the rectangle by the number of squares on one of its sides.

In dividing 12 by 4, the latter is not 4 linear inches, but the number of square inches in a rectangle 4 in. long and 1 in. wide. See figure, Art. **68**.

1. A floor containing 132 square feet, is 11 feet wide: what is its length?

2. A floor is 18 feet long, and contains 30 square yards: what is its width?

3. A field containing 9 acres, is 45 rods in length: what is its width?

4 A field 35 rods wide, contains 21 acres: what is its length?

SOLID OR CUBIC MEASURE.

70. **Solid or Cubic Measure** is used in measuring things having length, breadth, and thickness; that is, *three dimensions.*

A **Cube** is a solid, having 6 equal faces, which are squares.

REM.—If each side of a cube is 1 inch long, it is called a cubic inch; if each side is 3 feet (1 yard) long, as represented in the figure, it is a cubic or solid yard.

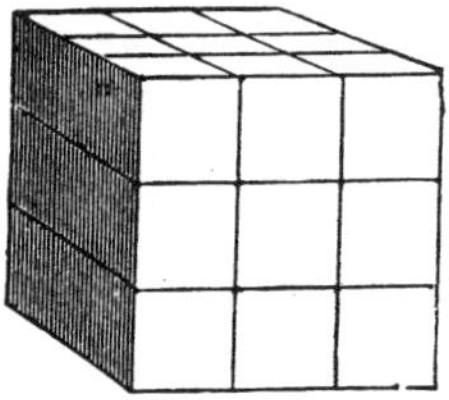

The base of a cube, being 1 square yard, contains $3 \times 3 = 9$ square feet; and 1 foot high on this base, contains 9 solid feet; 2 feet high contains $9 \times 2 = 18$ solid feet; 3 feet high contains $9 \times 3 = 27$ solid feet. Also, it may be shown that 1 solid or *cubic* foot contains $12 \times 12 \times 12 = 1728$ solid or *cubic* inches.

Hence, the number of small cubes in any large cube, is equal to the length, breadth, and thickness, multiplied together.

REM.—Any solid, whose corners resemble a cube, is a rectangular solid; boxes and cellars are generally of this form.

The solid contents of a rectangular solid are found, as in the cube, by multiplying together the length, breadth, and thickness.

TABLE.

1728 cubic inches (cu. in.)	make 1 cubic foot,	marked	cu. ft.
27 cubic feet	" 1 cubic yard,	"	cu. yd.
128 cubic feet $= 8 \times 4 \times 4 =$ 8 ft. long, 4 ft. wide, and 4 ft. high, make	1 cord,	"	C.

REM. 1.—A cord foot is 1 foot in length of the pile which makes a cord. It is 4 feet wide, 4 feet high, and 1 foot long; hence, it contains 16 cubic feet, and 8 cord feet make 1 cord.

REM. 2.—A perch of stone is a mass $16\frac{1}{2}$ ft. long, $1\frac{1}{2}$ ft. wide, and 1 ft. high, and contains $24\frac{3}{4}$ cu. ft.

1. Reduce 2 cu. yd. to cubic inches.
2. Reduce 28 cords of wood to cu. ft.
3. Reduce 34 cords of wood to cu. in.
4. Reduce 1 cord of wood to cu. in.
5. Reduce 63936 cu. in. to cu. yd.
6. How many cubic feet in a rectangular solid, 8 ft. long, 5 ft. wide, 4 ft. thick?
7. How many cubic yards of excavation in a cellar 8 yd. long, 5 yd. wide, 2 yd. deep?
8. How many cubic yards in a cellar, 18 feet long, 15 feet wide, 7 feet deep?
9. In a pile of wood 40 feet long, 12 feet wide, and 8 feet high, how many cords?
10. What will be the cost of a pile of wood 80 feet long, 8 feet high, and 4 feet thick, at $5.50 per cord?

11. What will be the cost of excavating a cellar 24 ft. long, 15 ft. wide, and 6 ft. deep, at $1.25 per cubic yard or load?

TIME MEASURE.

71. **Time Measure** is used in measuring time.

TABLE.

60 seconds (sec.)	make	1 minute,	marked min.
60 minutes	"	1 hour,	" hr.
24 hours	"	1 day,	" da.
365 days, 6 hours	"	1 year,	" yr.
100 years	"	1 century,	" cen.

Also, 7 days	make	1 week,	marked wk.
4 weeks	"	1 month (nearly),	" mon
12 calendar months	"	1 year,	" yr.
365 days	"	1 common year.	
366 days	"	1 leap year.	

REM. 1.—The exact length of the mean solar, or tropical year, is 365 days, 5 hours, 48 minutes, 46 seconds.

To correct the error of considering 365 days as the length of the year, the following rule has been adopted:

Every year whose number is not divisible by 4, consists of 365 days.

Every year whose number is divisible by 100, but not by 400, consists of 365 days.

Every year, except the even centuries, whose number is divisible by 4, and the even centuries divisible by 400, consist of 366 days.

The year containing 366 days is called Leap year, and the extra day is added to February, giving it 29, instead of 28 days.

REM. 2.—Among nearly all civilized nations, the year is divided into 12 calendar months, numbered, in their order, as follows:

January,	1st month,	31 days.		July,	7th month,	31 days.
February,	2d "	28 "		August,	8th "	31 "
March,	3d "	31 "		September,	9th "	30 "
April,	4th "	30 "		October,	10th "	31 "
May,	5th "	31 "		November,	11th "	30 "
June,	6th "	30 "		December,	12th "	31 "

1. Reduce 2 hr. to seconds. 7200 sec.
2. Reduce 7 da. to minutes. 10080 min.
3. Reduce 1 da. 3 hr. 44 min. 3 sec. to seconds. 99843 sec.
4. Reduce 9 wk. 6 da. 10 hr. 40 min. to minutes. 100000 min.
5. Reduce 4 wk. 3 da. 4 min. to minutes. 44644 min.
6. Reduce 10800 seconds to hours. 3 hr.
7. Reduce 432000 seconds to days. 5 da.
8. Reduce 7322 seconds to hours. 2 hr. 2 min. 2 sec.
9. Reduce 4323 minutes to days. 3 da. 3 min.
10. Reduce 20280 minutes to weeks. 2 wk. 2 hr.
11. Reduce 41761 min. to months. 1 mo. 1 da. 1 min.

MISCELLANEOUS TABLES.

I. MEASURES OF WEIGHT.

72. Troy Weight is used in weighing gold, silver, and jewels.

24 grains (gr.)	make	1 pennyweight,	marked	pwt.
20 pennyweights	"	1 ounce,	"	oz.
12 ounces	"	1 pound,	"	lb.

The *Standard Unit* of all weight in the United States is the *Troy pound,* containing 5760 grains.

Apothecaries Weight is used only in *compounding* medicines.

20 grains (gr.)	make	1 scruple,	marked	℈.
3 scruples	"	1 dram,	"	ʒ.
8 drams	"	1 ounce,	"	℥.
12 ounces	"	1 pound,	"	℔.

The following are also used by apothecaries:

60 minims (or drops) ♏,	make	1 fluid drachm,	marked	f. ʒ.
8 fluid drachms	"	1 fluid ounce,	"	f. ℥.
16 fluid ounces	"	1 pt. (octarius)	"	O.
8 pints	"	1 gal. (congius)	"	cong.

II. MEASURES OF LENGTH.

The following measures are often mentioned and most of them are still used in special professions:

12 lines	=1 inch.	3 feet	=1 pace.
3 barleycorns	=1 inch.	6 feet	=1 fathom.
4 inches	=1 hand.	3 miles	=1 league.
9 inches	=1 span.	$69\frac{1}{6}$ miles (nearly)	=1 degree.

Surveyors use a chain four rods long, divided into 100 links of $7\frac{92}{100}$ inches each.

Engineers divide the foot into tenths and hundredths. The yard is also divided similarly in estimating duties at the custom houses.

A degree is divided into 60 nautical or geographic miles.

A nautical mile or *knot* is, therefore, nearly $1\frac{1}{6}$ common miles.

Circular Measure is used in measuring circles.

60 seconds (″)	make	1 minute,	marked	′.
60 minutes	"	1 degree,	"	°.
360 degrees	"	1 circle.		

REM.—The circumference is also divided into *quadrants* of 90° each, and into *signs* of 30° each.

III. MISCELLANEOUS TABLE.

12 things	make	1 dozen,	marked doz.
12 dozen	"	1 gross,	" gr.
12 gross	"	1 great gross.	
20 things	"	1 score.	

100 pounds of nails,	make	1 keg.
196 pounds of flour	"	1 barrel.

200 pounds of pork or beef	make	1 barrel
240 pounds of lime	"	1 cask.

24 sheets of paper	make	1 quire.
20 quires	"	1 ream.
2 reams	"	1 bundle.

A sheet folded in

2 leaves	is called	a folio.
4 "	" "	a quarto, or 4to.
8 "	" "	an octavo, or 8vo.
12 "	" "	a duodecimo, or 12mo.
16 "	" "	a 16mo.

Examples in Miscellaneous Tables.

73. 1. Reduce 5 lb. 4 oz. Troy to ounces.

2. Reduce 9 lb. 3 oz. 5 pwt. to pwt.

3. Reduce 8 lb. 9 oz. 13 pwt. 17 gr. to gr.

4. Reduce 805 pwt. to pounds.

5. Reduce 12530 gr. to pounds.

6. Reduce 4 lb. 5 ℥ 2 gr. to grains.

7. Reduce 7 lb. 2 ℥ 1 ℈ to grains.

8. Reduce 431 ʒ to pounds.

9. Reduce 975 ℈ to pounds.

10. Reduce 6321 gr. to pounds.

11. Reduce 4 cong. 7 f. ℥ to fluid drams.

12. Reduce 5 O. 6 f. ℥ 3 f. ʒ to minims.

13. Reduce 2469 f. ʒ to gallons.

14. Reduce 3 yd. to barleycorns.

15. How many lines in 1 foot 6 inches?

16. What is the height of a horse of 16½ hands?

17. A field measures 24 chains in length and 15 chains in breadth: how many acres in it?

18. A cistern contains 267 cubic feet 624 cubic inches: how many gallons does it hold? (Art. **64**, Rem.).

19. Reduce 8° 41′ 45″ to seconds.

20. Reduce 61° 59′ 28″ to seconds.

21. Reduce 915′ to degrees.

22. Reduce 3661″ to degrees.

23. What cost 6 gross of screws at 5 cents a dozen?

24. A man is 4 score and 10: how old is he?

25. At 18 cents a quire, what will 3 bundles of paper cost?

26. How many sheets of paper will be required for a a 12mo. book of 336 pages?

27. An octavo work in 5 volumes has 512 pages in Vol. 1, 528 in Vol. 2, 528 in Vol. 3, 512 in Vol. 4, and 496 in Vol. 5: how much paper was used for one copy of the whole work?

PROMISCUOUS EXAMPLES.

74. 1. What cost 2 bu. of plums, at 5 ct. a pint?

2. What cost 3 bu. 2 pk. of peaches, at 50 ct. a peck?

3. What cost 3 pk. 3 qt. of barley, at 3 ct. a pint?

4. At 15 ct. a peck, how many bushels of apples can be bought for $3?

5. If salt cost 2 ct. a pint, how much can be bought with $1.66?

6. I put 91 bu. of wheat into bags containing 3 bu. 2 pk. each: how many bags were required?

REM.—Reduce both quantities to pecks, and then divide.

7. How many spikes, weighing 4 oz. each, are in a parcel weighing 15 lb. 12 oz.?

8. I bought 44 cwt. 52 lb. of cheese; each cheese weighed 9 lb. 15 oz.: how many cheeses did I buy?

9. How many kegs, of 84 lb. each, can be filled from a hogshead of sugar weighing 14 cwt. 28 lb.?

10. How many boxes, containing 12 lb. each, can be filled from 7 cwt. 56 lb. of tomatoes?

11. If a family use 3 lb. 13 oz. of sugar a week, how long will 6 cwt. 10 lb. last them?

12. What will 2 acres 125 square rods of land cost, at 20 cents a square rod?

13. A farmer has a field of 16 A. 53 sq. rd. to divide into lots of 1 A. 41 sq. rd. each: how many lots will it make?

14. How many cu. in. in a block of marble 2 ft. long, 2 ft. high, 2 ft. wide?

15. One cu. ft. of water weighs 1000 oz. avoirdupois: what do 5 cu. ft. weigh?

16. What is the weight of a quantity of water occupying the space of 1 cord of wood, each cubic foot of water weighing 1000 ounces avoirdupois?

17. A cubic foot of oak weighs 950 oz. avoirdupois: what do 2 cords of oak weigh?

18. Find the cost of 63 gallons of milk, at 20 cents a pint.

19. Find the cost of 5 barrels of molasses, each containing 31 gal. 2 qt., at 10 cents a quart.

20. At 5 cents a pint, what quantity of molasses can be bought for $2?

21. How many dozen bottles, each bottle holding 3 qt. 1 pt., can be filled from 63 gal. of cider?

22. How many kegs, of 4 gal. 3 qt. 1 pt. each, can be filled from 58 gal. 2 qt.?

23. If a human heart beat 70 times a minute, how many times will it beat in a day?

24. How many seconds in the month of February, 1876?

25. If a ship sail 8 miles an hour, how many miles will it sail in 3 wk. 2 da. 3 hr.?

26. A horse is fed 1 peck of oats daily. If oats cost 44 cents a bushel, how much will it cost to feed him a year of 365 days?

27. A flour dealer bought 40 barrels of flour for 3 ct. a pound, and sold it for 5 ct. a pound: how much did he gain?

ADDITION OF COMPOUND NUMBERS.

75. When the numbers to be added are compound, the operation is called *Addition of Compound Numbers.*

1. A farmer sold three lots of wheat: the first lot contained 25 bu. 3 pk.; the second, 14 bu. 2 pk.; the third, 32 bu. 1 pk.: how much did he sell?

Solution.—Place units of the same denomination in the same column (Art. **17**). Beginning with pecks, and adding, the sum is 6, which is reduced to bushels by dividing by 4, the number of pecks in a bushel, and there being 2 pecks left, write the 2 under the column of pecks, and carry the 1 bushel to the column of bushels; adding this to the bushels, the sum is 72, which write under the column of bushels.

OPERATION.

bu.	pk.
25	3
14	2
32	1
72	2

(2)

bu.	pk.	qt.	pt.
3	2	0	1
4	0	6	1
1	3	7	1
9	2	6	1

(3)

bu.	pk.	qt.	pt.
7	3	7	1
6	2	0	0
9	2	4	1
24	0	4	0

Rule.—1. *Write the numbers to be added, placing units of the same denomination in the same column.*

2. *Begin with the lowest denomination, add the numbers, and divide their sum by the number of units of this denomination which make a unit of the next higher.*

3. *Write the remainder under the column added, and carry the quotient to the next column.*

4. *Proceed in the same manner with all the columns to the last, under which write its entire sum.*

Proof.—The same as in Addition of Simple Numbers.

Rem. 1.—In writing compound numbers, if any intermediate denomination is wanting, supply its place with a cipher.

Rem. 2.—In adding simple numbers we carry one for every ten, because ten units of a lower order always make one of the next higher; but, in compound numbers, the scale varies, and we carry one for the number of the lower order, which makes one of the next higher.

Examples.

DRY MEASURE.

(4)

bu.	pk.	qt.
4	3	7
5	2	2
7	1	6

(5)

bu.	pk.	qt.	pt.
8	1	7	1
7	3	2	1
9	2	7	1

LIQUID MEASURE.

(6)

qt.	pt.	gi.
7	1	3
6	0	2
9	1	3

(7)

gal.	qt.	pt.	gi.
40	3	1	3
16	1	0	2
71	2	1	2

AVOIRDUPOIS WEIGHT.

(8)

T.	cwt.	lb.	oz.
45	3	53	10
14	14	75	15
19	17	18	13

(9)

cwt.	lb.	oz.
16	85	14
15	90	13
18	74	12

LONG MEASURE.

(10)

mi.	rd.
28	129
64	280
17	275

(11)

yd.	ft.	in.
4	2	11
3	1	9
5	1	8

SQUARE MEASURE.

(12)

A.	sq. rd.
41	51
64	104
193	155

(13)

sq. yd.	sq. ft.	sq. in.
15	8	115
20	7	109
14	5	137

CUBIC MEASURE.

(14)

C.	cu. ft.	cu. in.
13	28	390
15	90	874
20	67	983

(15)

cu. yd.	cu. ft.	cu. in.
50	18	900
45	17	828
46	20	990

TIME MEASURE.

(16)

da.	hr.	min.	sec.
16	18	28	47
13	15	49	59
19	16	53	42

(17)

mo.	wk.	da.	hr.	min.	sec.
3	0	0	23	51	40
1	2	4	19	30	37
3	1	5	13	27	18

18. Five loads of wheat measured thus: 21 bu. 3 pk.; 14 bu. 1 pk.; 23 bu. 2 pk.; 18 bu. 1 pk.; 22 bu. 1 pk.: how many bushels in all?

19. A farmer raised of oats 200 bu. 3 pk.; barley, 143 bu. 1 pk.; corn, 400 bu. 3 pk.; wheat, 255 bu. 1 pk.: how much in all?

20. A grocer sold 5 hogsheads of sugar: the first weighed 8 cwt. 36 lb.; the second, 4 cwt. 64 lb.; the third, 5 cwt. 19 lb.; the fourth, 7 cwt. 75 lb.; the fifth, 7 cwt. 84 lb.: what did all weigh?

21. Add 13 lb. 11 oz.; 17 lb. 13 oz.; 14 lb. 14 oz.; 16 lb.; 19 lb. 7 oz.; and 17 lb. 9 oz.

22. Two men depart from the same place: one travels 104 mi. 50 rd. due east; the other, 95 mi. 270 rd. due west: how far are they apart?

23. A man has 3 farms: in the first are 186 A. 134 sq. rd.; in the second, 286 A. 17 sq. rd.; in the third, 113 A. 89 sq. rd.: how much in all?

24. Add 17 sq. yd. 3 sq. ft. 119 sq. in.; 18 sq. yd. 141 sq. in.; 23 sq. yd. 7 sq. ft.; 29 sq. yd. 5 sq. ft. 116 sq. in.

25. A has 4 piles of wood: in the first, 7 C. 78 cu. ft.; the second, 16 C. 24 cu. ft.; the third, 35 C. 127 cu. ft.; the fourth, 29 C. 10 cu. ft.: how much in all?

26. I sold 4642 gal. 3 qt. 1 pt. of milk to A; 945 gal. to B; 1707 gal. 1 pt. to C; 10206 gal. 1 qt. to D: how many hogsheads of 63 gal. each did I sell?

SUBTRACTION OF COMPOUND NUMBERS.

76. When two given numbers are compound, the operation of finding their difference is called *Subtraction of Compound Numbers.*

1. I have 67 bu. 2 pk. of wheat: how much will remain after selling 34 bu. 3 pk.?

SOLUTION.—Write the less number under the greater, placing units of the same denomination in the same column. 3 pk. can not be taken from 2 pk., but 1 bu. being taken from 67 bu. reduced to pk., and added to the 2 pk., gives 6 pk.; 3 pk. from 6 pk. leaves 3 pk.; 34 bu. from 66 bu. leaves 32 bu. The difference is, therefore, 32 bu. 3 pk.

OPERATION.

bu.	pk.
67	2
34	3
32	3

REM.—Instead of diminishing the 67 bu. by 1, the result will be the same to increase the lower number 84 bu. by 1, as is done in subtraction of simple numbers.

(2)

	bu.	pk.	qt.	pt.
From	12	0	1	0
Take	8	2	1	1
	3	1	7	1

(3)

bu.	pk.	qt.	pt.
5	0	0	0
1	0	0	1
3	3	7	1

Rule.—1. *Write the less number under the greater, placing units of the same denomination in the same column.*

2. *Begin with the lowest denomination, and, if possible, take the lower number from the one above it.*

3. *But, if the lower number of any denomination be greater than the upper, increase the upper number by as many units of that denomination as make one of the next higher; subtract as before, and carry one to the lower number of the next higher denomination.*

4. *Proceed in the same manner with each denomination.*

PROOF.—The same as in Subtraction of Simple Numbers.

REM.—The resemblance between subtraction of simple, and of compound numbers, is the same as in Addition **75**, Rem. 2.

EXAMPLES.

LIQUID MEASURE.

(4)

	gal.	qt.	pt.
From	17	2	1
Take	13	3	0

(5)

gal.	qt.	pt.	gi.
43	1	1	2
23	3	1	3

AVOIRDUPOIS WEIGHT.

(6)

	T.	cwt.	lb.
From	14	12	50
Take	10	13	75

(7)

T.	cwt.	lb.	oz.
16	7	18	14
5	6	75	15

LONG MEASURE.

(8)

	mi.	rd.
From	18	198
Take	11	236

(9)

yd.	ft.	in.
4	1	10
2	1	11

SQUARE MEASURE.

(10)

	A.	sq. rd.
From	327	148
Take	77	155

(11)

sq. yd.	sq. ft.	sq. in.
19	6	72
16	6	112

CUBIC MEASURE.

(12)

	C.	cu. ft.
From	28	116
Take	19	119

(13)

cu. yd.	cu. ft.	cu. in.
18	7	927
9	15	928

TIME MEASURE.

(14)

	hr.	min.	sec.
From	18	43	27
Take	17	51	45

(15)

da.	hr.	min.	sec.
245	17	40	37
190	11	44	42

16. If 2 bu. 1 pk. 1 qt. be taken from a bag containing 4 bushels of hickory nuts, what quantity will remain?

17. From 100 bu. take 24 bu. 1 pt.

18. I bought 46 lb. 4 oz. of rice: after selling 19 lb. 8 oz., how much remained?

19. A wagon loaded with hay weighs 32 cwt. 66 lb.; the wagon alone weighs 8 cwt. 67 lb.: what is the weight of the hay?

20. It is 24899 miles round the earth: after a man has traveled 100 mi. 41 rd. what distance will remain?

21. I had a farm containing 146 A. 80 sq. rd. of land. I gave my son 86 A. 94 sq. rd.: how much was left?

22. From 8 C. 50 cu. ft. of wood, 3 C. 75 cu. ft. are taken: how much is left?

23. A cask of wine containing 63 gal. leaked; only 51 gal. 1 qt. 2 gi. remained: how much was lost?

24. From 5 da. 10 hr. 27 min. 15 sec. take 2 da. 4 hr. 13 min. 29 sec.

77. In finding the time between any two dates, consider 30 days 1 month, and 12 months 1 year.

1. A note, dated April 14, 1875, was paid February 12, 1877: find the time between these dates.

Solution.—In writing the dates, observe that February is the 2d month of the year and April the 4th; then, from 1877 yr. 2 mo. 12 da. subtract 1875 yr. 4 mo. 14 da. The remainder is 1 yr. 9 mo. 28 da.

OPERATION.

yr.	mon.	da.
1877	2	12
1875	4	14
1	9	28

2. The Independence of the United States was declared July 4, 1776: what length of time had elapsed on the 1st of September, 1876?

3. The first crusade ended July 15, 1099; the third crusade, July 12, 1191: find the difference of time between these dates.

4. Magna Charta was signed June 15, 1215; Mary, Queen of Scots, was beheaded February 8, 1587: find the difference of time between these dates.

5. The battle of Hastings was fought Oct. 14, 1066; William, Prince of Orange, landed at Tor Bay Nov. 5, 1688: what was the difference of time between the two events?

6. The battle of Austerlitz was fought December 2, 1805; the battle of Waterloo, June 18, 1815: find the difference of time.

78. To find the time between two dates in days.

1. Find the number of days from May 10 to Oct. 21.

SOLUTION.—Of May, there remains 31 — 10 = 21 days; there are 30 days in June, 31 in July, 31 in August, 30 in September, and 21 in October; then the number of days from May 10 to October 21, is 21 + 30 + 31 + 31 + 30 + 21 = 164.

OPERATION.

	31
	10
May,	21
June,	30
July,	31
Aug.,	31
Sept.,	30
Oct.,	21
	164

2. Find the number of days from March 17 to September 12.

3. A note dated April 18, 1877, is due June 20, 1877: how many days does it run?

4. A note dated Sept. 5, 1877, is due Dec. 7, 1877: how many days does it run?

5. Find the number of days from Oct. 12, 1877, to May 25, 1878.

6. Find the number of days from Aug. 20, 1875, to March 8, 1876.

MULTIPLICATION OF COMPOUND NUMBERS.

79. When the multiplicand is a compound number, the operation is called *Multiplication of Compound Numbers.*

1. A farmer takes to mill 5 bags of wheat, each containing 2 bu. 3 pk.: how much had he in all?

SOLUTION.—Begin at the lowest denomination for convenience. Multiply the 3 pk. by 5, making 15 pk., which, reduced, gives 3 bu. and 3 pk.; write the 3 pk. under the pecks, and carry the 3 bu. Then, multiply the 2 bu. by 5, add to the product the 3 bu., and write the 13 bu. under the bushels.

bu.	pk.
2	3
	5
13	3

Rule.—1. *Write the multiplier under the lowest denomination of the multiplicand.*

2. *Multiply the lowest denomination first, and divide the product by the number of units of this denomination which make a unit of the next higher, write the remainder under the denomination multiplied, and carry the quotient to the product of the next higher denomination.*

3. *Proceed in like manner with all the denominations, writing the entire product at the last.*

PROOF.—The same as in Simple Multiplication.

Rem.—There are *two* differences between multiplication of simple and of compound numbers: 1. In simple numbers it is more convenient to use *one* figure of the multiplier at a time; in compound numbers it is better to use the *entire multiplier* each time. 2. In simple numbers the scale is *uniform;* in compound numbers it *varies with the table.*

Examples.

2. Multiply 2 bu. 1 pk. 1 qt. 1 pt. by 6.

3. Multiply 2 bu. 2 pk. 2 qt. by 9.

4. If 4 bu. 3 pk. 3 qt. 1 pt. of wheat make 1 bl. of flour, how much will make 12 bl.?

5. Find the weight of 9 hogsheads of sugar, each weighing 8 cwt. 62 lb.

6. How much hay in 7 loads, each weighing 10 cwt. 89 lb.?

7. If a ship sail 208 mi. 176 rd. a day, how far will it sail in 15 days?

8. Multiply 23 cu. yd. 9 cu. ft. 228 cu. in. by 12.

9. Multiply 16 cwt. 74 lb. by 119.

10. Multiply 47 gal. 3 qt. 1 pt. by 59.

11. A travels 27 mi. 155 rd. in 1 day: how far will he travel in one month of 31 days?

12. In 17 piles of wood, each pile containing 7 C. 98 cu. ft.: what is the quantity of wood?

13. Multiply 2 wk. 4 da. 13 hr. 48 min. 39 sec. by 75.

14. A planter sold 75 hogsheads of sugar, each weighing 10 cwt. 84 lb., to a refiner, for 6 ct. a pound. The refiner sold the sugar for 8 ct. a pound: how much did he gain?

15. A cotton-factor sold 425 bales of cotton, each weighing 4 cwt. 85 lb., for 13 ct. a pound. He paid $24735 for the cotton: how much did he gain?

DIVISION OF COMPOUND NUMBERS.

80. When the dividend is a compound number, the operation is called *Division of Compound Numbers.*

The *divisor* may be either a Simple or a Compound Number. This gives rise to two cases:

FIRST.—To find how often one Compound Number is contained in another Compound Number.

This is done by reducing both divisor and dividend to the same denomination before dividing (Examples 6 and 8, Art. **74**).

SECOND.—To divide a Compound Number into a given number of equal parts. This is properly Compound Division.

1. Divide 14 bu. 2 pk. 1 qt. by 3.

OPERATION.

	bu.	pk.	qt.
3)	14	2	1
	4	3	3

SOLUTION.—Divide the highest denomination first, so that, if there be a remainder, it may be reduced to the next lower denomination, and added to it. 3 in 14 is contained 4 times, and 2 bu. are left; write the 4 under the bushels, and reduce the remaining 2 bu. to pk., to which add the 2 pk., making 10 pk. This, divided by 3, gives a quotient of 3 pk., with 1 pk. remaining; which, reduced to qt., and 1 qt. added, gives 9 qt. This, divided by 3, gives a quotient 3, which is written under the quarts.

(2)

	bu.	pk.	qt.
7)	33	2	6
	4	3	2

(3)

	da.	hr.	min.	sec.
5)	17	12	56	15
	3	12	11	15

Rule.—1. *Write the quantity to be divided in the order of its denominations, beginning with the highest; place the divisor on the left.*

2. *Begin with the highest denomination, divide each number separately, and write the quotient beneath.*

3. *If a remainder occurs after any division, reduce it to the next lower denomination, and, before dividing, add to it the number of its denomination.*

PROOF.—The same as in Simple Division.

REM.—Each *partial* quotient is of the same denomination as that part of the dividend from which it is derived.

4. Divide 67 bu. 3 pk. 4 qt. 1 pt. by 5.

5. Eleven casks of sugar weigh 35 cwt. 44 lb. 12 oz.: what is the average weight of each?

6. I traveled 39 mi. 288 rd. in 7 hr.: at what rate per hour did I travel?

7. Divide 69 A. 64 sq. rd. by 16.

8. 490 bu. 2 pk. 4 qt. ÷ 100.

9. 265 lb. 10 oz. ÷ 50.

10. 45 T. 18 cwt. ÷ 17.

11. 114 da. 22 hr. 45 min. 18 sec. ÷ 54.

12. 10 cwt. 27 lb. 13 oz. ÷ 23.

13. 309 bu. 2 pk. 2 qt. ÷ 78.

14. 127 gal. 3 qt. 1 pt. 3 gi. ÷ 63.

15. 788 mi. 169 rd. ÷ 319.

16. A farmer has two farms, one of 104 A. 117 sq. rd.; the other, 87 A. 78 sq. rd. He reserves 40 A. 40 sq. rd., and divides the remainder equally among his 3 sons: what is the share of each son?

17. A farmer's crop consisted of 5000 bu. 3 pk. of corn one year, and 7245 bu. 2 pk. the year following. He sold 8022 bu. 1 pk. and placed the remainder in 8 cribs, each crib containing an equal amount: how many bushels in each crib?

18. A speculator bought 6 adjoining pieces of land, each containing 4 A. 80 sq. rd. He divided the whole into 54 lots, and sold them at $5 a sq. rd.: how much did he get for each lot?

19. Add 35 lb. 9 oz., 75 lb. 14 oz., 85 lb. 15 oz.; from the sum take 186 lb. 14 oz.; multiply the remainder by 8; divide the product by 64: what is the result?

LONGITUDE AND TIME.

81. Difference of longitude and time between different places.

The circumference of the earth, like other circles, is divided into 360 equal parts, called *degrees of longitude.*

The sun appears to pass entirely round the earth, 360°, once in 24 hours, *one day;* and in 1 hour it passes over 15°. ($360° \div 24 = 15°$).

As 15° equal 900′, and 1 hour equals 60 minutes of *time,* therefore, the sun in 1 minute of *time* passes over 15′ of a *degree.* ($900' \div 60 = 15'$).

As 15′ equal 900″, and 1 minute of *time* equals 60 seconds of *time,* therefore, in 1 second of *time* the sun passes over 15″ of a *degree.* ($900'' \div 60 = 15''$).

Table for Comparing Longitude and Time.

15° of longitude = 1 hour of time.
15′ of longitude = 1 min. of time.
15″ of longitude = 1 sec. of time.

1. How many hr. min. and sec. of time correspond to 18° 25′ 30″ of longitude?

Analysis.—By inspection of the table, it is evident that,

Degrees (°) of longitude, divided by 15, give hours of *time*.
Minutes (′) of longitude, divided by 15, give minutes of *time*.
Seconds (″) of longitude, divided by 15, give seconds of *time*.

Hence, if 18° 25′ 30″ of lon. be divided by 15, the quotient will be the *time* in hr. min. and sec. corresponding to that longitude.

To find the time corresponding to any difference of longitude:

Rule.—*Divide the longitude by* 15, *according to the rule for Division of Compound Numbers, and mark the quotient* hr. min. sec., *instead of* ° ′ ″.

Conversely: **To find the longitude corresponding to** any difference of time.

Rule.—*Multiply the time by* 15, *according to the rule for Multiplication of Compound Numbers, and mark the product* ° ′ ″ *instead of* hr. min. sec.

2. The difference of longitude between two places is 30°: what is their difference of time?

3. The difference of longitude between two places is 71° 4′: what is the difference of time?

4. The difference of longitude between New York and Cincinnati is 10° 35′: what is the difference of time?

5. The difference of time between Cincinnati and Philadelphia is 37 min. 20 sec.: what is the difference of longitude?

6. The difference of time between New York and St. Louis is 1 hr. 4 min. 56 sec.: what is the difference of longitude?

7. The difference of time between London and Washington is 5 hr. 8 min. 4 sec.: what is the difference of longitude?

DIFFERENCE IN TIME.

82. It is noon (12 o'clock), at any place when the sun is on the meridian of that place.

As the sun appears to travel from the east *toward* the west, when it is noon at any place, it is *after* noon *east* of that place, and *before* noon *west* of that place.

Hence, a place has *later* or *earlier time* than another, according as it is *east* or *west* of it. Therefore,

When the time at one place is given, the time at another, if EAST *of this, is found by* ADDING *their difference of time; if* WEST, *by* SUBTRACTING *their difference of time.*

8. When it is noon at Cincinnati, what is the time at Philadelphia?

9. When it is 11 o'clock A. M. at New York, what is the time in longitude 30° east of New York?

10. When 12 o'clock (noon) at Philadelphia, what is the time at Cincinnati?

11. When it is 11 o'clock A. M. at New York, what is the time at St. Louis?

12. Wheeling, W. Va., is in longitude 80° 42′ west: the mouth of the Columbia river, in longitude 124° west: when it is 1 o'clock P. M. at Wheeling, what is the time at the mouth of Columbia river?

FACTORING

DEFINITIONS.

83. 1. **Factors** of a number are two or more numbers, the product of which equals the given number (Art. **28,** 2).

Thus, 2 and 3 are factors of 6, because $2 \times 3 = 6$; 2, 3, and 5 are factors of 30, because $2 \times 3 \times 5 = 30$.

REM. 1.—One and the number itself are not considered factors of a number.

REM. 2.—A number may be the product of more than one set of factors. Thus, $2 \times 6 = 12$, $3 \times 4 = 12$, and $2 \times 2 \times 3 = 12$.

2. A **multiple** of a number is a product of which the number is a factor.

Thus, 6 is a multiple of 3; 30 is a multiple of 5.

3. Numbers are divided into two classes, *prime* and *composite.*

4. A **prime number** has no factors.

Thus, 5, 11, 17 are prime numbers.

5. A **composite number** has two or more factors.

Thus, 6, 12, 30 are composite numbers.

6. A **prime factor** is a factor which is a prime number.

Thus, 3 is a prime factor of 12.

7. A factor is **common** to two or more **numbers when it** is a factor of each of them.

Thus, 3 is a common factor of 12 and 15.

REM.—Sometimes the smallest of two or more numbers may be the common factor. Thus, 6 is a common factor of 6, 12, and 18.

8. Two or more numbers are *prime to each other*, **when** they have no common factor.

Thus, 9 and 10 are prime to each other.

9. A **common divisor** (C. D.) of two or more **numbers** is any common factor.

Thus, 2, 3, and 6 are each a common divisor of 12 and 18.

10. The **greatest common divisor** (G. C. D.) **of two or** more numbers is the greatest common factor.

Thus, 6 is the greatest common divisor of 12 and 18.

11. A **common multiple** (C. M.) of two or more **numbers** is any multiple of all of them.

Thus, 6, 12, 18, etc., are common multiples of 2 and 3.

12. The **least common multiple** (L. C. M.) of two or more numbers is the least multiple of all of them.

Thus, 6 is the least common multiple of 2 and 3.

13. **Factoring** is the process of resolving composite numbers into their factors.

To Find the Prime Numbers.

84. All the prime numbers except 2 are odd **numbers.**

Rule.—1. *Write the odd numbers in a series* 1, 3, 5, 7, 9, *etc.*

2. *After* 3 *erase every* 3*d number; after* 5 *erase every* 5*th number; after* 7 *erase every* 7*th number; after* 11 *erase every* 11*th number, etc.*

3. *Then* 2 *and the numbers that remain are the prime numbers.*

EXERCISE.—Find the prime numbers from 1 to 100.

85. The operations of Factoring depend upon the following

PRINCIPLES.

1. *A factor of a number exactly divides it.*

Thus, 5 is a factor of 30 and is contained in it 6 times.

2. *A multiple of a number exactly contains it.*

Thus, 30 is a multiple of 5 and contains it 6 times.

3. *A factor of a number is a factor of any multiple of that number.*

Thus, 3 being a factor of 6 is a factor of 12, 18, 24, etc.

4. *A composite number is equal to the product of all its prime factors.*

Thus, the prime factors of 30 are 2, 3, and 5; $2 \times 3 \times 5 = 30$.

86. In resolving numbers into their prime factors it will be found convenient to remember the following facts in reference to the prime numbers 2, 3, and 5.

1. *Two is a factor of every even number.*

Thus, 2 is a factor of 4, 6, 8, 10, etc.

2. *Three is a factor of a number when the sum of its digits is* 3 *or some multiple of* 3.

Thus, 3 is a factor of 2457; for $2+4+5+7=18$, which is 6 times 3.

3. *Five is a factor of every number whose unit figure is* 0 *or* 5.

Thus, 5 is a factor of 10, 15, 20, 25, etc.

REM.—Whether the prime numbers 7, 11, 13, etc., are factors of a number or not is best ascertained by trial.

To Resolve a Number into its Prime Factors.

87. 1. Resolve 30 into its prime factors.

SOLUTION.—2 is a factor of 30 (Art. **86, 1**). Dividing 30 by 2, the quotient is 15. 3 being a factor of 15 (Art. **86,** 2) is also a factor of 30 (Art. **85,** Prin. 3). Dividing 15 by 3 the quotient is 5, a prime number. Then, 2, 3 and 5 are the prime factors of 30.

OPERATION.

$$\begin{array}{r|l} 2 & 30 \\ \hline 3 & 15 \\ \hline & 5 \end{array}$$

Rule.—1. *Divide the given number by any prime number that will exactly divide it.*

2. *Divide the quotient in the same manner; and so continue to divide, until a quotient is obtained which is a prime number.*

3. *The several divisors and the last quotient will be the prime factors of the given number.*

REM.—It will be most convenient to divide each time by the *smallest* prime number.

Resolve the following into their prime factors:

2. 4. 2, 2.
3. 8.
4. 9.
5. 10.
6. 12.
7. 14.
8. 15.
9. 16.
10. 18.
11. 20.
12. 22.
13. 24.
14. 25.
15. 26.
16. 27.
17. 28.
18. 32.
19. 34.
20. 35.
21. 36.
22. 38.
23. 39. 3, 13.
24. 40.
25. 42.
26. 44.
27. 45.
28. 46.
29. 48.
30. 49.
31. 50.
32. 70.
33. 77.
34. 91.
35. 105.
36. 119.
37. 133.
38. 154.
39. 210.
40. 231.
41. 330.
42. 462.
43. 2310.

88. To find the prime factors common to two or more numbers.

1. What prime factors are common to 30 and 42?

Solution.—Write the numbers in a line. 2 is a prime factor of both 30 and 42 (Art. **86,** 1). Dividing by 2, the quotients are 15 and 21. 3 is a prime factor of both 15 and 21 (Art. **86,** 2); and consequently of both 30 and 42 (Art. **85,** Prin. 3). Dividing by 3, the quotients 5 and 7 are prime to each other (Art. **83,** 8). Then 2 and 3 are the common factors.

OPERATION.

```
2)30  42
 ‾‾‾‾‾‾‾
3)15  21
 ‾‾‾‾‾‾‾
   5   7
```

Rule.—1. *Write the given numbers in a line.*

2. *Divide by any prime number that will exactly aivide all of them; divide the quotients in the same manner; and so continue to divide until two or more of the quotients are prime to each other.*

3 *Then the several divisors will be the common factors*

What prime factors are common to

2. 60 and 90?
3. 56 and 88?
4. 72 and 84?
5. 54 and 90?
6. 81 and 108?
7. 80 and 100?
8. 84 and 126?
9. 52, 68 and 76?
10. 66, 78 and 102?
11. 63, 99 and 117?
12. 50, 70 and 110?
13. 45, 75 and 105?
14. 75, 125 and 175?
15. 42, 70 and 98?
16. 33, 55, 77 and 121?
17. 39, 65, 91 and 104?
18. 34, 51, 85 and 102?
19. 38, 57, 95 and 114?
20. 46, 69, 92 and 115?

89. Finding the G. C. D. **of two or more** numbers depends upon the following

PRINCIPLE.—*The G. C. D. of two or more numbers contains all the prime factors common to the numbers, and no other factor.*

Thus, the G. C. D. of 12 and 18 is 6; it contains the common factors 2 and 3; it must contain both of them, else it would not be the *greatest* C. D.; it can contain no other factor, else it would not divide both 12 and 18.

1. Find the G. C. D. of 30 and 42.

FIRST METHOD.

SOLUTION.—The prime factors common to 30 and 42 are 2 and 3 (Art. **88**); their product is 6; then the G. C. D. of 30 and 42 is 6 (Prin.).

OPERATION.

```
2)30  42
3)15  21
   5   7
```

Rule.—1. *Find the prime factors common to the given numbers.*

2. *Multiply them together.*

3. *The product will be the greatest common divisor.*

SECOND METHOD.

SOLUTION.—Dividing 42 by 30, the remainder is 12; dividing 30 by 12, the remainder is 6; dividing 12 by 6, the remainder is 0. Then 6 is the G. C. D. of 30 and 42. For, $30 = 6 \times 5$ and $42 = 6 \times 7$; then, because 5 and 7 are prime to each other, 6 must contain all the prime factors common to 30 and 42; it is, therefore, their G. C. D. (Prin.).

OPERATION.

```
30)42(1
   30
   12)30(2
      24
       6)12(2
         12
```

Rule.—1. *Divide the greater number by the less, the divisor by the remainder, and so on, always dividing the last divisor by the last remainder, until nothing remains.*

2. *The last divisor will be the greatest common divisor.*

REM.—To find the G. C. D. of more than two numbers, first find the G. C. D. of two of them, then of that common divisor and one of the remaining numbers, and so on for all the numbers; the last common divisor will be the G. C. D. of all the numbers.

Find the greatest common divisor of the following numbers:

2. 16, 24 and 40.
3. 24, 36 and 60.
4. 36, 54 and 90.
5. 40, 60 and 100.
6. 54, 81 and 108.
7. 60, 90 and 120.
8. 32, 48, 80 and 112.
9. 48, 72, 96 and 120.
10. 72, 108, 144 and 180.
11. 62 and 93.
12. 78 and 130.
13. 161 and 253.
14. 247 and 323.
15. 391 and 697.
16. 2145 and 3471.
17. 16571 and 38363.
18. 72, 120 and 132.
19. 75, 125 and 165.
20. 64, 96, 112 and 136.

90. Finding the L. C. M. of two or more numbers depends upon the following

PRINCIPLE.—*The L. C. M. of two or more numbers contains all the prime factors of each number and no other factor.*

Thus, the L. C. M. of 12 and 18 is 36; its prime factors are 2, 2, 3, and 3; it must contain all these factors, else it would not contain both the numbers; it must contain no other factor, else it would not be the *least* C. M.

1. Find the L. C. M. of 4, 6, 9 and 12.

SOLUTION.—The prime factors of 4 are 2 and 2; those of 6 are 2 and 3; of 9, 3 and 3; and of 12, 2, 2, and 3. Then, the prime factors of the L. C. M. are 2, 2, 3, 3, and no other factor (Prin.). Hence, 36 is the L. C. M.

OPERATION.

$$4 = 2 \times 2$$
$$6 = 2 \times 3$$
$$9 = 3 \times 3$$
$$12 = 2 \times 2 \times 3$$
$$2 \times 2 \times 3 \times 3 = 36$$

The process of factoring and selecting the prime factors for the L. C. M. is very much simplified by the operation in the form of Short Division, as shown.

OPERATION.

```
2)4  6  9  12
 ------------
2)2  3  9   6
 ------------
   3)3  9   3
   ---------
        3
```

$$2 \times 2 \times 3 \times 3 = 36.$$

Rule.—1. *Write the given numbers in a line.*

2. *Divide by any prime number that will exactly divide two or more of them.*

3. *Write the quotients and undivided numbers in a line beneath.*

4. *Divide these numbers in the same manner, and so continue the operation until a line is reached in which the numbers are all prime to each other.*

5. *Then the product of the divisors and the numbers in the last line will be the least common multiple.*

REM.—When the quotient is 1 it need not be written.

Find the least common multiple of

2. 4, 6 and 8.
3. 6, 9 and 12.
4. 4, 8 and 10.
5. 6, 10 and 15.
6. 6, 8, 9 and 12.

7. 10, 12, 15 and 20.
8. 9, 15, 18 and 30.
9. 12, 18, 27 and 36.
10. 15, 25, 30 and 50.
11. 14, 21, 30 and 35.
12. 15, 20, 21 and 28.
13. 20, 24, 28 and 30.
14. 45, 30, 35 and 42.
15. 36, 40, 45 and 50.
16. 42, 56 and 63.
17. 78, 104 and 117.
18. 125, 150 and 200.
19. 10, 24, 25, 32 and 45.
20. 2, 3, 4, 5, 6, 7, 8 and 9.
21. 16, 27, 42, and 108.
22. 13, 29, 52, and 87.
23. 120, 360, 144, 720, and 72.

CANCELLATION.

91. 1. I bought 3 oranges at 5 cents each, and paid for them with pears at 3 cents each: how many pears did it take?

OPERATION.

$$\begin{array}{r} 5 \\ 3 \\ \hline 3)\,15 \\ \hline 5 \end{array}$$

SOLUTION I.—5 cents multiplied by 3 are 15 cents, the price of the oranges. 15 divided by 3 is 5, the number of pears.

From a consideration of this example and its solution we have the following.

PRINCIPLE.—*A number is not changed by multiplying it and then dividing the product by the multiplier.*

For the example, then, we may offer the following solution and operation:

SOLUTION II.—Indicate the multiplication and division; then, erase or *cancel* the multiplier 3 and the divisor 3 by drawing a line across them; and write the result, equal to 5.

OPERATION.

$$\frac{5 \times \not{3}}{\not{3}} = 5$$

REM.—The product 5×3 forms a dividend of which 3 is the divisor.

2. If I buy 10 pears at 3 cents each, and pay for them with oranges at 5 cents each: how many oranges will it take?

SOLUTION.—5 is a factor of 10, for $10 = 5 \times 2$; then, cancel the divisor 5 and also the factor 5 in 10 by canceling 10 and writing the remaining factor 2 above it. The product of the remaining factors is 6.

OPERATION.

$$\frac{\overset{2}{\not{10}} \times 3}{\not{5}} = 6$$

3. Divide 15×21 by 14×10.

SOLUTION.—5 is a common factor of 15 and 10; then, cancel 15, writing 3 above it, and 10, writing 2 below it. 7 is a common factor of 14 and 21; then, cancel 14, writing 2 below it, and 21, writing 3 above it. The product of the factors remaining in the dividend is 9, and of those remaining in the divisor is 4; the quotient of 9 divided by 4 is $2\frac{1}{4}$. Therefore,

OPERATION.

$$\frac{\overset{3}{\not{15}} \times \overset{3}{\not{21}}}{\underset{2}{\not{14}} \times \underset{2}{\not{10}}} = \frac{9}{4} = 2\frac{1}{4}$$

Cancellation is a process of abbreviation by omitting the common factors of the dividend and divisor.

Rule.—1. *Cancel the factors common to both the dividend and divisor.*

2. *Divide the product of the factors remaining in the dividend by the product of the factors remaining in the divisor.*

3. *The result will be the quotient required.*

4. How many barrels of molasses, at $13 a barrel, will pay for 13 barrels of flour, at $4 a barrel?

5. Multiply 17 by 18, and divide by 6.

6. In 15 times 8, how many times 4?

7. In 24 times 4, how many times 8?

8. In 37 times 15, how many times 5?

9. Multiply 36 by 40, and divide the product by 30 multiplied by 8.

10. In 36 times 5, how many times 15?

11. Multiply 42, 25, and 18 together, and divide the product by 21×15.

12. I sold 23 sheep, at $10 each, and was paid in hogs, at $5 each: how many did I receive?

13. How many yards of flannel, at 35 cents a yard, will pay for 15 yards of calico, at 14 cents?

14. What is the quotient of $21 \times 11 \times 6 \times 26$, divided by $13 \times 3 \times 14 \times 2$?

15. The factors of a dividend are 21, 15, 33, 8, 14, and 17; the divisors, 20, 34, 22 and 27: required the quotient.

16. I bought 21 kegs of nails of 95 pounds each, at 6 cents a pound; paid for them with pieces of muslin of 35 yards each, at 9 cents a yard: how many pieces of muslin did I give?

17. What is the quotient of $35 \times 39 \times 40$ divided by $26 \times 30 \times 42$?

18. What is the quotient of $26 \times 33 \times 35$ divided by $4 \times 9 \times 25$?

19. What is the quotient of $6 \times 9 \times 15 \times 21$ divided by $4 \times 6 \times 10 \times 14$?

20. What is the quotient of $21 \times 24 \times 28 \times 35$ divided by $14 \times 18 \times 20 \times 25$?

FRACTIONS.

92. A unit may be divided into equal parts; thus,

1st. An apple may be divided equally between two boys, by cutting it into *two equal parts.*

2d. An apple may be divided equally among three boys, by cutting it into *three equal parts.*

3d. In like manner, an apple may be divided into *four, five, six, or any number of equal parts.*

These equal parts into which a unit may be divided are called *fractions.*

DEFINITIONS.

93. 1. A **fraction** is one or more equal parts of a unit.

2. To express fractions by words and figures.

When a unit is divided into two equal parts,
Each part is called *one-half,* written $\frac{1}{2}$.
Both parts are called *two-halves,* " $\frac{2}{2}$.
When a unit is divided into three equal parts,
Each part is called *one-third,* written $\frac{1}{3}$.
Two parts are called *two-thirds,* " $\frac{2}{3}$.
All the parts are called *three-thirds,* " $\frac{3}{3}$.
When a unit is divided into four equal parts,
Each part is called *one-fourth,* written $\frac{1}{4}$.
Two parts are called *two-fourths,* " $\frac{2}{4}$.
Three parts are called *three-fourths,* " $\frac{3}{4}$.
All the parts are called *four-fourths,* " $\frac{4}{4}$.

When a unit is divided into five equal parts,

Each part is called *one-fifth*, written $\frac{1}{5}$.
Two parts are called *two-fifths*, " $\frac{2}{5}$.
Three parts are called *three-fifths*, " $\frac{3}{5}$.
Four parts are called *four-fifths*, " $\frac{4}{5}$.
All the parts are called *five-fifths*, " $\frac{5}{5}$.

When a unit is divided into six, seven, eight, etc., equal parts, each part is called *one-sixth*, $\frac{1}{6}$, *one-seventh*, $\frac{1}{7}$, *one-eighth*, $\frac{1}{8}$, etc.

94. 1. A fraction is expressed *in words* by two numbers; the first *numbers* the parts, the second *names* them; the first number is called the **numerator**, the second is called the **denominator**.

2. A fraction is expressed *in figures*, by writing the numerator above the denominator with a line between them.

3. The numerator and denominator are styled the **terms** of the fraction.

4. The denominator shows into how many equal parts the unit is divided, and the numerator, how many of the parts are taken.

95. When a unit is divided into equal parts, the size of each part depends upon the number of the parts.

Thus, if apples of equal size be divided, one into *two* equal parts, another into *three* equal parts, a third into *four* equal parts, etc., a *half* will be larger than a *third*, a *third* larger than a *fourth*, etc. Hence,

1st. The less the number of parts into which a unit is divided, the greater the size of each part.

2d. The greater the number of parts into which a unit is divided, the less the size of each part.

96. 1. A fraction may also be regarded as a part of one or more units.

Thus:

1st. Two apples may be divided equally among three boys.

Each boy will receive, either *one-third* of each of the two apples, or *two-thirds* of one of the apples; therefore, $\frac{1}{3}$ of 2 is $\frac{2}{3}$. Hence, $\frac{2}{3}$ may be considered either as *two-thirds* or as *one-third of two.*

2d. Two apples may be divided equally between two boys.

Each boy will receive, either *one-half* of each of the two apples, or *one* of the two apples; therefore, $\frac{1}{2}$ of 2 is $\frac{2}{2}$, or 1. Hence, $\frac{2}{2}$ may be considered either as *two halves* or as *one-half of two.*

3d. Three apples may be divided equally between two boys.

Each boy will receive, either *one-half* of each of the three apples, or *one apple* and *one-half* of another; therefore, $\frac{1}{2}$ of 3 is $\frac{3}{2}$, or $1\frac{1}{2}$. Hence, $\frac{3}{2}$ may be considered either as *three halves* or as *one-half of three.*

2. A **fraction** is a part of one or more units.

3. The **numerator** expresses the number of units.

4. The **denominator** expresses the part of each to be taken.

97. 1. A fraction may also be regarded as an expression of division, in which the numerator is the *dividend* and the denominator the *divisor.*

Thus:

1st. $\frac{2}{3}$ is 2 divided by 3; here, the division can only be indicated.

2d. $\frac{4}{2}$ is 4 divided by 2; in this case, the division can be performed exactly, giving a *quotient* 2.

3d. $\frac{5}{2}$ is 5 divided by 2; in this case, the division can not be performed exactly, the *quotient* being $2\frac{1}{2}$.

2. A **fraction** is an indicated division. The numerator is the dividend and the denominator is the divisor.

3. A whole number may be expressed in the form of a fraction, by writing the number for the numerator and 1 for the denominator.

Thus, 2 may be written $\frac{2}{1}$; for 2 divided by 1 is 2; 3 may be written $\frac{3}{1}$; 4 may be written $\frac{4}{1}$, etc.

98. The **value** of a fraction is its relation to a unit.

1. When the numerator is less than the denominator, the value of the fraction is less than 1.

Thus, $\frac{1}{2}$, $\frac{1}{3}$, $\frac{2}{3}$, etc., are less than 1.

2. When the numerator is equal to the denominator, the value of the fraction is equal to 1.

Thus, $\frac{2}{2}$, $\frac{3}{3}$, $\frac{4}{4}$, etc., equal 1.

3. When the numerator is greater than the denominator, the value of the fraction is greater than 1.

Thus, $\frac{3}{2}$, $\frac{4}{3}$, $\frac{5}{4}$, etc., are greater than 1.

4. A **proper** fraction is one whose value is less than 1.

5. An **improper** fraction is one whose value is equal to or greater than 1.

6. A **mixed** number is a whole number and a fraction.

99. 1. A fraction may be divided into equal parts.

Thus, after an apple has been divided into two equal parts, each half may be divided into two equal parts; the whole apple will then be divided into four equal parts; therefore, $\frac{1}{2}$ of $\frac{1}{2}$ is $\frac{1}{4}$.

Such expressions as $\frac{1}{2}$ of $\frac{1}{2}$, $\frac{1}{2}$ of $\frac{1}{3}$, etc., are termed *compound fractions.*

2. A **compound** fraction is a fraction of a fraction.

100. 1. Fractions sometimes occur in which the numerator, the denominator or both are fractional.

Thus, $\frac{3\frac{1}{2}}{4}$, $\frac{1}{2\frac{1}{4}}$, $\frac{2\frac{1}{4}}{3\frac{1}{2}}$, are such expressions; they are called *complex* fractions. They are read $3\frac{1}{2}$ *divided by* 4, etc.

2. A **simple** fraction is one in which both terms are entire.

3. A **complex** fraction is one in which one or both of the terms are fractional.

101. The operations with fractions depend upon the following

PRINCIPLES.

1. *A fraction is multiplied by multiplying the numerator.*

Thus, if the numerator of $\frac{2}{7}$ be multiplied by 3, the result will be $\frac{6}{7}$; in $\frac{6}{7}$ the parts are of the same size as in $\frac{2}{7}$, but there are *three times* as many.

2. *A fraction is divided by dividing the numerator.*

Thus, if the numerator of $\frac{6}{7}$ be divided by 3, the result will be $\frac{2}{7}$; in $\frac{2}{7}$ the parts are of the same size as in $\frac{6}{7}$, but there are only *one-third* as many.

3. *A fraction is divided by multiplying the denominator.*

Thus, if the denominator of $\frac{2}{3}$ be multiplied by 3, the result will be $\frac{2}{9}$; in $\frac{2}{9}$ there are the same number of parts as in $\frac{2}{3}$, but the parts are only *one-third* as large.

4. *A fraction is multiplied by dividing the denominator.*

Thus, if the denominator of $\frac{2}{9}$ be divided by 3, the result will be $\frac{2}{3}$; in $\frac{2}{3}$ there are the same number of parts as in $\frac{2}{9}$, but the parts are *three times* as large.

5. *Multiplying both terms of a fraction by the same number does not change its value.*

Thus, if both terms of $\frac{3}{5}$ be multiplied by 2, the result is $\frac{6}{10}$; in $\frac{6}{10}$ there are *twice* as many parts as in $\frac{3}{5}$, but they are only *one-half* as large.

6. *Dividing both terms of a fraction by the same number does not change its value.*

Thus, if both terms of $\frac{6}{10}$ be divided by 2, the result will be $\frac{3}{5}$; in $\frac{3}{5}$ there are only *one-half* as many parts as in $\frac{6}{10}$, but they are *twice* as large.

These six principles may be stated more briefly, as follows:

I. A fraction is multiplied,

1st. *By multiplying the numerator.*
2d. *By dividing the denominator.*

II. A fraction is divided,

1st. *By dividing the numerator.*
2d. *By multiplying the denominator.*

III. The value of a fraction is not changed,

1st. *By multiplying both terms by the same number.*
2d. *By dividing both terms by the same number.*

The operations with fractions are *Reduction*, *Addition*, *Subtraction*, *Multiplication* and *Division*.

REDUCTION OF FRACTIONS.

102. Reduction of Fractions is changing their form without altering their value. There are *six cases.*

CASE I.

103. To reduce an integer to an improper fraction, having a given denominator.

1. In 3 apples, how many halves?

OPERATION.

$\frac{2}{2} \times 3 = \frac{6}{2}$

SOLUTION.—In 1 apple there are 2 halves; then, in 3 apples there are 3×2 halves $=$ 6 halves.

Rule.—1. *Multiply the integer by the given denominator; under the product write the denominator.*

2. In 4 apples, how many halves?
3. In 2 apples, how many thirds?
4. In 3 apples, how many fourths?
5. In 4 apples, how many fifths?
6. In 6 inches, how many tenths?
7. In 8 feet, how many twelfths?
8. Reduce 4 to sevenths.
9. Reduce 8 to ninths.
10. Reduce 19 to thirteenths.
11. Reduce 25 to twentieths.
12. Reduce 37 to twenty-thirds.

CASE II.

104. To reduce a mixed number to an improper fraction.

1. In $3\frac{1}{2}$ apples, how many halves?

OPERATION.

$\frac{2}{2} \times 3 = \frac{6}{2}$

$\frac{6}{2} + \frac{1}{2} = \frac{7}{2}$

SOLUTION.—In 1 apple there are 2 halves; then, in 3 apples there are 3×2 halves $= 6$ halves. 6 halves and 1 half are 7 halves.

Rule.—1. *Multiply the integer by the denominator of the fraction; to the product add the numerator, and under the sum write the denominator.*

2. In $4\frac{1}{2}$ apples, how many halves?
3. In $2\frac{1}{3}$ apples, how many thirds?
4. In $2\frac{2}{3}$ apples, how many thirds?
5. In $5\frac{3}{4}$ dollars, how many fourths?
6. Reduce $8\frac{3}{4}$ to an improper fraction.
7. Reduce $12\frac{3}{5}$ to an improper fraction.
8. Reduce $15\frac{5}{6}$ to an improper fraction.
9. Reduce $26\frac{13}{24}$ to an improper fraction.
10. Reduce $3\frac{17}{55}$ to an improper fraction.
11. Reduce $46\frac{5}{8}$ to an improper fraction.
12. Reduce $21\frac{117}{583}$ to an improper fraction.
13. Reduce $1\frac{999}{1000}$ to an improper fraction.
14. Reduce $14\frac{6}{71}$ to an improper fraction.
15. Reduce $10\frac{1}{111}$ to an improper fraction.

CASE III.

105. To reduce an improper fraction to an integer or mixed number.

1. In $\frac{6}{2}$ of an apple, how many apples?

OPERATION.

$$2\,)\,\underline{6}$$
$$3$$

SOLUTION.—There are 2 halves in 1 apple; then, in 6 halves, there are $6 \div 2 = 3$ apples.

2. In $\frac{9}{4}$ of a dollar, how many dollars?

OPERATION.

$4\,)\,9$

$2\frac{1}{4}$

SOLUTION.—There are 4 fourths in 1 dollar; then, in 9 fourths, there are $9 \div 4 = 2\frac{1}{4}$ dollars.

Rule.—1. *Divide the numerator by the denominator; the quotient will be the integer or the mixed number.*

3. In $\frac{6}{3}$ of an apple, how many apples?
4. In $\frac{12}{4}$ of an apple, how many apples?
5. In $\frac{15}{4}$ of a dollar, how many dollars?
6. In $\frac{17}{5}$ of a dollar, how many dollars?
7. In $\frac{19}{7}$ of a bushel, how many bushels?
8. In $\frac{23}{10}$ of a dollar, how many dollars?
9. In $\frac{25}{3}$ of an ounce, how many ounces?
10. In $\frac{53}{4}$ of a dollar, how many dollars?
11. Reduce $\frac{75}{4}$ to a mixed number.
12. Reduce $\frac{125}{8}$ to a mixed number.
13. Reduce $\frac{611}{24}$ to a mixed number.
14. Reduce $\frac{3000}{75}$ to an integer.
15. Reduce $\frac{775}{25}$ to an integer.
16. Reduce $\frac{171}{12}$ to a mixed number.
17. Reduce $\frac{509}{11}$ to a mixed number.
18. Reduce $\frac{6437}{298}$ to a mixed number.
19. Reduce $\frac{7536}{125}$ to a mixed number.
20. Reduce $\frac{3781}{19}$ to an integer.
21. Reduce $\frac{1325}{101}$ to a mixed number.

CASE IV.

106. To reduce a fraction to higher terms.

A fraction is reduced to higher terms by multiplying both terms by the same number. This does not change its value (Art. **101**, Prin. 5).

1. Reduce $\frac{4}{5}$ to thirtieths.

OPERATION.

$30 \div 5 = 6$
$6 \times 4 = 24$
$\frac{4}{5} = \frac{24}{30}$

SOLUTION.—30 divided by 5 is 6. Multiplying both terms of $\frac{4}{5}$ by 6, the result is $\frac{24}{30}$.

Rule.—1. *Divide the required denominator by the denominator of the given fraction.*

2. *Multiply both terms of the fraction by the quotient; the result will be the required fraction.*

2. Reduce $\frac{1}{2}$ to fourths.
3. Reduce $\frac{2}{3}$ to sixths.
4. Reduce $\frac{3}{4}$ to twelfths.
5. Reduce $\frac{5}{6}$ to twenty-fourths.
6. Reduce $\frac{5}{7}$ to twenty-eighths.
7. Reduce $\frac{4}{21}$ to eighty-fourths.
8. Reduce $\frac{7}{8}$ to seventy-seconds.
9. Reduce $\frac{3}{5}$ to sixtieths.
10. Reduce $\frac{9}{10}$ to hundredths.
11. Reduce $\frac{9}{20}$ to a fraction whose denominator is 720.
12. Reduce $\frac{13}{14}$ to a fraction whose denominator is 2016.
13. Reduce $\frac{22}{43}$ to a fraction whose denominator is 1935.
14. Reduce $\frac{35}{41}$ to a fraction whose denominator is 8118.
15. Reduce $\frac{16}{17}$ to a fraction whose denominator is 5134.
16. Reduce $\frac{77}{81}$ to a fraction whose denominator is 23328.
17. Reduce $\frac{13}{21}$ to a fraction whose denominator is 2541.

CASE V.

107. **To reduce a fraction to its lowest terms.**

1. A fraction is reduced to lower terms by dividing both terms by the same number. This does not change its value. (Art. **101**, Prin. 6).

2. A fraction is in its lowest terms when the numerator and denominator are prime to each other. (Art. **83**, 8).

1. Reduce $\frac{24}{30}$ to its lowest terms.

First Method.

OPERATION.

$$2)\frac{24}{30}=\frac{12}{15}$$

$$3)\frac{12}{15}=\frac{4}{5}$$

Solution.—2 is a common factor of 24 and 30 (**86**, 1). Dividing both terms of $\frac{24}{30}$ by 2, the result is $\frac{12}{15}$. 3 is a common factor of 12 and 15 (**86**, 2). Dividing both terms of $\frac{12}{15}$ by 3, the result is $\frac{4}{5}$. 4 and 5 are prime to each other.

Rule.—1. *Divide both terms of the given fraction by any common factor.*

2. *Divide the resulting fraction in the same manner.*

3. *So continue to divide until a fraction is obtained whose terms are prime to each other.*

Second Method.

OPERATION.

```
24)30(1
   24
    6)24(4
      24
```

$$6)\frac{24}{30}=\frac{4}{5}$$

Solution.—The greatest common divisor of 24 and 30 is 6. Dividing both terms of $\frac{24}{30}$ by 6, the result is $\frac{4}{5}$.

Rule.—1. *Divide both terms of the given fraction by their greatest common divisor.*

2. *The resulting fraction will be in its lowest terms.*

2. Reduce $\frac{18}{30}$ to its lowest terms.
3. Reduce $\frac{60}{90}$ to its lowest terms.
4. Reduce $\frac{12}{18}$ to its lowest terms.
5. Reduce $\frac{30}{45}$ to its lowest terms.
6. Reduce $\frac{60}{150}$ to its lowest terms.
7. Reduce $\frac{42}{70}$ to its lowest terms.
8. Reduce $\frac{96}{112}$ to its lowest terms.
9. Reduce $\frac{60}{125}$ to its lowest terms.
10. Reduce $\frac{126}{198}$ to its lowest terms.
11. Reduce $\frac{182}{196}$ to its lowest terms.
12. Reduce $\frac{615}{915}$ to its lowest terms.
13. Reduce $\frac{873}{1067}$ to its lowest terms.
14. Reduce $\frac{777}{1998}$ to its lowest terms.
15. Reduce $\frac{909}{2323}$ to its lowest terms.
16. Reduce $\frac{391}{667}$ to its lowest terms.
17. Reduce $\frac{585}{1287}$ to its lowest terms.
18. Reduce $\frac{796}{14129}$ to its lowest terms.
19. Reduce $\frac{1457}{5921}$ to its lowest terms.
20. Reduce $\frac{6465}{7335}$ to its lowest terms.

CASE VI.

108. To reduce two or more fractions to their least common denominator.

1. Two or more fractions have a *common denominator* when they have the same denominator.

2. A **common denominator** of two or more fractions is a common multiple of their denominators (**83, 11**).

3. The least common denominator of two or more fractions is the least common multiple of their denominators (83, 12).

1. Reduce $\frac{3}{4}$, $\frac{5}{6}$, $\frac{8}{9}$, and $\frac{11}{12}$ to their least common denominator.

OPERATION.

$$\begin{array}{r|rrrr} 2 & 4 & 6 & 9 & 12 \\ \hline 2 & 2 & 3 & 9 & 6 \\ \hline 3 & & 3 & 9 & 3 \\ \hline & & & 3 & \end{array}$$

$$2 \times 2 \times 3 \times 3 = 36$$

$$\begin{array}{ll} 36 \div 4 = 9 & 36 \div 6 = 6 \\ 9 \times 3 = 27 & 6 \times 5 = 30 \\ \frac{3}{4} = \frac{27}{36} & \frac{5}{6} = \frac{30}{36} \end{array}$$

$$\begin{array}{ll} 36 \div 9 = 4 & 36 \div 12 = 3 \\ 4 \times 8 = 32 & 3 \times 11 = 33 \\ \frac{8}{9} = \frac{32}{36} & \frac{11}{12} = \frac{33}{36} \end{array}$$

SOLUTION.—The least common multiple of the denominators 4, 6, 9, and 12 is 36 (**90**). Each fraction, then, must be reduced to thirty-sixths (**106**). $\frac{3}{4} = \frac{27}{36}$, $\frac{5}{6} = \frac{30}{36}$, $\frac{8}{9} = \frac{32}{36}$, and $\frac{11}{12} = \frac{33}{36}$.

Rule.—1. *Find the L. C. M. of the denominators of the fractions for their least common denominator.*

2. *Reduce each fraction to another having this denominator.*

REM. 1.—Integers must be reduced to the common denominator by Art. **103**, Rule.

REM. 2.—Before commencing the operation, mixed numbers must be reduced to improper fractions (**104**).

REM. 3.—Each fraction must be in its lowest terms (**107**).

REM. 4.—Two or more fractions may be reduced to any common denominator in the same way.

Reduce to their least common denominator:

2. $\frac{1}{2}$, $\frac{2}{3}$, $\frac{3}{4}$.
3. $\frac{2}{3}$, $\frac{5}{6}$, $\frac{7}{9}$.
4. $\frac{1}{2}$, $\frac{3}{4}$, $\frac{4}{5}$.

5. $\frac{3}{8}$, $\frac{4}{5}$, $\frac{9}{10}$.
6. $\frac{2}{3}$, $\frac{3}{4}$, $\frac{7}{8}$.
7. $\frac{3}{4}$, $\frac{5}{8}$, $\frac{5}{9}$.
8. $\frac{1}{2}$, $\frac{3}{4}$, $\frac{7}{8}$.
9. $\frac{2}{3}$, $\frac{5}{6}$, $\frac{7}{12}$.
10. $\frac{3}{4}$, $\frac{5}{8}$, $\frac{11}{16}$.
11. $\frac{1}{2}$, $\frac{2}{3}$, $\frac{3}{4}$, $\frac{4}{5}$.
12. $\frac{2}{3}$, $\frac{2}{5}$, $\frac{3}{7}$, $\frac{5}{8}$.
13. $\frac{2}{7}$, $\frac{5}{14}$, $\frac{9}{21}$, $\frac{11}{28}$.
14. $\frac{2}{5}$, $\frac{3}{4}$, $\frac{6}{9}$, $\frac{15}{18}$.
15. 2, $\frac{3}{4}$, $\frac{5}{9}$, $\frac{7}{12}$.
16. $2\frac{2}{3}$, $\frac{3}{5}$, 4, $5\frac{5}{6}$.
17. $2\frac{1}{2}$, $3\frac{1}{3}$, $4\frac{1}{4}$, 5.
18. $\frac{7}{16}$, $\frac{11}{18}$, $\frac{17}{24}$, $\frac{19}{36}$, $\frac{25}{48}$.
19. $\frac{4}{7}$, $\frac{3}{10}$, $\frac{5}{12}$, $\frac{17}{35}$, $\frac{4}{63}$, $\frac{15}{28}$.
20. $\frac{3}{5}$, $\frac{7}{10}$, $\frac{6}{25}$, $\frac{11}{30}$, $\frac{13}{45}$, $\frac{23}{60}$.

ADDITION OF FRACTIONS.

109. Addition of Fractions is the process of finding the sum of two or more fractional numbers. There are *two cases.*

CASE I.

110. When the fractions have a common denominator.

1. Add $\frac{1}{5}$, $\frac{2}{5}$, and $\frac{3}{5}$.

OPERATION.

$\frac{1}{5}+\frac{2}{5}+\frac{3}{5}=\frac{6}{5}$

$\frac{6}{5}=1\frac{1}{5}$

SOLUTION.—The sum of 1 fifth, 2 fifths, and 3 fifths, is 6 fifths. $\frac{6}{5}$ are equal to $1\frac{1}{5}$ (Art. **105**).

EXPLANATION.—Since the denominators are the same, the numerators express parts of the same size; therefore, add 1 fifth, 2 fifths, and 3 fifths, as you would add 1 cent, 2 cents, and 3 cents; the sum, in one case, being 6 fifths, in the other, 6 cents.

Rule.—1. *Add the numerators; under the sum write the common denominator.*

REM. 1—The result, if an improper fraction, must be reduced to an integer, or a mixed number (Art. **105**).

REM. 2.—The result must be reduced to its lowest terms (Art. **107**).

2. Add $\frac{1}{4}$, $\frac{2}{4}$, $\frac{3}{4}$.
3. Add $\frac{1}{5}$, $\frac{2}{5}$, $\frac{3}{5}$, $\frac{4}{5}$.
4. Add $\frac{1}{7}$, $\frac{2}{7}$, $\frac{3}{7}$, $\frac{6}{7}$.
5. Add $\frac{4}{9}$, $\frac{5}{9}$, $\frac{7}{9}$, $\frac{8}{9}$.
6. Add $\frac{3}{11}$, $\frac{7}{11}$, $\frac{8}{11}$, $\frac{10}{11}$.
7. Add $\frac{5}{13}$, $\frac{8}{13}$, $\frac{9}{13}$, $\frac{11}{13}$.
8. Add $\frac{7}{15}$, $\frac{8}{15}$, $\frac{11}{15}$, $\frac{13}{15}$.
9. Add $\frac{9}{20}$, $\frac{11}{20}$, $\frac{13}{20}$, $\frac{17}{20}$.
10. Add $\frac{12}{25}$, $\frac{16}{25}$, $\frac{18}{25}$, $\frac{24}{25}$.

CASE II.

111. When the fractions have not a common denominator.

1. Add $\frac{5}{6}$, $\frac{8}{9}$, and $\frac{11}{12}$.

SOLUTION.—Reducing the fractions to a common denominator (Art. **108**), $\frac{5}{6}=\frac{30}{36}$, $\frac{8}{9}=\frac{32}{36}$, and $\frac{11}{12}=\frac{33}{36}$; then, the sum of $\frac{30}{36}$, $\frac{32}{36}$, and $\frac{33}{36}$ is $\frac{95}{36}$. $\frac{95}{36}$ are equal to $2\frac{23}{36}$.

OPERATION.

$$\frac{5}{6}=\frac{30}{36} \quad \frac{8}{9}=\frac{32}{36} \quad \frac{11}{12}=\frac{33}{36}$$
$$\frac{30}{36}+\frac{32}{36}+\frac{33}{36}=\frac{95}{36}$$
$$\frac{95}{36}=2\frac{23}{36}$$

EXPLANATION.—Since the denominators are different, the numerators do not express parts of the same size; therefore, the fractions can not be added till they are reduced to a common denominator.

Rule.—1. *Reduce the fractions to a common denominator.*

2. *Add the numerators, and under the sum write the common denominator.*

REM. 1.—Integers and fractions may be added separately and their sums then united.

REM. 2.—The integral and the fractional parts of mixed numbers may be added separately and their sums then united.

2. Add $\frac{1}{2}$ and $\frac{1}{3}$.
3. Add $\frac{1}{3}$ and $\frac{1}{4}$.
4. Add $\frac{1}{2}$ and $\frac{3}{5}$.
5. Add $\frac{5}{6}$ and $\frac{1}{9}$.
6. Add $\frac{3}{4}$ and $\frac{5}{6}$.
7. Add $\frac{7}{8}$ and $\frac{11}{12}$.
8. Add $2\frac{1}{2}$ and $3\frac{2}{3}$.

SOLUTION.—The sum of $\frac{1}{2}$ and $\frac{2}{3}$ is $\frac{7}{6}$; $\frac{7}{6} = 1\frac{1}{6}$; write the $\frac{1}{6}$ under the column of fractions and carry the 1 to the column of integers. The sum of 1, 3, and 2 is 6.

OPERATION.

$2\frac{1}{2}$
$3\frac{2}{3}$
$6\frac{1}{6}$ *Ans.*

9. Add $\frac{2}{3}$, $\frac{3}{4}$, $\frac{5}{6}$.
10. Add $\frac{1}{4}$, $\frac{7}{8}$, $\frac{11}{12}$.
11. Add $\frac{1}{8}$, $\frac{1}{9}$, $\frac{2}{11}$.
12. Add $\frac{4}{5}$, $7\frac{1}{2}$, $8\frac{3}{4}$.
13. Add $\frac{1}{12}$, $\frac{1}{13}$, $\frac{1}{14}$, $\frac{1}{15}$.
14. Add $\frac{13}{18}$, $\frac{8}{15}$, $\frac{11}{20}$, $\frac{13}{30}$.
15. Add $\frac{7}{12}$, $2\frac{5}{6}$, $3\frac{3}{8}$, $3\frac{4}{9}$.
16. Add $16\frac{2}{3}$, $12\frac{3}{4}$, $8\frac{3}{5}$, $2\frac{1}{4}$.
17. Add $\frac{1}{2}$, $\frac{1}{3}$, $\frac{1}{4}$, $\frac{1}{5}$, $\frac{1}{6}$.
18. Add $\frac{2}{5}$, $\frac{7}{16}$, $\frac{7}{50}$, $\frac{3}{140}$, $\frac{3}{2800}$.
19. Add $\frac{1}{20}$, $\frac{7}{16}$, $\frac{11}{12}$, $1\frac{2}{15}$, $2\frac{11}{18}$.
20. Add $\frac{2}{3}$, $2\frac{1}{2}$, $4\frac{1}{5}$, $6\frac{1}{3}$, $8\frac{1}{4}$.
21. Add $1\frac{1}{3}$, $4\frac{2}{7}$, $2\frac{1}{5}$, $2\frac{1}{21}$.

SUBTRACTION OF FRACTIONS.

112. Subtraction of Fractions is the process of finding the difference between two fractional numbers. There are *two cases.*

CASE I.

113. When the fractions have a common denominator.

1. From $\frac{5}{7}$ subtract $\frac{2}{7}$.

OPERATION.

SOLUTION.—2 sevenths from 5 sevenths leaves 3 sevenths.

$\frac{5}{7}-\frac{2}{7}=\frac{3}{7}$

EXPLANATION.—Since the denominators are the same, the numerators express parts of the same size; therefore, subtract 2 sevenths from 5 sevenths as you would subtract 2 cents from 5 cents; the remainder, in one case, being 3 sevenths, in the other 3 cents.

Rule.—1. *From the greater numerator subtract the less; under the remainder write the common denominator.*

2. From $\frac{3}{4}$ subtract $\frac{1}{4}$.
3. From $\frac{7}{8}$ subtract $\frac{5}{8}$.
4. From $\frac{5}{9}$ subtract $\frac{2}{9}$.
5. From $\frac{8}{10}$ subtract $\frac{3}{10}$.
6. From $3\frac{1}{8}$ subtract $1\frac{3}{8}$.

OPERATION.

SOLUTION.—$\frac{3}{8}$ can not be taken from $\frac{1}{8}$; so borrow 1 from 3. 1 equals $\frac{8}{8}$; $\frac{8}{8}$ and $\frac{1}{8}$ are $\frac{9}{8}$; $\frac{3}{8}$ from $\frac{9}{8}$ leaves $\frac{6}{8}$; $\frac{6}{8}=\frac{3}{4}$. 2 from 3 leaves 1. (25, Rem. 5.)

$$\begin{array}{r} 3\frac{1}{8} \\ 1\frac{3}{8} \\ \hline 1\frac{3}{4} \end{array} \textit{ Ans.}$$

7. From $4\frac{1}{4}$ subtract $2\frac{3}{4}$.
8. From $8\frac{1}{8}$ subtract $3\frac{2}{8}$.
9. From $23\frac{7}{20}$ subtract $17\frac{11}{20}$.

CASE II.

114. When the fractions have not a common denominator.

1. From $\frac{9}{10}$ subtract $\frac{5}{6}$.

SOLUTION.—Reducing the fractions to a common denominator (Art. **108**), $\frac{5}{6}=\frac{25}{30}$ and $\frac{9}{10}=\frac{27}{30}$; then, $\frac{25}{30}$ from $\frac{27}{30}$ leaves $\frac{2}{30}$ $\frac{2}{30}=\frac{1}{15}$.

OPERATION.

$\frac{9}{10}=\frac{27}{30}$ $\frac{5}{6}=\frac{25}{30}$

$\frac{27}{30}-\frac{25}{30}=\frac{2}{30}$

$\frac{2}{30}=\frac{1}{15}$

EXPLANATION.—Since the denominators are different, the numerators do not express parts of the same size; therefore, one fraction can not be subtracted from the other till they are reduced to a common denominator.

Rule.—1. *Reduce the fractions to a common denominator.*

2. *From the greater numerator subtract the less, and under the remainder write the common denominator.*

2. From $\frac{1}{2}$ subtract $\frac{1}{3}$.
3. From $\frac{1}{3}$ subtract $\frac{1}{4}$.
4. From $\frac{3}{4}$ subtract $\frac{2}{3}$.
5. From $\frac{4}{5}$ subtract $\frac{1}{2}$.
6. From $\frac{5}{6}$ subtract $\frac{3}{10}$.
7. From $\frac{5}{6}$ subtract $\frac{3}{8}$.
8. From $\frac{5}{9}$ subtract $\frac{1}{6}$.
9. From $\frac{4}{15}$ subtract $\frac{1}{10}$.
10. From $\frac{16}{21}$ subtract $\frac{5}{14}$.
11. From $3\frac{1}{2}$ subtract $1\frac{2}{3}$.

SOLUTION.—$\frac{1}{2}$ equals $\frac{3}{6}$, and $\frac{2}{3}$ equals $\frac{4}{6}$. $\frac{4}{6}$ can not be taken from $\frac{3}{6}$; so borrow 1 from the 3. 1 equals $\frac{6}{6}$; $\frac{6}{6}$ and $\frac{3}{6}$ are $\frac{9}{6}$; $\frac{4}{6}$ from $\frac{9}{6}$ leaves $\frac{5}{6}$. 2 from 3 leaves 1.

OPERATION.

$$\begin{array}{r} 3\frac{1}{2} \\ 1\frac{2}{3} \\ \hline 1\frac{5}{6} \end{array}$$ *Ans.*

12. From 5 subtract $\frac{2}{3}$.
13. From $5\frac{2}{8}$ subtract $4\frac{1}{2}$.
14. From $7\frac{2}{3}$ subtract $4\frac{3}{4}$.
15. From $14\frac{1}{4}$ subtract $12\frac{2}{3}$.
16. From $5\frac{3}{14}$ subtract $2\frac{10}{21}$.
17. From $4\frac{1}{24}$ subtract $3\frac{1}{16}$.
18. From $56\frac{1}{3}$ subtract $42\frac{1}{4}$.
19. From $60\frac{4}{5}$ subtract $41\frac{3}{10}$.
20. From $97\frac{1}{2}$ subtract $48\frac{5}{6}$.

MULTIPLICATION OF FRACTIONS.

115. Multiplication of Fractions is the process of finding the product of two or more fractional numbers.

1. If 1 apple cost $\frac{4}{5}$ of a cent, what will 3 apples cost?

OPERATION.
$\frac{4}{5} \times \frac{3}{1} = \frac{12}{5}$
$\frac{12}{5} = 2\frac{2}{5}$

Solution.—They will cost 3 times $\frac{4}{5}$ of a cent $= \frac{12}{5}$ of a cent (Art. **101**, Prin. 1). $\frac{12}{5}$ equals $2\frac{2}{5}$.

Explanation.—3 apples will cost $\frac{4}{5} + \frac{4}{5} + \frac{4}{5} = \frac{12}{5}$ of a cent; hence, 3 times $\frac{4}{5} = \frac{12}{5}$.

2 At 12 ct. a yard, what will $\frac{2}{5}$ of a yard of ribbon cost?

OPERATION.
$\frac{12}{1} \times \frac{2}{5} = \frac{24}{5}$
$\frac{24}{5} = 4\frac{4}{5}$

Solution.—$\frac{1}{5}$ of a yard will cost $\frac{1}{5}$ of $12 = \frac{12}{5}$ ct. then, $\frac{2}{5}$ of a yard will cost 2 times $\frac{12}{5} = \frac{24}{5}$ ct. (Ex. 1). $\frac{24}{5} = 4\frac{4}{5}$.

3. What will $\frac{4}{7}$ of a yard of cloth cost, at $\frac{3}{5}$ of a dollar per yard?

OPERATION.
$\frac{3}{5} \times \frac{4}{7} = \frac{12}{35}$

Solution.—$\frac{1}{7}$ of a yard will cost $\frac{1}{7}$ of $\frac{3}{5} = \frac{3}{35}$ of a dollar; then, $\frac{4}{7}$ of a yard will cost 4 times $\frac{3}{35} = \frac{12}{35}$ of a dollar.

EXPLANATION.—$\frac{1}{7}$ of $\frac{1}{5}$ of a dollar is $\frac{1}{35}$ of a dollar (Art. **99**) then, $\frac{1}{7}$ of $\frac{3}{5}$ of a dollar is 3 times $\frac{1}{35}=\frac{3}{35}$ of a dollar (Ex. 1).

4. Multiply $\frac{2}{3}$ by $\frac{4}{5}$.

SOLUTION.—$\frac{4}{5}$ is the same as $\frac{1}{5}$ of 4 (Art. **96**). $\frac{2}{3}$ multiplied by 4 is $\frac{8}{3}$ (Art. **101**, Prin. 1); then, $\frac{2}{3}$ multiplied by $\frac{1}{5}$ of 4 is $\frac{1}{5}$ of $\frac{8}{3}=\frac{8}{15}$ (Ex. 3, Explanation).

OPERATION.
$\frac{2}{3}\times\frac{4}{5}=\frac{8}{15}$

Rule.—1. *Multiply together the numerators of the given fractions for the numerator of the product.*

2. *Multiply together the denominators of the given fractions for the denominator of the product.*

REM. 1.—Express integers in the form of fractions (Art. **97**, 3).

REM. 2.—Reduce mixed numbers to improper fractions (Art. **104**). Sometimes it may be more convenient to multiply by the integral and fractional parts separately.

REM. 3.—Indicate the operation and apply the Rule for Cancellation wherever it is practicable (Art. **91**, Rule).

5. Multiply $\frac{3}{4}$ by 3.
6. Multiply 8 by $\frac{2}{3}$.
7. Multiply $\frac{3}{4}$ by $\frac{5}{7}$.
8. Multiply $\frac{2}{3}$ by 4.
9. Multiply 5 by $\frac{3}{4}$.
10. Multiply $\frac{8}{9}$ by $\frac{3}{4}$.

SOLUTION.—Indicating the operation and applying the Rule for Cancellation (Art. **91**), the result is $\frac{2}{3}$.

OPERATION.
$\frac{\overset{2}{\cancel{8}}}{\underset{3}{\cancel{9}}}\times\frac{\cancel{3}}{\cancel{4}}=\frac{2}{3}$

11. Multiply $\frac{2}{3}$ by 6.
12. Multiply 20 by $\frac{3}{4}$.
13. Multiply $\frac{8}{13}$ by $\frac{11}{16}$.
14. Multiply $\frac{3}{5}$ by 10.

15. Multiply 12 by $\frac{2}{3}$.
16. Multiply $\frac{9}{13}$ by $\frac{3}{7}$.
17. Multiply $\frac{3}{7}$ by 6.
18. Multiply 7 by $\frac{2}{3}$.
19. Multiply $2\frac{1}{4}$ by $3\frac{1}{2}$.

SOLUTION.—Reducing $2\frac{1}{4}$ and $3\frac{1}{2}$ to improper fractions (Art. **104**), they are $\frac{9}{4}$ and $\frac{7}{2}$. Multiplying together $\frac{9}{4}$ and $\frac{7}{2}$, the result is $\frac{63}{8} = 7\frac{7}{8}$.

OPERATION.

$$2\frac{1}{4} = \frac{9}{4} \quad 3\frac{1}{2} = \frac{7}{2}$$
$$\frac{9}{4} \times \frac{7}{2} = \frac{63}{8}$$
$$\frac{63}{8} = 7\frac{7}{8}$$

20. Multiply $18\frac{3}{4}$ by 8.

SOLUTION.—8 times 18 is 144. 8 times $\frac{3}{4}$ is 6. $144 + 6 = 150$.

OPERATION.

$$\begin{array}{r} 18\frac{3}{4} \\ 8 \\ \hline 144 \\ 6 \\ \hline 150 \end{array}$$

21. Multiply 8 by $3\frac{2}{3}$.
22. Multiply $2\frac{1}{2}$ by $2\frac{1}{2}$.
23. Multiply $10\frac{7}{9}$ by 7.
24. Multiply 25 by $8\frac{3}{5}$.
25. Multiply $\frac{9}{10}$ by $17\frac{3}{11}$.
26. Multiply $10\frac{5}{6}$ by 9.
27. Multiply 64 by $8\frac{7}{8}$.
28. Multiply $8\frac{3}{4}$ by $\frac{3}{7}$.

Multiply together:

29. $\frac{5}{12}$, $\frac{9}{16}$, $2\frac{2}{11}$.
30. $2\frac{1}{16}$, $\frac{3}{11}$, $1\frac{7}{9}$.
31. $6\frac{3}{4}$, $2\frac{8}{9}$, 21.
32. $2\frac{1}{2}$, $3\frac{2}{3}$, $4\frac{3}{4}$, $1\frac{1}{7}$.
33. $2\frac{1}{5}$, $2\frac{3}{26}$, $3\frac{1}{4}$, $1\frac{5}{11}$.
34. $\frac{7}{8}$, $\frac{3}{10}$, $\frac{8}{9}$, $\frac{5}{6}$, $\frac{2}{3}$, $\frac{6}{7}$.
35. $\frac{1}{4}$, $\frac{9}{7}$, $\frac{4}{5}$, $\frac{7}{9}$, $\frac{5}{4}$, $\frac{2}{3}$, 6.

36. $\frac{6}{7}$, $\frac{4}{9}$, $1\frac{3}{4}$, $\frac{1}{6}$, $\frac{3}{4}$, $\frac{5}{6}$, $\frac{2}{5}$, 20.
37. $2\frac{1}{2}$, $6\frac{2}{5}$, $3\frac{1}{4}$, $\frac{7}{18}$, 2, $\frac{3}{7}$.

116. Fractional parts of integers are obtained by multiplication.

1. What is $\frac{2}{3}$ of 2?

OPERATION.
$\frac{2}{3} \times \frac{2}{1} = \frac{4}{3}$
$\frac{4}{3} = 1\frac{1}{3}$

SOLUTION.—$\frac{1}{3}$ of 2 is $\frac{2}{3}$ (Art. **96**); then, $\frac{2}{3}$ of 2 is 2 times $\frac{2}{3} = \frac{4}{3}$. $\frac{4}{3} = 1\frac{1}{3}$.

2. What is $\frac{3}{4}$ of 5?
3. What is $\frac{2}{5}$ of 7?
4. What is $\frac{4}{5}$ of 10?
5. What is $\frac{5}{6}$ of 12?
6. What is $\frac{5}{6}$ of 15?
7. What is $\frac{8}{9}$ of 21?
8. What is $\frac{7}{10}$ of 25?
9. What is $\frac{5}{12}$ of 27?
10. What is $\frac{7}{12}$ of 28?

117. Compound fractions (Art. **99**) are reduced to simple fractions by multiplication.

1. Reduce $\frac{2}{3}$ of $\frac{4}{5}$ to a simple fraction.

OPERATION.
$\frac{2}{3} \times \frac{4}{5} = \frac{8}{15}$.

SOLUTION.—Multiplying $\frac{2}{3}$ by $\frac{4}{5}$ (Art. **115**, Rule), the result is $\frac{8}{15}$.

2. Reduce $\frac{2}{3}$ of $\frac{5}{7}$ to a simple fraction.
3. Reduce $\frac{3}{5}$ of $\frac{7}{8}$ to a simple fraction.
4. Reduce $\frac{1}{2}$ of $\frac{3}{5}$ of $2\frac{3}{4}$ to a simple fraction.
5. Reduce $\frac{7}{11}$ of $\frac{2}{3}$ to a simple fraction.
6. Reduce $\frac{3}{4}$ of $\frac{5}{8}$ to a simple fraction.
7. Reduce $\frac{2}{3}$ of $\frac{5}{7}$ of $1\frac{4}{9}$ to a simple fraction.

8. Reduce $\frac{2}{3}$ of $\frac{3}{4}$ of $\frac{4}{5}$ to a simple fraction.
9. Reduce $\frac{1}{3}$ of $\frac{3}{4}$ of $\frac{5}{6}$ to a simple fraction.
10. Reduce $\frac{3}{5}$ of $\frac{5}{7}$ of $\frac{7}{8}$ to a simple fraction.
11. Reduce $\frac{3}{5}$ of $\frac{4}{9}$ of $\frac{7}{12}$ of $\frac{18}{35}$ to a simple fraction.

12. Reduce $\frac{1}{3}$ of $\frac{3}{4}$ of $\frac{4}{9}$ to a simple fraction.
13. Reduce $\frac{1}{9}$ of $\frac{3}{4}$ of $1\frac{1}{3}$ to a simple fraction.
14. Reduce $\frac{3}{5}$ of $\frac{6}{7}$ of $1\frac{17}{18}$ to an integer.
15. Reduce $\frac{3}{7}$ of $2\frac{2}{3}$ of $1\frac{3}{4}$ to an integer.
16. Reduce $\frac{9}{13}$ of $\frac{7}{18}$ of $1\frac{6}{7}$ to a simple fraction.
17. Reduce $\frac{1}{2}$ of $\frac{4}{5}$ of $\frac{1}{8}$ of 5 to a simple fraction.
18. Reduce $\frac{1}{2}$ of $\frac{2}{3}$ of $\frac{3}{4}$ of $\frac{4}{5}$ of $\frac{5}{8}$ of $\frac{5}{9}$ of $\frac{9}{10}$ to a simple fraction.

Miscellaneous Examples.

118. What will be the cost

1. Of $2\frac{1}{3}$ lb. of meat, at $13\frac{1}{5}$ ct. a lb.?
2. Of 3 yd. linen, at $\$\frac{2}{3}$ a yd.? Of 5 yd.? Of 7 yd.? Of $6\frac{1}{2}$ yd.? $5\frac{3}{4}$ yd.?
3. Of $3\frac{1}{3}$ lb. of rice, at $4\frac{4}{5}$ ct. a lb.?
4. Of $3\frac{1}{5}$ tons of iron, at $\$18\frac{3}{4}$ per T.?
5. Of $1\frac{2}{3}$ yd. of muslin, at $\$\frac{3}{20}$ per yd.?
6. Of $2\frac{1}{2}$ lb. of tea, at $\$\frac{4}{5}$ per lb.?
7. Of $5\frac{5}{9}$ cords of wood, at $\$1\frac{1}{5}$ per C.?
8. At the rate of $5\frac{1}{2}$ miles an hour, how far will a man travel in $7\frac{3}{4}$ hours?
9. I own $\frac{2}{3}$ of a steamboat, and sell $\frac{3}{5}$ of my share: what part of the boat do I sell?
10. At $\$6\frac{3}{4}$ per yard, what cost $\frac{2}{9}$ of a piece of cloth containing $5\frac{1}{2}$ yards?
11. $\frac{3}{7}$ of $\frac{5}{9}$ of $16\frac{1}{2} \times \frac{3}{8}$ of $\frac{7}{8}$ of $15 =$ what?
12. What is the sum of $\frac{2}{3} + \frac{3}{4}$ and $\frac{2}{3} \times \frac{3}{4}$?

DIVISION OF FRACTIONS.

119. Division of Fractions is the process of finding the quotient of two fractional numbers.

1. If 3 yards of ribbon cost $\frac{6}{7}$ of a dollar, what will 1 yard cost?

OPERATION.

SOLUTION.—1 yard will cost $\frac{1}{3}$ of $\frac{6}{7}=\frac{2}{7}$ of a dollar (Art. **117**).

$$\frac{\overset{2}{\cancel{6}}}{7}\times\frac{1}{\cancel{3}}=\frac{2}{7}$$

EXPLANATION.—$\frac{6}{7}$ is to be divided into 3 equal parts. Each part will be $\frac{2}{7}$ (Art. **101**, Prin. 2); for $\frac{6}{7}=\frac{2}{7}+\frac{2}{7}+\frac{2}{7}$.

2. At 2 dollars a yard, what part of a yard of cloth can be bought for $\frac{3}{5}$ of a dollar?

SOLUTION.—For 1 dollar $\frac{1}{2}$ a yard can be bought, and for $\frac{1}{5}$ of a dollar $\frac{1}{5}$ of $\frac{1}{2}=\frac{1}{10}$ of a yard (Art. **117**); then, for $\frac{3}{5}$ of a dollar 3 times $\frac{1}{10}=\frac{3}{10}$ of a yard can be bought.

OPERATION.

$$\frac{3}{5}\times\frac{1}{2}=\frac{3}{10}$$

EXPLANATION.—Were it required to find how many yards, at \$2 a yard, could be bought for \$6, then 6 would be divided by 2; hence, to find the part of a yard that \$$\frac{3}{5}$ will pay for, $\frac{3}{5}$ must be divided by 2. To divide $\frac{3}{5}$ by 2, multiply the denominator (Art. **101**, Prin. 3).

3. At $\frac{2}{3}$ of a cent for 1 apple, how many can be bought for 4 cents?

SOLUTION.—For $\frac{1}{3}$ of a cent $\frac{1}{2}$ an apple can be bought, and for $\frac{3}{3}$, or 1 cent, 3 times $\frac{1}{2}=\frac{3}{2}$ of an apple; then, for 4 cents, there can be bought 4 times $\frac{3}{2}=6$ apples.

OPERATION.

$$\frac{\overset{2}{\cancel{4}}}{1}\times\frac{3}{\cancel{2}}=6$$

4. At $\frac{2}{3}$ of a cent for 1 apple, how many apples can be bought for $\frac{3}{4}$ of a cent?

SOLUTION.—For $\frac{1}{3}$ of a cent $\frac{1}{2}$ an apple can be bought, and for $\frac{3}{3}$, or 1 cent, 3 times $\frac{1}{2}=\frac{3}{2}$ of an apple; then, for $\frac{1}{4}$ of a cent $\frac{1}{4}$ of $\frac{3}{2}=\frac{3}{8}$ of an apple can be bought (Art. **117**), and for $\frac{3}{4}$ of a cent 3 times $\frac{3}{8}=1\frac{1}{8}$ apples.

OPERATION.

$\frac{3}{4}\times\frac{3}{2}=\frac{9}{8}$

$\frac{9}{8}=1\frac{1}{8}$

5. Divide $\frac{3}{4}$ by $\frac{4}{5}$.

SOLUTION.—$\frac{4}{5}$ is the same as $\frac{1}{5}$ of 4 (Art. **96**). $\frac{3}{4}$ divided by 4 is $\frac{3}{16}$ (Art. **101,** Prin. 3); then, $\frac{3}{4}$ divided by $\frac{1}{5}$ of 4 is 5 times $\frac{3}{16}=\frac{15}{16}$ (Art. **115,** Ex. 1).

OPERATION.

$\frac{3}{4}\times\frac{5}{4}=\frac{15}{16}$

Rule.—*Multiply the dividend by the divisor with its terms inverted.*

REM. 1.—Express integers in the form of fractions (Art. **97,** 3).

REM. 2.—Reduce mixed numbers to improper fractions (Art. **104**).

REM. 3.—Indicate the operation and apply the Rule for Cancellation whenever it is practicable (Art. **91,** Rule).

6. If 4 yards of muslin cost $\frac{8}{9}$ of a dollar, what will 1 yard cost?

7. At $\frac{1}{2}$ a cent each, how many apples can be bought for 3 cents?

8. At $\frac{1}{5}$ of a dollar per yard, how many yards of muslin can be bought for $\$\frac{9}{10}$?

9. If 1 orange cost 3 cents, what part of an orange could be purchased for $\frac{1}{2}$ a cent?

10. At $\frac{3}{4}$ of a dollar per yard, how many yards of cloth can you buy for 6 dollars?

11. At $\frac{1}{5}$ of a dollar per yard, how many yards of ribbon can be purchased for $\frac{3}{4}$ of a dollar?

12. If 7 pounds of rice cost $\frac{14}{25}$ of a dollar, what will 1 pound cost?

13. Divide $4\frac{1}{2}$ by $1\frac{1}{3}$.

OPERATION.

$4\frac{1}{2}=\frac{9}{2}$

$1\frac{1}{3}=\frac{4}{3}$

$\frac{9}{2}\times\frac{3}{4}=\frac{27}{8}$

$\frac{27}{8}=3\frac{3}{8}$

SOLUTION.—Reducing $4\frac{1}{2}$ and $1\frac{1}{3}$ to improper fractions (Art. **104**), we have $\frac{9}{2}$ and $\frac{4}{3}$. Dividing $\frac{9}{2}$ by $\frac{4}{3}$, the result is $3\frac{3}{8}$.

14. Divide $2\frac{2}{5}$ by 6.
15. Divide 22 by $5\frac{1}{2}$.
16. Divide $2\frac{1}{2}$ by $\frac{1}{16}$.
17. Divide $4\frac{4}{5}$ by 8.
18. Divide 6 by $2\frac{2}{5}$.
19. Divide $4\frac{3}{4}$ by $5\frac{1}{8}$.
20. Divide $12\frac{4}{7}$ by 11.
21. Divide 30 by $3\frac{3}{4}$.
22. Divide $2\frac{1}{4}$ by $7\frac{1}{2}$.
23. Divide $3\frac{2}{3}$ by 7.
24. Divide 50 by $4\frac{3}{7}$.
25. Divide $\frac{1}{2}$ by $\frac{1}{50}$.
26. Divide $47\frac{2}{5}$ by 15.
27. Divide 56 by $5\frac{4}{9}$.
28. Divide $\frac{14}{15}$ by 21.
29. Divide $130\frac{2}{3}$ by 18.
30. Divide $\frac{1}{2}$ of $\frac{2}{3}$ by $\frac{3}{4}$ of $\frac{4}{5}$.

OPERATION.

$\frac{1}{2}\times\frac{2}{3}\times\frac{4}{3}\times\frac{5}{4}=\frac{5}{9}$

EXPLANATION.—Invert the terms of both $\frac{3}{4}$ and $\frac{4}{5}$ as in the case of the divisor being a simple fraction.

31. Divide $\frac{3}{5}$ of $\frac{8}{9}$ by $\frac{6}{7}$ of $\frac{3}{4}$.
32. Divide $\frac{1}{3}$ of $5\frac{1}{8}$ by $\frac{3}{4}$ of $17\frac{1}{2}$.
33. Divide $\frac{5}{18}$ of $\frac{2}{5}$ of $12\frac{3}{10}$ by $\frac{1}{5}$ of $8\frac{1}{5}$.
34. Divide $\frac{2}{7}$ of $\frac{7}{8}$ by $\frac{3}{4}$ of $\frac{1}{3}$ of 5.
35. Divide $\frac{5}{18}$ of $\frac{2}{5}$ of $12\frac{3}{10}$ by $\frac{1}{5}$ of $4\frac{1}{10}$ of 20.

120. What part one number is of another is found by division.

1. 1 is what part of 2?

SOLUTION.—1 is $\frac{1}{2}$ of 2; for $\frac{1}{2}$ of 2 is $\frac{2}{2}$, or 1 (Art. **96,** 2d).

OPERATION: $\frac{1}{1} \times \frac{1}{2} = \frac{1}{2}$

2. 2 is what part of 3?

SOLUTION.—1 is $\frac{1}{3}$ of 3; then, 2 is 2 times $\frac{1}{3} = \frac{2}{3}$ of 3.

OPERATION: $\frac{2}{1} \times \frac{1}{3} = \frac{2}{3}$

3. $\frac{1}{2}$ is what part of 3?

SOLUTION.—1 is $\frac{1}{3}$ of 3; then, $\frac{1}{2}$ is $\frac{1}{2}$ of $\frac{1}{3} = \frac{1}{6}$ of 3.

OPERATION. $\frac{1}{2} \times \frac{1}{3} = \frac{1}{6}$

4. $\frac{2}{3}$ is what part of $\frac{3}{4}$?

SOLUTION.—$\frac{1}{4}$ is $\frac{1}{3}$ of $\frac{3}{4}$, and $\frac{4}{4}$, or 1, is 4 times $\frac{1}{3} = \frac{4}{3}$ of $\frac{3}{4}$; then, $\frac{1}{3}$ is $\frac{1}{3}$ of $\frac{4}{3} = \frac{4}{9}$ of $\frac{3}{4}$, and $\frac{2}{3}$ is 2 times $\frac{4}{9} = \frac{8}{9}$ of $\frac{3}{4}$.

OPERATION. $\frac{2}{3} \times \frac{4}{3} = \frac{8}{9}$

5. 3 is what part of 4?
6. $\frac{3}{4}$ is what part of 5?
7. $\frac{1}{4}$ is what part of $\frac{1}{2}$?
8. $\frac{2}{3}$ is what part of $\frac{5}{6}$?
9. $3\frac{3}{4}$ is what part of 5?
10. $\frac{5}{6}$ is what part of $\frac{8}{9}$?
11. $8\frac{5}{9}$ is what part of 11?
12. $\frac{21}{32}$ is what part of $\frac{35}{48}$?

121. Complex fractions, (Art. **100**) are reduced to simple fractions by division.

1. Reduce $\dfrac{1\frac{1}{4}}{2\frac{1}{3}}$ to a simple fraction.

SOLUTION.—Reducing $1\frac{1}{4}$ and $2\frac{1}{3}$ to improper fractions (Art. **104**), we have $\frac{5}{4}$ and $\frac{7}{3}$. Dividing $\frac{5}{4}$ by $\frac{7}{3}$ (Art. **119**), the result is $\frac{15}{28}$.

OPERATION.

$1\frac{1}{4} = \frac{5}{4}$

$2\frac{1}{3} = \frac{7}{3}$

$\frac{5}{4} \times \frac{3}{7} = \frac{15}{28}$

2. Reduce $\frac{\frac{6}{7}}{\frac{11}{5}}$ to a simple fraction.

3. Reduce $\frac{\frac{2}{3}}{5}$ to a simple fraction.

4. Reduce $\frac{2}{3\frac{2}{3}}$ to a simple fraction.

5. Reduce $\frac{3\frac{1}{8}}{4\frac{5}{7}}$ to a simple fraction.

6. Reduce $\frac{2\frac{1}{3}}{4\frac{1}{2}}$ to a simple fraction.

7. Reduce $\frac{3\frac{3}{4}}{5\frac{5}{8}}$ to a simple fraction.

8. Reduce $\frac{9\frac{7}{9}}{2\frac{1}{27}}$ to a mixed number.

9. Reduce $\frac{8\frac{3}{4}}{5\frac{5}{8}}$ to a mixed number.

10. Reduce $\frac{7\frac{5}{6}}{8\frac{9}{11}}$ to a simple fraction.

Miscellaneous Examples.

122. 1. At $\frac{1}{2}$ a dollar per yard, how many yards of silk can be bought for \$$3\frac{1}{4}$?

2. At $\frac{3}{5}$ of a dollar per pound, how many pounds of tea can be purchased for \$$2\frac{3}{10}$?

3. At $3\frac{3}{4}$ dollars per yard for cloth, how many yards can be purchased with \$$42\frac{1}{2}$?

4. By what must $\frac{3}{8}$ be multiplied that the product may be 10?

5. Divide $3\frac{3}{7}$ by $\frac{3}{7}$ of $1\frac{1}{2}$.

6. Divide $\frac{4}{11}$ of $27\frac{1}{2}$ by $\frac{3}{10}$ of $21\frac{1}{4}$.

7. Multiply $\frac{1\frac{1}{2}}{2\frac{1}{3}}$ by $\frac{\frac{3}{7}}{4\frac{1}{2}}$.

8. Multiply $\frac{7\frac{8}{15}}{9\frac{5}{12}}$ of $\frac{2\frac{1}{9}}{3\frac{2}{15}}$ by $\frac{1\frac{1}{4}}{\frac{5}{6}}$.

9. Divide $\frac{1\frac{1}{2}}{\frac{2}{3}}$ by $\frac{2\frac{2}{5}}{2\frac{1}{6}}$.

10. Divide $\frac{1\frac{2}{3}}{2\frac{1}{2}}$ by $\frac{5\frac{1}{7}}{84\frac{6}{7}}$.

FRACTIONAL COMPOUND NUMBERS.

123. 1. Add $\$16\frac{1}{16}$; $\$9\frac{1}{8}$; $\$5\frac{7}{16}$; $\$2\frac{13}{16}$.

2. I paid for books $\$9\frac{1}{8}$; for paper, $\$4\frac{7}{16}$; for a slate, $\$\frac{3}{8}$; for pens, $\$1\frac{5}{8}$; what amount did I expend?

3. Having $\$50\frac{1}{4}$, I paid a bill of $\$27\frac{3}{16}$: how much had I left?

4. From $\$32.31\frac{1}{4}$ take $\$15.12\frac{1}{2}$.

5. From $\$5.81\frac{1}{4}$ take $\$1.18\frac{3}{4}$.

Find the cost of

6. 9 yd. of muslin, at $12\frac{1}{2}$ ct. a yd.
7. 21 lb. of sugar, at $6\frac{1}{4}$ ct. a lb.
8. 15 yd. of cloth, at $\$3.18\frac{3}{4}$ per yd.
9. $5\frac{1}{2}$ yd. of linen, at $\$0.62\frac{1}{2}$ per yd.
10. $12\frac{1}{2}$ yd. of ribbon, at $18\frac{3}{4}$ ct. per yd.
11. $13\frac{1}{2}$ yd. of calico, at $16\frac{2}{3}$ ct. per yd.
12. $10\frac{1}{4}$ yd. of cloth, at $\$3.37\frac{1}{2}$ a yard.
13. $17\frac{2}{3}$ dozen books, at $\$3.75$ per dozen.

14. At $18\frac{3}{4}$ ct. per yard, how many yards of muslin can be purchased for $2.25?

15. At $37\frac{1}{2}$ ct. per bushel, how many bushels of barley can you buy for $\$5.81\frac{1}{4}$?

16. If 5 yards of cloth cost $\$11.56\frac{1}{4}$, what cost one yard?

17. Seven men share $\$31.06\frac{1}{4}$ equally: what is the share of each man?

18. Reduce 5 mi. to inches.

19. Reduce 2 mi. 2 rd. 2 ft. to feet.

20. Reduce 20 yd. to rods.

21. Reduce 15875 ft. to miles.

22. Reduce 142634 in. to miles.

23. How many steps, of 2 ft. 8 in. each, will a man take in walking 2 miles?

24. How many revolutions will a wheel, of 9 ft. 2 in. circumference, make in running 65 miles?

25. Reduce 1 A. 136 sq. rd. 25 sq. yd. to square yards.

26. Reduce 7506 sq. yd. to A.

27. Reduce 5 chains 15 links to in.

28. How many acres in a field $40\frac{1}{2}$ rd. long and 32 rd. wide?

29. Reduce 4 years to hours.

30. Reduce 914092 hr. to cen.

31. In what time will a body move from the earth to the moon, at the rate of 31 miles per day, the distance being 238545 miles?

124. A fraction is reduced to a lower denomination by multiplication (Art. **63,** Rule I).

1. Reduce $\frac{1}{24}$ of a peck to the fraction of a pint.

SOLUTION.—To reduce $\frac{1}{24}$ of a peck to the fraction of a pint, multiply by 8 and by 2. The result is $\frac{2}{3}$ of a pint.

OPERATION.

$$\frac{1}{24} \times \frac{8}{1} \times \frac{2}{1} = \frac{2}{3}$$
(24 cancelled to 3, 8 cancelled)

2. Reduce $\frac{1}{40}$ bu. to the fraction of a quart.

3. Reduce $\frac{1}{28}$ lb. to the fraction of an ounce.

4. Reduce $\frac{1}{16}$ lb. Troy to the fraction of an ounce.

5. Reduce $\frac{1}{20}$ rd. to the fraction of a foot.

6. Reduce $\frac{7}{1280}$ A. to the fraction of a square rod.

7. Reduce $\$\frac{3}{350}$ to the fraction of a cent.
8. Reduce $\frac{1}{1584}$ da. to the fraction of a minute.
9. Reduce $\frac{3}{320}$ bu. to the fraction of a pint.

125. In reducing a fraction to a lower denomination, when the result is a mixed number, proceed only with the reduction of the fractional part. This is called finding the value of a fraction *in integers.*

1. Find the value of $\frac{2}{5}$ of a day in integers.

Solution.—To reduce $\frac{2}{5}$ of a day to hours, multiply by 24; the result is $9\frac{3}{5}$ hr. To reduce $\frac{3}{5}$ of an hour to minutes, multiply by 60; the result is 36 min. $\frac{2}{5}$ of a day, then, is 9 hr. 36 min.

OPERATION.

$\frac{2}{5} \times \frac{24}{1} = 9\frac{3}{5}$

$\frac{3}{5} \times \frac{60}{1} = 36$

2. Find the value of $\frac{4}{5}$ mi. in integers.
3. Find the value of $\$\frac{3}{5}$ in integers.
4. Find the value of $\frac{2}{5}$ mi. in integers.
5. Find the value of $\frac{4}{5}$ lb. Troy in integers.
6. Find the value of $\frac{7}{16}$ T. in integers.
7. Find the value of $\frac{5}{8}$ A. in integers.
8. Find the value of $\frac{7}{8}$ of 63 gallons of wine in integers.

126. A fraction is reduced to a higher denomination by division (Art. **63**, Rule II).

1. Reduce $\frac{2}{3}$ of a pint to the fraction of a peck.

Solution.—To reduce $\frac{2}{3}$ of a pint to the fraction of a peck, divide by 2 and by 8. The result is $\frac{1}{24}$ of a peck.

OPERATION.

$\frac{2}{3} \times \frac{1}{2} \times \frac{1}{8} = \frac{1}{24}$

2. Reduce $\frac{4}{5}$ qt. to the fraction of a bushel.
3. Reduce $\frac{4}{5}$ ft. to the fraction of a rod.

4. Reduce $\frac{3}{80}$ oz. to the fraction of a pound.
5. Reduce $\frac{4}{9}$ lb. to the fraction of a ton.
6. Reduce $\frac{3}{5}$ pt. to the fraction of a bushel.
7. Reduce $\frac{4}{7}$ oz. to the fraction of a hundred-weight.

8. Reduce $\frac{3}{4}$ in. to the fraction of a rod.
9. Reduce $\frac{8}{9}$ min. to the fraction of a day.
10. Reduce $\frac{5}{112}$ oz. to the fraction of a hundred-weight.

127. To find what part one compound number is of another, reduce them to the same denomination and proceed as in Art. **120.**

1. 2 ft. 3 in. is what part of a yard?

OPERATION.

2 ft. 3 in. = 27 in.
1 yd. = 36 in.
$\frac{27}{36} = \frac{3}{4}$

SOLUTION.—2 ft. 3 in. equals 27 in. 1 yd. equals 36 in. 27 in. are $\frac{27}{36}$ of 36 in. $\frac{27}{36}$ equals $\frac{3}{4}$. 2 ft. 3 in., then, is $\frac{3}{4}$ of a yard.

2. 2 ft. 6 in. is what part of 6 ft. 8 in.?
3. 2 pk. 4 qt. is what part of a bushel?
4. What part is 2 yd. 9 in. of 8 yd. 2 ft. 3 in.?
5. What part of a day is 13 hr. 30 min.?
6. What part of a mile is 145 rd.?
7. What part of a yard is 2 ft. 8 in.?
8. 15 mi. 123 rd. is what part of 35 mi. 287 rd.?
9. A man has a farm of 168 A. 28 sq. rd.; if he sell 37 A. 94 sq. rd., what part of his farm will he dispose of?
10. What part of a pound is $7\frac{1}{9}$ oz.?
11. 2 qt. $1\frac{1}{3}$pt. is what part of 1 bu. 1 qt. $1\frac{3}{8}$ pt.?

12. 1 yd. 1 ft. $1\frac{9}{11}$ in. is what part of 3 yd. 2 ft. $8\frac{6}{7}$ in.?

128. To add and subtract fractional compound numbers, find the value of the fractions in integers and then proceed as in Addition and Subtraction of Compound Numbers.

1. Add $\frac{3}{4}$ yd. and $\frac{5}{6}$ ft.

OPERATION.

$\frac{3}{4}$ yd. = 2 ft. 3 in.
$\frac{5}{6}$ ft. = 10 in.
3 ft. 1 in.

SOLUTION.—$\frac{3}{4}$ yd. equals 2 ft. 3 in.; $\frac{5}{6}$ ft. equals 10 in.; the sum of 2 ft. 3 in. and 10 in. is 3 ft. 1 in. (Art. **75**).

2. From $\frac{2}{9}$ da. subtract $\frac{5}{6}$ hr.

OPERATION.

$\frac{2}{9}$ da. = 5 hr. 20 min.
$\frac{5}{6}$ hr. = 50 min.
4 hr. 30 min.

SOLUTION.—$\frac{2}{9}$ da. equals 5 hr. 20 min.; $\frac{5}{6}$ hr. equals 50 min.; 50 min. subtracted from 5 hr. 20 min. leaves 4 hr. 30 min. (Art. **76**).

3. Add $\frac{2}{3}$ da. and $\frac{3}{4}$ hr.
4. Add $\frac{1}{4}$ wk. $\frac{1}{4}$ da. and $\frac{1}{4}$ hr.
5. Add $\frac{2}{3}$ wk. $\frac{5}{9}$ da. $\frac{2}{3}$ hr. and $\frac{2}{3}$ min.

6. Add $\frac{11}{12}$ gal. and $\frac{1}{12}$ qt.
7. From $\frac{7}{9}$ da. subtract $\frac{1}{18}$ hr.
8. From $\$\frac{5}{8}$ subtract $\$\frac{3}{40}$.
9. From $\frac{3}{8}$ lb. subtract $\frac{7}{8}$ oz.
10. From $\frac{1}{7}$ da. subtract $\frac{6}{7}$ hr.

129. Promiscuous Examples.

1. Reduce $\frac{32989}{56981}$ to its lowest terms.
2. Add $\frac{5}{14}$, $\frac{8}{21}$, $2\frac{1}{2}$, $3\frac{2}{3}$.
3. From $3\frac{4}{7}$ subtract $1\frac{4}{5}$.
4. From $3\frac{5}{8}$ subtract $\frac{1}{3}$ of $3\frac{1}{2}$.
5. Add $\frac{5}{9}$ of $\frac{7}{10}$ and $\frac{2}{5}$ of $\frac{7}{12}$.

6. Add $1\frac{3}{4} \div 2\frac{1}{2}$ and $5\frac{1}{2} \div 3\frac{1}{8}$.

7. What number divided by $\frac{3}{5}$ will give 10 for a quotient?

8. What number multiplied by $\frac{3}{5}$ will give 10 for a product?

9. What number is that, from which if you take $\frac{3}{7}$ of itself, the remainder will be 16?

10. What number is that, to which if you add $\frac{3}{7}$ of itself, the sum will be 20?

11. A boat is worth \$900; a merchant owns $\frac{5}{8}$ of it, and sells $\frac{1}{3}$ of his share: what part has he left, and what is it worth?

12. I own $\frac{7}{12}$ of a ship, and sell $\frac{1}{3}$ of my share for \$1944$\frac{4}{9}$: what is the whole ship worth?

13. What part of 3 cents is $\frac{2}{3}$ of 2 cents?

14. What part of 368 is 176?

15. From $\frac{25}{37}$ subtract the sum of $\frac{1}{8}$, $\frac{1}{18}$, and $\frac{13}{111}$.

16. From 1 subtract $\frac{3}{10}$ of $\frac{7}{12}$ of $4\frac{9}{14}$.

17. From $\frac{2}{3} \div \frac{5}{7}$ subtract $\frac{5}{8} \div \frac{10}{11}$.

18. If I ride 2044 rods in $\frac{7}{15}$ of an hour, at that rate how far will I ride in $1\frac{14}{15}$ hr.?

19. What part of $1\frac{1}{4}$ feet are $3\frac{1}{3}$ inches?

20. Two men bought a barrel of flour; one paid \$3$\frac{1}{5}$, and the other \$3$\frac{2}{3}$: what part of it should each have?

21. A has \$2400; $\frac{5}{8}$ of his money, + \$500, is $\frac{5}{4}$ of B's: what sum has B?

22. John Jones divided his estate among 2 sons and 3 daughters, the latter sharing equally with each other. The younger son received \$2200, which was $\frac{5}{12}$ of the share of the elder, whose share was $\frac{16}{35}$ of the whole estate: find the share of each daughter.

PRACTICE.

130. An **aliquot part** is an exact divisor of a number.

ALIQUOT PARTS OF 100.

$5 = \frac{1}{20}$	$12\frac{1}{2} = \frac{1}{8}$	$25 = \frac{1}{4}$
$6\frac{1}{4} = \frac{1}{16}$	$16\frac{2}{3} = \frac{1}{6}$	$33\frac{1}{3} = \frac{1}{3}$
$10 = \frac{1}{10}$	$20 = \frac{1}{5}$	$50 = \frac{1}{2}$

The following multiples of aliquot parts of 100 are often used: $18\frac{3}{4} = \frac{3}{16}$, $37\frac{1}{2} = \frac{3}{8}$, $40 = \frac{2}{5}$, $60 = \frac{3}{5}$, $62\frac{1}{2} = \frac{5}{8}$, $75 = \frac{3}{4}$, $87\frac{1}{2} = \frac{7}{8}$.

1. What will 24 yd. of muslin cost at 25 ct. a yd.?

OPERATION.

$$\begin{array}{r} 4\,)\,24 \\ \hline \$\,6 \end{array}$$

SOLUTION.—Since 25 ct. is $\frac{1}{4}$ of a dollar, the cost will be $\frac{1}{4}$ as many dollars as there are yards. $\frac{1}{4}$ of \$24 is \$6.

2. I spent $\$1.12\frac{1}{2}$ for muslin at $12\frac{1}{2}$ ct. a yd.: how many yd. did I buy?

OPERATION.

$$\begin{array}{r} 1\frac{1}{8} \\ 8 \\ \hline 9 \text{ yd.} \end{array}$$

SOLUTION.—Since $12\frac{1}{2}$ ct. is $\frac{1}{8}$ of a dollar, there will be 8 times as many yards as there are dollars. 8 times $1\frac{1}{8} = 9$ yd.

3. What cost $12\frac{1}{2}$ yd. of ribbon at $18\frac{3}{4}$ ct. a yd? $\$2.34\frac{3}{8}$.

4. Paid \$2.25 for muslin at $18\frac{3}{4}$ ct. a yd. how many **yd.** did I buy?

5. What will $5\frac{1}{2}$ yd. of linen cost at \$0.62$\frac{1}{2}$ a yd.?

6. Paid \$66.25 for books at \$3.75 a dozen: how many doz. books did I buy?

7. What will 80 gal. of milk cost at \$2.37$\frac{1}{2}$ a gal.?

8. A number of men divide \$39 so that each one receives \$4.87$\frac{1}{2}$: how many men are there?

9. What will 36 barrels of flour cost at \$8.33$\frac{1}{3}$ a barrel?

10. How many yd. of cloth at \$1.33$\frac{1}{3}$ a yd. can be bought for \$246.66$\frac{2}{3}$?

11. What will 4 A. 60 sq. rd. of land cost at \$16.50 an acre?

SOLUTION.—Since 1 A. costs \$16.50, 4 A. cost $\$16.50 \times 4 = \$66$. Since 160 sq. rd. = 1 A., 40 sq. rd. = $\frac{1}{4}$ A. The cost of 40 sq. rd. will be $\frac{1}{4}$ of \$16.50 = \$4.12$\frac{1}{2}$. The cost of 20 sq. rd. will be $\frac{1}{2}$ of the cost of 40 sq. rd., or \$2.06$\frac{1}{4}$. The total cost is \$66 + \$4.12$\frac{1}{2}$ + \$2.06$\frac{1}{4}$ = \$72.18$\frac{3}{4}$.

OPERATION.

	\$16.50
	4
	66.00
$\frac{1}{4}$ of \$16.50 =	4.12$\frac{1}{2}$
$\frac{1}{2}$ of 4.12$\frac{1}{2}$ =	2.06$\frac{1}{4}$
	\$72.18$\frac{3}{4}$

12. At \$18.33$\frac{1}{3}$ per acre, how much land can be bought for \$229.16$\frac{2}{3}$?

13. What will 11 A. 120 sq. rd. of land cost, at \$125.60 per acre?

14. At \$250 a lot, containing 50×150 ft., how much land can be bought for \$10000?

15. What will 83 bu. 3 pk. 2 qt. of grass seed cost, at \$6.20 a bu.?

16. At $0.75 a bushel, how many bushels can be bought for $167.50?

17. What will $3\frac{1}{2}$ yd. cost, at $1.75 a yard?

18. At $1.50 a yard, how much cloth can be bought for 7.12\frac{1}{2}$?

19. What will 45 lb. 12 oz. of butter cost, at 0.37\frac{1}{2}$ per pound?

20. At 0.12\frac{1}{2}$ per pound, how much sugar can be bought for 2.93\frac{3}{4}$?

21. What is the cost of 2 T. 9 cwt. of wool at $37\frac{1}{2}$ ct. a pound?

22. What is the cost of 100 readers at $3.90 a dozen?

23. What is the cost of $3\frac{3}{4}$ dozen knives at $5.40 a dozen?

24. A farmer sold $6\frac{1}{2}$ doz. chickens, at 0.33\frac{1}{3}$ apiece, and $37\frac{1}{2}$ lb. butter, at 0.37\frac{1}{2}$ per pound: he received $36 in money, and the remainder in sugar, at 0.12\frac{1}{2}$ per pound: how many pounds of sugar did he get?

DECIMAL FRACTIONS.

131. The orders of integers decrease from left to right in a *tenfold* ratio.

Thus, in the number 1111, 1 thousand is 10 times 1 hundred, 1 hundred is 10 times 1 ten, and 1 ten is 10 times 1 unit.

ORDERS OF DECIMALS.

132. 1. The orders may be continued from the order units toward the right by the same law of decrease.

2. Let the order units be separated from the order that follows by a point (.).

3. Then, in the number 1.111,

1st. Since the 1 to the left of the point is 1 unit, the 1 to the right of the point is 1 tenth; for 1 unit is 10 times $\frac{1}{10}$.

2d. Since the first order from the unit is 1 tenth, the second order from the unit is 1 hundredth; for $\frac{1}{10}$ is 10 times $\frac{1}{100}$.

3d. Since the second order from the unit is 1 hundredth, the third order from the unit is 1 thousandth; for $\frac{1}{100}$ is 10 times $\frac{1}{1000}$.

4th. In like manner it may be shown that 1 in the fourth order to the right from the unit is 1 ten-thousandth; 1 in the fifth order to the right is 1 hundred-thousandth; 1 in the sixth order is 1 millionth, etc.

Rem.—A number consisting of figures other than 1, might be used as well for the purpose of illustration.

4. The position of the integral and decimal places relative to the unit is exhibited in the following

DIAGRAM.

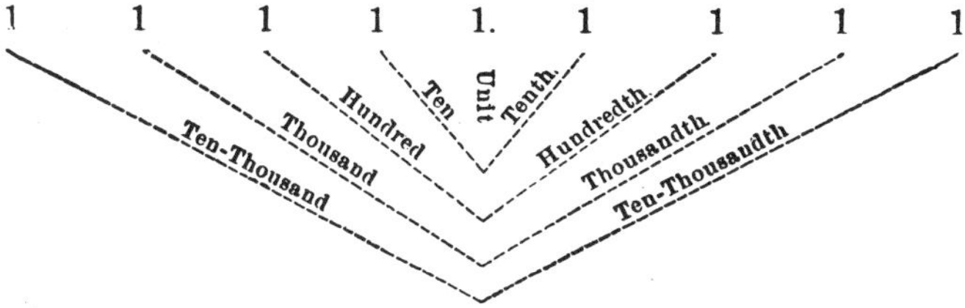

5. The first order on the *left* of the unit is *tens*, the first order on the *right* of the unit is *tenths;* the second order on the *left* is *hundreds;* the second order on the *right* is *hundredths*, etc.

DEFINITIONS.

133. 1. A **decimal fraction,** or *decimal,* is one or more *tenths, hundredths, thousandths,* etc., written like the orders of integers.

2. A **decimal point** (.) is placed before the order tenths to distinguish the fraction.

3. The decimal orders increase from right to left, and decrease from left to right the same as the orders of integers.

4. The names of the orders of decimals are similar to the names of the corresponding orders of integers.

134. Conversion of the common fractions $\frac{1}{10}$, $\frac{1}{100}$, $\frac{1}{1000}$, etc., to decimals.

1. $\frac{1}{10}$ is written .1

$\frac{2}{10}$	are	written	.2	$\frac{6}{10}$	are	written	.6
$\frac{3}{10}$	"	"	.3	$\frac{7}{10}$	"	"	.7
$\frac{4}{10}$	"	"	.4	$\frac{8}{10}$	"	"	.8
$\frac{5}{10}$	"	"	.5	$\frac{9}{10}$	"	"	.9

Hence, *when the denominator is* 10, *there is one decimal order.*

2. $\frac{1}{100}$ is written .01; there being no tenths, a cipher is written in the vacant order.

$\frac{2}{100}$	are	written	.02	$\frac{6}{100}$	are	written	.06
$\frac{3}{100}$	"	"	.03	$\frac{7}{100}$	"	"	.07
$\frac{4}{100}$	"	"	.04	$\frac{8}{100}$	"	"	.08
$\frac{5}{100}$	"	"	.05	$\frac{9}{100}$	"	"	.09

Hence, *when the denominator is* 100, *there are two decimal orders.*

3. $\frac{1}{1000}$ is written .001; there being no tenths and no hundredths, ciphers are written in the vacant orders.

$\frac{2}{1000}$	are	written	.002	$\frac{6}{1000}$	are	written	.006
$\frac{3}{1000}$	"	"	.003	$\frac{7}{1000}$	"	"	.007
$\frac{4}{1000}$	"	"	.004	$\frac{8}{1000}$	"	"	.008
$\frac{5}{1000}$	"	"	.005	$\frac{9}{1000}$	"	"	.009

Hence, *when the denominator is* 1000, *there are three decimal orders.*

4. In like manner:

$\frac{1}{10000}$	is	written	.0001
$\frac{1}{100000}$	"	"	.00001
$\frac{1}{1000000}$	"	"	.000001

Hence, *the number of orders in the decimal is always the same as the number of ciphers in the denominator of the common fraction.*

5. $\frac{1}{10}$ and $\frac{1}{100}$ are $\frac{11}{100}$ written .11
$\frac{1}{10}$, $\frac{1}{100}$, $\frac{1}{1000}$ are $\frac{111}{1000}$ " .111
$\frac{1}{10}$, $\frac{1}{100}$, $\frac{1}{1000}$, $\frac{1}{10000}$ are $\frac{1111}{10000}$ " .1111

Hence, tenths and hundredths are read as *hundredths;* tenths, hundredths, and thousandths are read as *thousandths;* tenths, hundredths, thousandths, and ten-thousandths are read as *ten-thousandths*, etc.

6. The **numerator** of a decimal is the number it expresses disregarding the decimal point.

7. If there are vacant orders before the numerator, ciphers are written in them.

8. The name of the right hand order is the name of the decimal.

To Write Decimals.

135. 1. Write two hundred and sixty-five *thousandths.*

NUMBER WRITTEN. .265.

EXPLANATION.—First, write the numerator, 265, as an integer. The figure 5 must stand in the order thousandths (**134,** 8); then, 6 must be hundredths and 2 must be tenths; the decimal point, therefore, is placed before the figure 2 (**133,** 2).

2. Write two hundred and sixty-five *millionths.*

NUMBER WRITTEN. .000265.

EXPLANATION.—Write the numerator, 265, as an integer. The figure 5 must stand in the order millionths (**134,** 8); then, 6 must be hundred-thousandths, 2 must be ten-thousandths, and ciphers must be written in the orders thousandths, hundredths, and tenths (**134,** 7); the decimal point is placed before 0 tenths (**133,** 2).

3. Write two hundred and sixty-five *hundredths*.

NUMBER WRITTEN. 2.65.

EXPLANATION.—Write the numerator, 265, as an integer. The figure 5 must stand in the order hundredths; then, 6 must be tenths; the decimal point, therefore, is placed between the figures 2 and 6.

4. Write four hundred and ninety-eight and two hundred and sixty-five *millionths*.

NUMBER WRITTEN. 498.000265.

EXPLANATION.—First write the decimal as in Ex. 2; then write the integer, placing it at the left of the decimal point.

Rule.—1. *Write the numerator as an integer.*

2. *Place the decimal point so that the name of the right hand order shall be the same as the name of the decimal.*

NOTE.—Pupils should be rendered familiar with the decimal orders so as to name them readily, in succession, both from left to right, and from right to left.

REM. 1.—When the decimal is a proper fraction it is sometimes necessary to prefix ciphers to the numerator (Ex. 2).

REM. 2.—When the decimal is an improper fraction, the decimal point is placed between two of the figures of the numerator (Ex. 3).

REM. 3.—In a mixed number, the decimal point is placed after the units order of the integer (Ex. 4).

Write the following decimal numbers:

5. Twenty-six *hundredths*.
6. Thirty-five *hundredths*.
7. Eighty-seven *hundredths*.
8. Four hundred and nineteen *hundredths*.
9. Five *thousandths*.
10. Fifty-four *thousandths*.
11. Three hundred and four *thousandths*.

12. Seven thousand two hundred and ninety-three *thousandths.*

13. Twenty-five and forty-seven *thousandths.*

14. Two hundred and five *ten-thousandths.*

15. Four thousand one hundred and twenty-five *ten-thousandths.*

16. Nine *hundred-thousandths.*

17. Nine hundred *thousandths.*

18. Six hundred and five *hundred-thousandths.*

19. Twenty thousand three hundred and four *hundred-thousandths.*

20. Seven *millionths.*

21. Two hundred and three *millionths.*

22. Three hundred thousand and four *millionths.*

23. Twenty-four *ten-millionths.*

24. Eighty thousand and six *ten-millionths.*

25. Two hundred *millionths.*

26. Two *hundred-millionths.*

27. Nine hundred and seven *hundred-millionths.*

28. Twenty million twenty thousand and three *hundred-millionths.*

29. One million ten thousand and one hundred *millionths.*

30. One million ten thousand and one *hundred-millionths.*

31. One hundred and six and thirty-seven *thousandths.*

32. One thousand and one *thousandth.*

33. Two hundred and twenty-five *thousandths.*

34. Two hundred *units* and twenty-five *thousandths.*

35. Two thousand nine hundred and twenty-nine *millionths.*

36. Two thousand nine hundred *units* and twenty-nine *millionths.*

37. One million and five *billionths.*

38. Two hundred and two *ten-billionths.*
39. Two hundred *units* and two *ten-billionths.*
40. Sixty-five and six thousand and five *millionths.*

Change the following common fractions to decimals:

41. $\frac{3}{10}$, $\frac{7}{10}$, $\frac{9}{100}$, $\frac{17}{100}$, $\frac{23}{100}$, $\frac{41}{100}$, $\frac{53}{100}$.
42. $\frac{87}{100}$, $\frac{97}{100}$, $\frac{123}{1000}$, $\frac{289}{1000}$, $\frac{487}{1000}$, $\frac{733}{1000}$.
43. $\frac{3}{1000}$, $\frac{101}{10000}$, $\frac{53}{100000}$, $\frac{503}{1000000}$.

To Read Decimals.

136. 1. Read .265.

NUMBER READ.—Two hundred and sixty-five thousandths.

EXPLANATION.—Disregarding the decimal point, the number is two hundred and sixty-five; this is the numerator of the decimal (**134,** 6). The right hand order of the decimal is thousandths; this is the name of the decimal (**134,** 8).

2. Read .000265.

NUMBER READ.—Two hundred and sixty-five millionths.

EXPLANATION.—Disregarding the decimal point, the number is two hundred and sixty-five; this is the numerator of the decimal. The right hand order is millionths; this is the name of the decimal.

3. Read 2.65.

NUMBER READ.—Two and sixty-five hundredths, or two hundred and sixty five hundredths.

Rule.—1. *Disregarding the decimal point, read the number as an integer.*

2. *Give the name of the right hand order.*

NOTE.—Before commencing to read the decimal, the name of the right hand order should be ascertained (**135**, Note, under Rule).

REM.—A mixed number may be read either as an integer and a fraction, or as an improper fraction (Ex. 3).

Read the following decimal numbers:

4. .028; .341; 2.327; 50.005; 184.173.
5. .0003; .0625; .2374; .2006; .0104.
6. 3.0205; 810.2406; 10720.0905.
7. .00004; .00137; .02376; .01007.
8. .001768; .040035; 70.360004.
9. .1010101; .00040005; .00100304.
10. .31456; .000133; 60.04; 45.1003.
11. 357.75; .4928; 5.945; 681.0002.
12. 70.1200764; 954.203; 38.027.
13. 1007.3154; 7496.35491768.
14. .00715; 3.00005; 28.10065701.
15. 13.0008241094710947.

Change the following decimals to common fractions:

16. .9; .13; .19; .29; .37; .73.
17. .91; .347; .513; .691; .851; .917.
18. .007; .0207; .00079; .001007.
19. 1.36; .3421; .03401; .0900.
20. .001; .5302; 8.01; .000053.

137. The operations with decimals are *Reduction, Addition, Subtraction, Multiplication* and *Division.*

REDUCTION OF DECIMALS.

138. Reduction of Decimals is changing their form without altering their value. There are *four cases.*

CASE I.

139. 1. *Annexing decimal ciphers to an integer does not change its value.*

Thus, 7.00 is the same as 7; for 7.00 is 7 and no hundredths (Art **136**, Rule).

2. Conversely: *Omitting decimal ciphers from the right of an integer does not change its value.*

Number 1 of this case evidently corresponds to Case I, Art. **103**, and 2 to Case III, Art. **105**.

CASE II.

140. 1. *Annexing ciphers to a decimal does not change its value.*

Thus, .70 is the same as .7; for $\frac{7}{10}=\frac{70}{100}$.

2. Conversely: *Omitting ciphers from the right of a decimal does not change its value.*

Number 1 of this case evidently corresponds to case IV, Art. **106**, and 2 to Case V, Art. **107**.

CASE III.

141. To reduce a decimal to a common fraction.

1. Reduce .75 to a common fraction.

SOLUTION.—75 hundredths written as a common fraction is $\frac{75}{100}$. $\frac{75}{100}$ reduced to its lowest terms (Art. **107**), is $\frac{3}{4}$.

OPERATION.

$.75=\frac{75}{100}$

$\frac{75}{100}=\frac{3}{4}$

Rule.—1. *Write the decimal as a common fraction.*

2. *Reduce the fraction to its lowest terms.*

2. Reduce .6 to a common fraction.
3. Reduce .25 to a common fraction.
4. Reduce .375 to a common fraction.
5. Reduce .035 to a common fraction.
6. Reduce .5625 to a common fraction.
7. Reduce .34375 to a common fraction.
8. Reduce .1484375 to a common fraction.
9. Express 4.02 as an integer and common fraction.

10. Express 8.415 as an integer and common fraction.

CASE IV.

142. To reduce a common fraction to a decimal

1. Reduce $\frac{3}{4}$ to a decimal.

SOLUTION.—Annexing a decimal cipher to 3, it is 3.0; 30 tenths divided by 4 is 7 tenths, and 2 tenths remaining. Annexing a cipher to .2 it is .20; 20 hundredths divided by 4 is 5 hundredths. The result is .75.

OPERATION.
$$\begin{array}{r} 4\,)\,3.00 \\ \hline .75 \end{array}$$

EXPLANATION.—$\frac{3}{4}$ is 3 divided by 4 (Art. **97**). Annexing a decimal cipher to 3 does not change its value (Art. **139**). Annexing a cipher to .2 does not change its value (Art. **140**).

Rule.—1. *Annex decimal ciphers to the numerator.*
2. *Divide by the denominator.*
3. *Point off as many decimal orders in the quotient as there are decimal ciphers annexed to the numerator.*

2. Reduce $\frac{4}{5}$ to a decimal.
3. Reduce $\frac{5}{8}$ to a decimal.
4. Reduce $\frac{7}{25}$ to a decimal.

5. Reduce $\frac{3}{40}$ to a decimal.
6. Reduce $\frac{15}{16}$ to a decimal.
7. Reduce $\frac{1}{1250}$ to a decimal.
8. Reduce $\frac{9}{400}$ to a decimal.
9. Reduce $\frac{1}{256}$ to a decimal.
10. Reduce $\frac{5}{6}$ to a decimal.
11. Reduce $\frac{1}{11}$ to a decimal.
12. Reduce $\frac{4}{33}$ to a decimal.

ADDITION OF DECIMALS.

143. Addition of Decimals is the process of finding the sum of two or more decimal numbers.

1. Add 375.83; 49.627; 5842.1963; 813.9762.

SOLUTION.—Write the numbers so that the four decimal points may be in a column, the units 5, 9, 2, 3 in the first column to the left, the tenths 8, 6, 1, 9 in the first column to the right, etc.; then, adding as in simple numbers, place the decimal point in the sum between 1 and 6 under the column of decimal points.

OPERATION.

```
 375.83
  49.627
5842.1963
 813.9762
---------
7081.6295
```

Rule.—1. *Write the numbers so that the decimal points and figures of the same order may stand in the same column.*

2. *Add as in simple numbers.*

3. *Place the decimal point in the sum under the column of decimal points.*

2. Add 37.1065; 432.07; 4.20733; 11.706.

3. Add 4 and 4 ten-thousandths; 28 and 35 thousandths; 8 and 7 hundredths; and 9404 hundred-thousandths.

4. Find the sum of 3 units and 25 hundredths; 6 units and 4 tenths; and 35 hundredths.

5. Add 21.611; 6888.32; 3.4167.

6. Add 6.61; 636.1; 6516.14; 67.1234; and 5.1233.

7. Add 4 and 8 tenths; 43 and 31 hundredths; 74 and 19 thousandths; 11 and 204 thousandths.

8. Add 45 and 19 thousandths; 7 and 71 hundred-thousandths; 93 and 4327 ten-thousandths; 6 and 401 ten-thousandths.

9. Add 432 and 432 thousandths; 61 and 793 ten-thousandths; 100 and 7794 hundred-thousandths; 6.009; 1000 and 1001 ten-thousandths.

10. Add 16 and 41 thousandths; 9 and 94 millionths; 33 and 27 hundredths; 8 and 969 thousandths; 32 and 719906 millionths.

11. Add 204 and 9 ten-thousandths; 103 and 9 hundred-millionths; 42 and 9099 millionths; 430 and 99 hundredths; 220.0000009.

12. Add 35 ten-thousandths; .00035; 35 millionths, and 35 ten-millionths.

SUBTRACTION OF DECIMALS.

144. Subtraction of Decimals is the process of finding the difference between two decimal numbers.

1. From 729.835 subtract 461.5738.

SOLUTION.—Write the numbers so that the two decimal points may be in a column, the units 9 and 1 in the first column to the left, the tenths 8 and 5 in the first column to the right, etc.; then, subtracting as in simple numbers, place the decimal point in the remainder between 8 and 2 under the column of decimal points.

OPERATION.

```
729.835
461.5738
--------
268.2612
```

REM.—The ten-thousandth place in the minuend may be regarded as occupied by a cipher (Art. **140**).

Rule.—1. *Write the numbers so that the decimal points and figures of the same order may stand in the same column.*

2. *Subtract as in simple numbers.*

3. *Place the decimal point in the remainder under the column of decimal points.*

2. From 97.5168 subtract 38.25942.
3. From 20.014 subtract 7.0021.
4. From 5.03 subtract 2.115.
5. From 24.0042 subtract 13.7013.
6. From 170.0035 subtract 68.00181.
7. From .0142 subtract .005.
8. From .05 subtract .0024.
9. From 13.5 subtract 8.037.
10. From 3 subtract .00003.
11. From 29.0029 subtract 19.003.
12. From 5 subtract .125.
13. From 1 *thousand* subtract 1 *ten-thousandth.*
14. From 1 subtract 1 *millionth.*
15. From 25 *thousandths* take 25 *millionths.*

MULTIPLICATION OF DECIMALS.

145. Multiplication of Decimals is the process of finding the product of numbers involving decimals.

146. Placing the decimal point in the product depends upon the following

PRINCIPLE.

The number of decimal orders in the product is equal to the number of decimal orders in both the factors.

Thus, let the factors be .2 and .03; then, the number of decimal orders in the product will be three. For, $.2 = \frac{2}{10}$ and $.03 = \frac{3}{100}$; then, the product of .2 by .03 will be the same as the product of $\frac{2}{10}$ by $\frac{3}{100}$. But, $\frac{2}{10} \times \frac{3}{100} = \frac{6}{1000}$; and $\frac{6}{1000} = .006$. Therefore, $.2 \times .03 = .006$, in which there are three decimal orders.

EXAMPLES.

147. 1. Multiply 2.149 by 6.34.

SOLUTION.—Multiply as in simple numbers, 2149 by 634.

There are three decimal orders in 2.149, and two decimal orders in 6.34; hence, there must be five decimal orders in the product (Art. **146**). Therefore, the product is 13.62466.

OPERATION.

```
    2.149
    6.34
   ------
     8596
    6447
  12894
 --------
 13.62466
```

2. Multiply .0276 by .035.

SOLUTION.—Multiply the numerator (Art. **134**, 6) 276 by the numerator 35; the result is 9660. There are four decimal orders in .0276, and three decimal orders in .035; hence, there must be seven decimal orders in the product (Art. **146**); three ciphers, then, must be prefixed to 9660. Therefore, omitting the cipher on the right (Art. **140**, 2) the product is .000966.

OPERATION.

```
    .0276
     .035
    -----
     1380
     828
 --------
 .0009660
```

3. Multiply 2.075 by 100.

SOLUTION.—Write 2075 and place the decimal point between 7 and 5, two places farther to the right than it is in 2.075.

OPERATION.

```
207.5
```

REM.—To multiply 207.5 by 100, annex a cipher and move the decimal point two places to the right.

Rule.—1. *Multiply together the numerators of the decimals as in Simple Numbers.*

2. *Point off as many decimal orders in the product as there are decimal orders in both factors.*

REM. 1.—When the number of figures in the product of the numerators is less than the number of decimal orders required, prefix ciphers. (Ex. 2.)

REM. 2.—After placing the decimal point, omit ciphers at the right of the decimal part of the product. (Ex. 2.)

REM. 3.—To multiply a decimal by 10, 100, 1000, etc., remove the decimal point as many places to the *right* as there are ciphers in the multiplier. If there be not enough figures annex ciphers.

4. Multiply 33.21 by 4.41.
5. Multiply 32.16 by 22.5.
6. Multiply .125 by 9.
7. Multiply .35 by 7.
8. Multiply .2 by .8.
9. Multiply .02 by .4.
10. Multiply .15 by .7.
11. Multiply 125.015 by .001.
12. Multiply .135 by .005.
13. Multiply 1.035 by 17.
14. Multiply 19 by .125.
15. Multiply 4.5 by 4.
16. Multiply .625 by 64.
17. Multiply 61.76 by .0071.
18. Multiply 1.325 by .0716.
19. Multiply 4.87 by 10.
20. Multiply 5.3 by 100.
21. Multiply 17.62 by 100.
22. Multiply 1.01 by 10.

23. Multiply .0001 by 100.
24. Multiply 1 *tenth* by 1 *hundredth.*
25. Multiply 1 *hundred* by 1 *ten-thousandth.*
26. Multiply 43 *thousandths* by 21 *ten-thousandths.*

27. Multiply 40000 by 1 *millionth.*
28. Multiply .09375 by 1.064.

DIVISION OF DECIMALS.

148. **Division of Decimals** is the process of finding the quotient of two numbers involving decimals.

149. Placing the decimal point in the quotient depends upon the following

PRINCIPLE.

The number of decimal orders in the quotient is equal to the number of decimal orders in the dividend, less the number in the divisor.

Thus, let .006 be divided by .03; then, the number of decimal orders in the quotient will be one. For $.006 = \frac{6}{1000}$ and $.03 = \frac{3}{100}$; then, the quotient of .006 by .03 will be the same as the quotient of $\frac{6}{1000}$ divided by $\frac{3}{100}$. But, $\frac{6}{1000} \div \frac{3}{100} = \frac{2}{10}$; and $\frac{2}{10} = .2$. Therefore, $.006 \div .03 = .2$, in which there is one decimal order.

EXAMPLES.

150. 1. Divide 2.125 by .5.

SOLUTION.—Divide as in simple numbers 2125 by 5. There are three decimal orders in 2.125, and one decimal order in .5; hence, there must be two decimal orders in the quotient (Art. **149**). Therefore, the quotient is 4.25.

OPERATION.

$$.5\,)\,\underline{2.125}$$
$$4.25$$

2. Divide .048 by .006.

SOLUTION.—Divide the numerator (Art. **134,** 6) 48 by the numerator 6. There are three decimal orders in .048, and three decimal orders in .006; hence, there will be no decimal orders in the quotient (Art. **149**). Therefore the quotient is 8.

OPERATION.

$$\begin{array}{r} .006\,)\,.048 \\ \hline 8 \end{array}$$

3. Divide .3 by .004.

SOLUTION.—Annex two ciphers to .3; then solve as in Ex. 2.

OPERATION.

$$\begin{array}{r} .004\,)\,.300 \\ \hline 75 \end{array}$$

4. Divide 83.1 by 4.

SOLUTION.—Annex two ciphers to the decimal (Art. **140,** 1) in order that the division may be performed exactly; then solve as in Ex. 1.

OPERATION.

$$\begin{array}{r} 4\,)\,83.100 \\ \hline 20.775 \end{array}$$

5. Divide 2.11 by 3.

SOLUTION.—Annex one or more ciphers to the decimal (Art. **140,** 1) in order to carry the division as far as is wanted; then solve as in Ex. 1.

OPERATION.

$$\begin{array}{r} 3\,)\,2.110 \\ \hline .703+ \end{array}$$

6. Divide 475.6 by 100.

SOLUTION.—Write 4756 and place the decimal point between 4 and 7, two places farther to the left than it is in 475.6.

OPERATION.

4.756

REM.—To divide 4.756 by 100 prefix a cipher; thus, .04756.

Rule.—1. *Divide the numerator of the dividend by the numerator of the divisor as in simple numbers.*

2. *Point off as many decimal orders in the quotient as the number of orders in the dividend exceeds the number in the divisor.*

REM. 1.—When the number of decimal orders in the dividend is the same as the number in the divisor, the quotient is an integer (Ex. 2).

REM. 2.—When the number of decimal orders in the dividend is less than the number in the divisor, for convenience in pointing off, make them the same by annexing ciphers to the dividend (Ex. 3).

REM. 3.—When the division is not exact, it may be continued to any required number of decimal places (Ex. 5).

REM. 4.—To divide a decimal by 10, 100, 1000, etc., remove the decimal point as many places to the left as there are ciphers in the divisor. If there be not enough figures, prefix ciphers (Ex. 6, Rem).

7. Divide 1.125 by .03.
8. Divide 86.075 by 27.5.
9. Divide 24.73704 by 3.44.
10. Divide 206.166492 by 4.123.
11. Divide .96 by .24.
12. Divide .0425 by .0085.
13. Divide 21 by .5.
14. Divide 2 by .008.
15. Divide 37.2 by 5.
16. Divide 100.8788 by 454.
17. Divide .000343 by 3.43.
18. Divide 9811.0047 by .108649.
19. Divide .21318 by .19.
20. Divide 102048 by .3189.
21. Divide .102048 by 3189.
22. Divide 9.9 by .0225.
23. Divide 872.6 by 100.
24. Divide 4.5 by 1000.
25. Divide 400 by 10000.
26. Divide 1 *tenth* by 10.
27. Divide 1 by 1 *tenth*.
28. Divide 10 by 1 *hundredth*.
29. Divide 1.7 by 64.

30. Divide .08 by 80.
31. Divide 1.5 by 7.
32. Divide 11.1 by 32.76.
33. Divide .0123 by 3.21.

DECIMAL COMPOUND NUMBERS.

151. A decimal is reduced to a lower denomination by multiplication (Art. **63**, Rule I).

1. Reduce .05 gal. to the decimal of a pint.

OPERATION.

$$\begin{array}{r} .05 \\ 4 \\ \hline .20 \\ 2 \\ \hline .4 \end{array}$$

SOLUTION.—To reduce .05 gal. to the decimal of a pint, multiply by 4 and by 2. The result is .4 pint.

2. Reduce .035 pk. to the decimal of a pint.
3. Reduce .0075 bu. to the decimal of a quart.
4. Reduce .005 yd. to the decimal of an inch.
5. Reduce .00546875 A. to the decimal of a square rod.

152. To find the value of a decimal in integers (Art. **125**).

1. Find the value of .3125 bu. in integers.

OPERATION.

$$\begin{array}{r} .3125 \\ 4 \\ \hline 1.2500 \\ 8 \\ \hline 2.00 \end{array}$$

SOLUTION.—To reduce .3125 bu. to pecks, multiply by 4; the result is 1.25 pk. To reduce .25 pk. to quarts, multiply by 8; the result is 2 qt. Therefore, .3125 bu. equals 1 pk. 2 qt.

2. Find the value of .75 yd. in integers.
3. Find the value of .3375 A. in integers.

4. Find the value of .7 lb. Troy in integers.

5. Find the value of .8125 bu. in integers.

6. Find the value of .44 mi. in integers.

7. Find the value of .33625 cwt. in integers.

153. A decimal is reduced to a higher denomination by division (Art. **63.** Rule II).

1. Reduce .64 pt. to the decimal of a gallon.

OPERATION.

$$\begin{array}{r} 2\,\underline{).6\,4} \\ 4\,\underline{).3\,2} \\ .0\,8 \end{array}$$

Solution.—To reduce .64 pt. to the decimal of a gallon, divide by 2 and by 4. The result is .08 gal.

2. Reduce .72 qt. to the decimal of a bushel.

3. Reduce .77 yd. to the decimal of a mile.

4. Reduce .25 pt. to the decimal of a gallon.

5. Reduce .6 pt. to the decimal of a bushel.

6. Reduce .7 rd. to the decimal of a mile.

Promiscuous Examples.

154. 1. What is the cost of 9 yd. flannel, at $0.40 per yard, and 12 yd., at $0.75 per yard?

2. What is the cost of 2.3 yd. of ribbon, at $0.45 per yard, and 1.5 yd., at $0.375 per yard?

3. What is the cost of 16.25 yd. of cloth, at $2.6875 per yard?

4. At $0.75 per bushel, how much wheat can be bought for $35.25?

5. At $2.5625 per yard, how much cloth can be bought for $98.40?

6. What will 6 cwt. 50 lb. of hops cost at $3.25 per hundred-weight?

7. What will 14 bu. 3 pk. 4 qt. of corn cost, at $0.625 per bushel?

8. What will 13 A. 115 sq. rd. of land cost, at $17.28 per acre?

9. At $0.3125 per bushel, how much corn can be bought for $9.296875?

10. At $4.32 per acre, how much land can be bought for $59.265?

11. If 63 gal. of milk cost $49, what will 464 gal. cost?

12. Add .34 yd., 1.07 ft. and 8.92 in.

13. Add .625 gal. and .75 qt.

14. From 1.53 yd. subtract 2 ft. 3.08 in.

15. From .05 yr. subtract .5 hr.

16. From .41 da. subtract .16 hr.

17. Find the value of .3 yr. in integers.

18. What is the cost of 343 yd. 2 ft. 3 in. of tubing, at $0.16 per yard?

19. At $690.35 per mile, what is the cost of a road 17 mi. 135 rd. long?

THE METRIC SYSTEM.

DEFINITIONS.

155. 1. The **Metric System** is so called from the *meter*, the unit upon which the system is based.

Rem.—The French originated this system of weights and measures at the close of the last century, and its use in France became obligatory in 1841. The metric system is now legal in nearly all civilized countries, and, in several, it is making its way rapidly into general use. In 1866, its use was legalized, in the United States, by act of Congress. It is in general use by scientific men throughout the world.

2. All the units of the other measures are derived in a simple manner from the meter. Thus,

1st. The **Meter** is the unit of Length. It is the base of the Metric System, and is very nearly one ten-millionth (.0000001) part of the quadrant extending through Paris from the equator to the pole.

2d. The **Ar** is the unit of Land Measure. It is a square whose side is 10 meters.

3d. The **Liter** is the unit of capacity. It is a vessel whose contents are equivalent to a cube the edge of which is .1 meter.

4th. The **Gram** is the unit of Weight. It is the weight of a cube of pure water whose edge is .01 meter.

3. The name of each denomination indicates at once its relation to the unit of the measure.

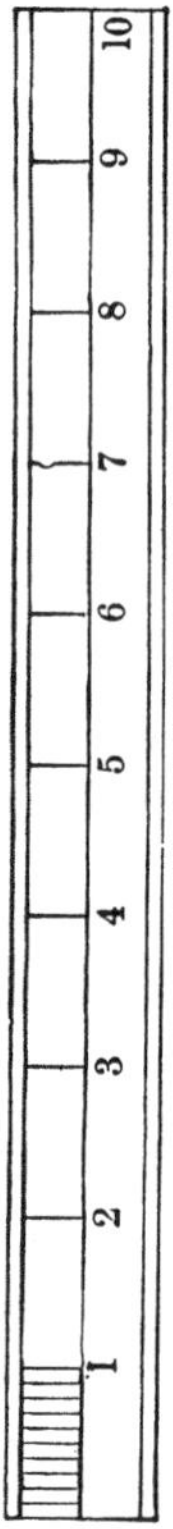

ONE DECIMETER.

Thus: 1st. The names of the *lower* denominations are formed by prefixing to the name of the unit the *Latin* numerals *milli* (.001), *centi* (.01), and *deci* (.1).

For example, a *millimeter* is one thousandth of a meter; a *centigram* is one hundredth of a gram; and a *deciliter* is one tenth of a liter.

2d. The names of the *higher* denominations are formed by prefixing to the unit the *Greek* numerals *deka* (10), *hekto* (100), *kilo* (1000), and *myria* (10000). For example, a *dekameter* is ten meters; a *hektoliter* is one hundred liters; a *kilogram* is one thousand grams; and a *myriameter* is ten thousand meters.

4. Since in the Metric System 10, 100, 1000, etc., units of a lower denomination make a unit of a higher denomination, it follows that,

1st. *A number is reduced to a* LOWER *denomination by removing the decimal point as many places to the* RIGHT *as there are ciphers in the multiplier.*

2d. *A number is reduced to a* HIGHER *denomination by removing the decimal point as many places to the* LEFT *as there are ciphers in the divisor.*

MEASURES OF LENGTH.

156. The **Meter** is the unit of length; it is legal in the United States at 39.37 inches.

REM. 1.—Its length is also a little less than 1.1 yards, or nearly 3 ft. $3\frac{3}{8}$ in., which may be remembered as *the rule of the three threes.*

REM. 2.—The decimeter and its divisions are shown in the engraving on the opposite page.

REM. 3.—Standard meters have been provided by the United States, and copies have been furnished to the several states.

TABLE.

10 millimeters, marked mm.,	are	1 centimeter,	marked	cm.
10 centimeters	"	1 decimeter,	"	dm.
10 decimeters	"	1 meter,	"	m.
10 meters	"	1 dekameter,	"	Dm.
10 dekameters	"	1 hektometer,	"	Hm.
10 hektometers	"	1 kilometer,	"	Km.
10 kilometers	"	1 myriameter,	"	Mm.

REM.—The measures chiefly used are the meter and kilometer. The meter, like the yard, is used in measuring cloth and short distances; the kilometer is used in measuring long distances.

1. Reduce 5.638 m. to centimeters.

SOLUTION.—To reduce meters to centimeters, multiply by 100. Write 5638 and place the decimal point between 3 and 8, two orders farther to the right than it is in 5.638 (Art. **155**, 4, 1st).

Ans. 563.8 cm.

2. Reduce 3642.9 m. to kilometers.

SOLUTION. — To reduce meters to kilometers, divide by 1000 Write 36429 and place the decimal point between 3 and 6, three orders farther to the left than it is in 3642.9 (Art. **155**, 4, 2d).

Ans. 3.6429 Km.

3. Reduce 4.27 Dm. to centimeters.

SOLUTION.—To reduce dekameters to centimeters, multiply by $10 \times 100 = 1000$. Write 427 and annex a cipher (Ex. 1).

Ans. 4270 cm.

4. Reduce 5.6 dm. to hektometers.

SOLUTION.—To reduce decimeters to hektometers, divide by $10 \times 100 = 1000$. Write 56, prefix two ciphers, and place the decimal point before them (Ex. 2). *Ans.* .0056 Hm.

5. Reduce 30.75 m. to centimeters.
6. Reduce 4.5 Km. to meters.
7. Reduce 75 mm. to meters.
8. Reduce .025 Dm. to decimeters.
9. Reduce 36.5 dm. to dekameters.
10. Reduce .4875 Km. to centimeters.

LAND OR SQUARE MEASURE.

157. The **Ar** is the unit of Land Measure; it is legal at 119.6 square yards.

TABLE.

100 centars, marked ca.,	are	1 ar,	marked a.
100 ars	"	1 hektar,	" Ha.

REM. 1.—An ar is 100 square meters, marked m². The hektar is very nearly $2\frac{1}{2}$ acres.

REM. 2.—For measuring other surfaces, squares of the meter and its subdivisions are used.

1. Reduce 2.625 a. to centars.
2. Reduce 397.8 a. to hektars.
3. Reduce 2500 ca. to hektars.
4. Reduce 3.8 a. to square meters.

MEASURES OF CAPACITY.

158. The **Liter** is the unit of Capacity; it is legal at 1.0567 quarts, Liquid measure.

TABLE.

10 centiliters, marked cl.,	are	1 deciliter,	marked dl.
10 deciliters	"	1 liter,	" l.
10 liters	"	1 dekaliter,	" Dl.
10 dekaliters	"	1 hektoliter,	" Hl.

REM. 1.—The measures commonly used are the liter and hektoliter. The liter is very nearly a quart; it is used in measuring milk, wine, etc., in moderate quantities. The hektoliter is about 2 bu. 3⅓ pk.; it is used in measuring grain, fruit, roots, etc., in large quantities.

REM. 2.—Instead of the milliliter and the kiloliter, it is customary to use the cubic centimeter and the cubic meter (marked m^3), which are their equivalents.

REM. 3.—For measuring wood the ster is used; it is a cubic meter

1. Reduce 2.456 l. to centiliters.
2. Reduce 873.5 l. to hektoliters.
3. Reduce 1.83 Hl. to deciliters.
4. Reduce 2400 cl. to dekaliters.
5. Reduce 1400 l. tc cubic meters.

MEASURES OF WEIGHT.

159. The **Gram** is the unit of Weight; it is legal at 15.432 grains.

TABLE.

10 milligrams, marked mg.,	are	1 centigram,	marked	cg.
10 centigrams	"	1 decigram,	"	dg.
10 decigrams	"	1 **gram**,	"	g.
10 grams	"	1 dekagram,	"	Dg.
10 dekagrams	"	1 hektogram,	"	Hg.
10 hektograms	"	1 kilogram,	"	Kg.
10 kilograms	"	1 myriagram,	"	Mg.
10 myriagrams	"	1 quintal,	"	Q.
10 quintals, or 1000 kilograms,	"	1 metric ton,	"	M.T.

REM.—The weights commonly used are the gram, kilogram, and metric ton. The gram is used in mixing medicines, in weighing the precious metals, and in all cases where great exactness is required. The kilogram—or, as it is commonly called, the "kilo"—is the usual weight for groceries and coarse articles generally; it is very nearly 2⅕ pounds Av. The metric ton is used for weighing hay and other heavy articles; it is about 204 lb. more than our ton.

1. Reduce 1428.06 g. to kilograms.
2. Reduce .28 Kg. to grams.
3. Reduce 1713.5 Kg. to metric tons.
4. Reduce .00654 Hg. to centigrams.
5. Reduce 192.7 dg. to dekagrams.

160. The legal and approximate values of those denominations of the Metric System which are in common use are presented in the following

TABLE:

DENOMINATION.	LEGAL VALUE.	APP. VALUE.
Meter.	39.37 inches.	3 ft. $3\frac{3}{8}$ inches.
Kilometer.	.62137 mile.	$\frac{5}{8}$ mile.
Square Meter.	1.196 sq. yards.	$10\frac{3}{4}$ sq. feet.
Ar.	119.6 sq. yards.	4 sq. rods.
Hektar.	2.471 acres.	$2\frac{1}{2}$ acres.
Cubic Meter.	1.308 cu. yards.	$35\frac{1}{3}$ cu. feet.
Ster.	.2759 cord.	$\frac{1}{4}$ cord.
Liter.	1.0567 quarts.	1 quart.
Hektoliter.	2.8375 bushels.	2 bu. $3\frac{1}{3}$ pecks.
Gram.	15.432 gr. T.	$15\frac{1}{2}$ grains.
Kilogram.	2.2046 lb. Av.	$2\frac{1}{5}$ pounds.
Tonneau.	2204.6 lb. Av.	1 T. 204 lb.

NOTE.—The legal value is used in solving the following examples.

1. How many yards, feet, etc., in 4 m.?

SOLUTION.—In 4 meters there are 4 times 39.37 in. which are 157.48 in., 157.48 in. reduced to integers of higher denominations are 4 yd. 1 ft. 1.48 in.

OPERATION.

```
     39.37
         4
12)157.48
 3)13 ft. 1.48 in.
   4 yd.  1 ft.
```

2. What is the value of 36 lb. in kilograms?

SOLUTION.—In 36 pounds there are as many kilograms as 2.2046 are contained times in 36 which are 16.329+.

OPERATION.

```
2.2046)36.0000(16.329+
       22046
       139540
       132276
         72640
         66138
          65020
          44092
          209280
          198414
```

3. What is the value of 20 Km.?
4. How many hektars in 160 acres?
5. What is the value of 49 m.?
6. What is the value of 15 g.?
7. How many hektoliters in 42 bu.?
8. How many cords in 500 sters?
9. How many square yards in a roll of paper 9 m. long and .5 m. wide?
10. 32 l. are how many gallons?

MISCELLANEOUS EXAMPLES.

161. 1. What is the sum of 127 dl., 4.87 l., 1563 cl., and 234.5 dl.?

2. What will be the cost of 45 Ha. of land, at $3.32 an ar?

3. A merchant paid $457.92 for cloth, at $3 a meter: how many meters did he buy?

4. A block of marble .72 m. long, .48 m. wide, and .5 m. thick cost $.864: what is the cost of the marble per cubic meter?

5. A manufacturer bought 380 sters of wood for $454.10: how much was that a ster?

6. How many hektoliters of oats in 4685 sacks, each containing 1.6 Hl.?

7. I bought 346.75 Kg. of coffee for $194.18: what did I pay per kilogram?

8. The nickel 5-cent coin weighs 5 g. and is 2 cm. in diameter: what would be the weight of enough of these coins laid in a row, to make a meter in length?

9. How much lining 1.85 m. wide will it take for a garment made of 6.5 m. of cloth 1.25 m. wide?

10. How many kilometers from Cincinnati to Dayton, the distance being 60 miles.

11. A map is 29 mm. long and 22.4 mm. wide: what space does it cover?

12. The distance between two towns is 13.24037 Km.: how many steps of .715 m. each, must I take to walk that distance?

NOTE.—To illustrate the difference between the metric system and our common system of measures, a similar example may be given, substituting 8 mi. 72 rd. 4 yd. 1.7 in. for the distance, and 28.15 in. for the length of one step.

PERCENTAGE.

162. 1. Any **per cent** of a number is so many hundredths of it.

Thus, 1 per cent of a number is $\frac{1}{100}$ of it, 2 per cent is $\frac{2}{100}$, etc.

REM.—Per cent is from the Latin *per centum,* by the hundred.

2. The sign of per cent is %, read *per cent.*

Thus, 5 % is read *five per cent.*

3. In all operations with per cent, it may be expressed in two ways: 1st. As a common fraction; 2d. As a decimal.

Thus the following expressions are equivalent:

One	per cent,	1 %,	is	$\frac{1}{100}$	or .01
Two	per cent,	2 %,	is	$\frac{2}{100}=\frac{1}{50}$,	or .02
Three	per cent,	3 %,	is	$\frac{3}{100}$	or .03
Four	per cent,	4 %,	is	$\frac{4}{100}=\frac{1}{25}$,	or .04
Five	per cent,	5 %,	is	$\frac{5}{100}=\frac{1}{20}$,	or .05
Six	per cent,	6 %,	is	$\frac{6}{100}=\frac{3}{50}$,	or .06

REM. 1.—Per cent, which is expressed as a mixed number, may be reduced to equivalent expressions by Arts. **121** and **142.** Thus, $4\frac{1}{2}\,\% = \frac{4\frac{1}{2}}{100}$, which may be reduced to $\frac{9}{200}$; also, $4\frac{1}{2}\,\% = .045$.

Express the following as common fractions and as decimals:

1. 10%	7. $6\frac{1}{4}$%
2. 15%	8. $12\frac{1}{2}$%
3. 20%	9. $18\frac{3}{4}$%
4. 30%	10. $37\frac{1}{2}$%
5. 50%	11. $56\frac{1}{4}$%
6. $2\frac{1}{2}$%	12. $87\frac{1}{2}$%

REM. 2.—Common fractions may be reduced to hundredths by Art. **106**, and then read as per cent. Thus, $\frac{1}{6}=.16\frac{2}{3}$ or $16\frac{2}{3}$%.

How many per cent are equivalent to the following fractions?

1. $\frac{2}{25}$.	6. $\frac{1}{4}$.
2. $\frac{3}{25}$.	7. $\frac{2}{5}$.
3. $\frac{4}{25}$.	8. $\frac{3}{4}$.
4. $\frac{1}{30}$.	9. $\frac{1}{8}$.
5. $\frac{1}{12}$.	10. $\frac{7}{16}$.

DEFINITIONS.

163. 1. **Percentage** embraces the various operations with per cent.

2. In Percentage three quantities are considered. (1) the *Base*, (2) the *Rate*, and (3) the *Percentage*.

3. The **Base** is the number upon which the per cent is estimated.

4. The **Rate** is the per cent when expressed as a common fraction or as a decimal.

5. The **Percentage** is the result of taking the per cent of the base.

6. Any two of these quantities being given, the third may be found. There are *four cases*.

CASE I.

164. Given the base and the rate, to find the percentage.

1. What is 25% of 32?

OPERATION.

Solution.—25% is $\frac{1}{4}$ (Art. **162**). $\frac{1}{4}$ of 32 is 8.

$$25\% = \frac{1}{4}$$
$$\frac{32}{1} \times \frac{1}{4} = 8$$

2. What is 7% of 162?

OPERATION.

Solution.—7% is .07 (Art. **162**). Multiplying 162 by .07, the result is 11.34.

$$\begin{array}{r} 162 \\ .07 \\ \hline 11.34 \end{array}$$

Rule.—*Multiply the base by the rate; the product will be the percentage.*

Rem.—Whether the rate should be expressed as a common fraction, or as a decimal, must be a matter of judgment. That form of expression is best which is simplest or most convenient in the given example.

3. What is 1% of 278?
4. What is 2% of 180?
5. What is 3% of 97?
6. What is $3\frac{1}{3}$% of 165?
7. What is $3\frac{3}{4}$% of 240?
8. What is 4% of 140?
9. What is 5% of 118?
10. What is $5\frac{1}{3}$% of 150?
11. What is 6% of 250?
12. What is $6\frac{2}{3}$% of 450?
13. What is 8% of 11?
14. What is $8\frac{1}{3}$% of 384?
15. What is 10% of 57?
16. What is $12\frac{1}{2}$% of 292?

17. What is 15% of 95?
18. What is 17% of 53.4?
19. What is $18\frac{3}{4}$% of 11.2?
20. What is 20% of 9.85?
21. What is 25% of 43?
22. What is $33\frac{1}{3}$% of 6.93?
23. What is 45% of 5.7?
24. What is 50% of 38.75?
25. What is $\frac{1}{2}$% of 456?
26. What is $\frac{3}{8}$% of 464?
27. What is $\frac{7}{16}$% of 144?
28. What is 125% of 36?
29. What is 208% of 650?
30. What is 450% of 12?
31. What is 1000% of 24.75?

CASE II.

165. Given the base and the percentage, to find the rate.

1. What per cent of 8 is 2?

OPERATION.

SOLUTION.—2 is $\frac{1}{4}$ of 8 (Art. **120**). $\frac{1}{4}$ is 25 %.

$\frac{2}{8}=\frac{1}{4}$
$\frac{1}{4}=25$ %

2. What per cent of 56 is 3.5?

OPERATION.

SOLUTION.—Dividing 3.5 by 56, the result is .0625. .0625 is $6\frac{1}{4}$ %.

$3.5 \div 56 = .0625$
$.0625 = 6\frac{1}{4}$ %

EXPLANATION.—One per cent of 56 is .56; then 3.5 is as many per cent as .56 is contained times in 3.5.

Rule.—1. *Divide the percentage by the base; the quotient will be the rate.*

3. What per cent of 15 is 3?
4. What per cent of 50 is 6?
5. What per cent of 75 is 4.5?
6. What per cent of 9 is 3?
7. What per cent of 25 is .25?
8. What per cent of 142.6 is 7.13?
9. What per cent of 9 is 9?
10. What per cent of 9 is 13.5?
11. What per cent of 243 is 8.505?
12. What per cent of 2 is .002?
13. What per cent of 3532 is 13.245?
14. What per cent of $\frac{4}{5}$ is $\frac{3}{25}$?
15. What per cent of $\frac{2}{3}$ is $\frac{2}{15}$?
16. What per cent of $\frac{16}{21}$ is $\frac{2}{7}$?
17. What per cent of $11\frac{2}{3}$ is $5\frac{1}{4}$?
18. What per cent of $57\frac{7}{9}$ is $10\frac{5}{6}$?

CASE III.

166. Given the rate and the percentage to find the base.

1. 15 is 25% of what number?

OPERATION.

SOLUTION.—25% is $\frac{1}{4}$ (Art. **162**). Since 15 is $\frac{1}{4}$ of some number, the number is $4 \times 15 = 60$.

$25\% = \frac{1}{4}$
$15 \times 4 = 60$

2. 4.93 is 17% of what number?

OPERATION.

SOLUTION.—17% is .17 (Art. **162**). Since some number multiplied by .17 gives the product 4.93, the number is 4.93 divided by .17 or 29.

$17\% = .17$
$4.93 \div .17 = 29$

Rule.—*Divide the percentage by the rate; the quotient will be the base.*

3. 60 is 20% of what number?
4. 90 is 75% of what number?
5. 85 is 125% of what number?
6. 7.13 is 23% of what number?
7. 20.23 is 34% of what number?
8. 23.5 is 47% of what number?
9. 45 is $1\frac{1}{2}$% of what number?
10. 2.25 is $12\frac{1}{2}$% of what number?
11. $\frac{3}{4}$ is 250% of what number?
12. $14\frac{2}{7}$ is $16\frac{2}{3}$% of what number?

CASE IV.

167. Given the rate and the sum or the difference of the base and percentage, to find the base.

1. A number, plus 35% of itself, equals 675: what is the number?

SOLUTION.—35% is .35. The number plus .35 of itself equals 1.35 of it; then, 1.35 of the number is 675, and the number itself is 675 divided by 1.35, or 500.

OPERATION.

35% = .35
1 + .35 = 1.35
675 ÷ 1.35 = 500

2. A number, minus 5% of itself, equals 57: what is the number?

SOLUTION.—5% is $\frac{1}{20}$. The number minus $\frac{1}{20}$ of itself equals $\frac{19}{20}$ of it; then, $\frac{19}{20}$ of the number is 57, $\frac{1}{20}$ of it is 3, and the number is 20 times 3 = 60.

OPERATION.

$5\% = \frac{1}{20}$
$\frac{20}{20} - \frac{1}{20} = \frac{19}{20}$
$\frac{\overset{3}{\cancel{57}}}{1} \times \frac{20}{\cancel{19}} = 60$

Rule.—*Divide the sum by* 1 *plus the rate, or divide the difference by* 1 *minus the rate; the quotient will be the base.*

3. 721 is 3% greater than a certain number; what is the number?

4. 68 is 66% less than what number?

5. What number, increased by 25% of itself, amounts to 2125?

6. What number, diminished by 6% of itself, is equal to 7.52?

7. 8250 is $37\frac{1}{2}$% greater than what number?

8. What fraction, less 10% of itself, equals $\frac{3}{8}$?

9. 6.6 is 20% more than what number?

168. Formulas for the Four Cases of Percentage.

Let b represent the base, r the rate, and p the percentage. Then,

Case I. $b \times r = p.$

Case II. $p \div b = r.$

Case III. $p \div r = b.$

Case IV. $\frac{b+p}{1+r} = b.$ $\frac{b-p}{1-r} = b.$

Miscellaneous Examples.

169. 1. I had \$800 in bank and drew out 36% of it: how much had I left?

2. A man had \$300; after he had spent \$225, what per cent did he have left?

3. A merchant withdrew 40% of his deposits, leaving \$3000 remaining in the bank: what amount did he withdraw?

4. A grain dealer sold corn for 56 ct. a bushel, which was 40% more than it cost him: what was the cost per bushel?

5. A man sold a horse for \$175, which was $12\frac{1}{2}$% less than the horse cost: what did the horse cost?

6. A grocer bought 4 sacks of coffee of 75 pounds each; $12\frac{1}{2}\%$ was lost by waste: what was the remainder worth at 35 cents per pound?

7. A man owed $500; he paid $425: what per cent of the debt remains unpaid?

8. A speculator invested 75% of his estate in bonds, and the remainder of it, amounting to $5000, in real estate: how much did he invest in bonds?

9. A farmer owned a farm of 250 A. 86 sq. rd., which was $12\frac{1}{2}\%$ more than his neighbor owned: how much land did his neighbor own?

10. A flock of 160 sheep increased 35% in one year: how many were then in the flock?

11. A miller takes for toll 6 qt. from every 5 bu. of wheat ground: what per cent does he take?

12. A farmer owning 45% of a tract of land, sold 540 acres, which was 60% of what he owned: how many acres were there in the tract?

13. When the gold dollar is worth 7% more than the greenback dollar, how much in gold are $371.29 in greenbacks worth?

14. A's salary is $800 a year; he spends 18% of it for rent, 15% for clothing, 23% for provisions, and 12% for sundries: how much does he save annually?

15. A pupil at an examination answered 17 of the 20 questions correctly: what per cent did he make?

16. 2 bu. 3 pk. are $33\frac{1}{3}\%$ of what number?

17. The number of pupils attending school on a certain day was 37; this was $7\frac{1}{2}\%$ less than the number enrolled: how many were enrolled?

18. A gold dollar weighs 25.8 grains Troy; 10% of it is alloy: how many grains of pure gold does it contain?

19. The five-cent piece weighs 5 grams, of which 1.25 G. are nickel and the remainder copper: what is the per cent of copper?

20. A man sold a horse for $150, which was 25% more than it cost him: if he had sold the horse for $200, how many per cent would it have been more than it cost him?

APPLICATIONS OF PERCENTAGE.

DEFINITIONS.

170. 1. The applications of Percentage may be divided into *two classes:* (1) Those *without* the element of time; (2) those *with* the element of time.

2. The most important applications of the first class are (1) *Mercantile Transactions,* (2) *Stock Transactions.*

3. The most important applications of the second class are (1) *Interest;* (2) *Discount.*

4. Percentage enters to a greater or less extent into the calculations of *Exchange, Insurance, Taxes, Equation of Payments, etc.*

5. The principles of Percentage apply directly to applications of the first class in accordance with the following

GENERAL RULE.

Rule.—1. *Ascertain the quantities which correspond to base, percentage, and their sum or their difference.*

2. *Note the quantities given and the quantities required.*

3. *Apply the proper case of Percentage to the given example.*

MERCANTILE TRANSACTIONS.

DEFINITIONS.

171. 1. **Mercantile Transactions** relate to the purchase and sale of merchandise.

2. **Price** is the value of any thing in money.

3. Merchandise is bought and sold at *wholesale* and at *retail* prices.

4. The **wholesale** price is the price of merchandise in quantities.

5. The **retail** price is the price of merchandise in small quantities.

REM.—Wholesale merchants buy and sell merchandise at wholesale prices. Retail dealers distribute merchandise of every description, to the users or consumers of it, at retail prices.

6. The chief Mercantile Transactions involving an application of Percentage are (1) *Commission;* (2) *Trade Discount*, and (3) *Profit and Loss.*

REM.—Wholesale merchants buy and sell merchandise largely through agents, who receive salaries, or a commission, for their services; buyers at wholesale are sometimes allowed discounts upon their purchases; and merchants usually make a profit, or suffer a loss, in their transactions.

COMMISSION.

172. 1. An **agent** is a person intrusted with the business of another.

REM.—The person who employs the agent, in reference to him, is called the principal.

2. A **commission merchant** buys and sells merchandise for another.

Rem. 1.—A factor is an agent who buys and sells merchandise in his own name, and is intrusted by his principal with the possession and control of it.

Rem. 2.—The person to whom merchandise is sent to be sold is termed the consignee; the person who sends it is termed the consignor; while the merchandise itself is called a consignment.

3. The **commission** is the sum paid an agent for transacting business.

4. The **charges** are expenses incurred by an agent in transacting business.

5. The **net proceeds** is the sum remaining after deducting the commission and charges.

6. The value of the materials in the business transacted is the *base;* the commission is the *percentage;* and the net proceeds is the *base less the percentage.*

Examples.

1. An agent whose commission is 5%, receives how much upon a sale of goods amounting to $240?

2. An auctioneer received $11.50 for selling a lot of goods amounting to $460: what per cent commission did he receive?

3. At a commission of $2\frac{1}{2}$% a commission merchant receives 8.12\frac{1}{2}$ for selling 25 barrels of molasses: for how much per barrel did he sell the molasses?

4. An agent receives $210 with which to buy goods: after deducting his commission of 5% what sum must he expend?

5. What are the net proceeds on a sale of goods amounting to $180, at 4% commission?

6. A lawyer received $11.25 for collecting a debt: his commission being 5%, what was the amount of the debt?

7. An agent receives $1323.54 to cover cost of goods and commission at 8%: what is his commission?

8. A commission merchant sells 250 bbl. pork, at $15 per bbl.; 175 bbl. flour, at $7 per bbl.; and 1456 lb. feathers, at 25 ct. per lb.; his commission is 3%: what sum does he remit the owner?

TRADE DISCOUNT.

173. 1. Merchandise may be sold at a *net price* or *at a discount* from an assumed *list*, or *regular*, *price*.

2. A **net price is a** fixed price from which no discount is allowed.

3. A **list, or regular, price** is an established price, assumed by the seller as a basis upon which to calculate discounts.

4. The **discount** is the deduction from the list, or regular, price.

Rem. 1.—In the wholesale trade, the amount of discount granted to a purchaser depends upon (1) the amount purchased, and (2) the time of payment.

Rem. 2.—In some lines of goods the discounts are made from the price-list of the dealer; in others, from the price-current of the market.

Rem. 3.—In regard to time, selling for cash means payment as soon as the goods can be delivered.

Time purchases means that the payments are to be made in a certain time after the purchase—the time varies with different lines of goods.

5. The discount is expressed as so many per cent *off* or as so many *off*.

Thus, 20% off, or 20 off, means at a discount of 20% from the price.

6. There may be: 1st. A single discount; as 5%, or 5 off. 2d. Two or more successive discounts.

Thus, the expression 20 and 5% off means, first, a discount of 20% from the price, and then a discount of 5% from the remainder. The expression 25, 10, and 5% off, means three successive discounts

REM.—The per cent is sometimes expressed as a common fraction. Thus, $\frac{1}{8}$ off means $12\frac{1}{2}$% off; $\frac{1}{3}$ and 5 off means $33\frac{1}{3}$ and 5 off.

7. The price of the seller is the *base;* the sum of all the discounts is the *percentage;* and the price of the buyer or price paid is the *base less the percentage.*

EXAMPLES.

1. A bill of goods amounted to $225.50 list; 20% off being allowed, what was paid for the goods?

2. A bill of articles amounted to $725.16, the purchaser being allowed $\frac{1}{3}$ and 5 off, what did he pay?

3. I paid $1430.75 for a lot of groceries, which was 3% discount from the face of the bill: what was the amount of the bill?

4. A bill of goods cost $390.45 at 25 and 5 off: what was the list price?

5. Sold 20 doz. feather dusters, giving the purchaser a discount of 10, 10, and 10%: his discounts amounting to $325.20, how much was my price per dozen?

6. Bought 100 doz. stay bindings, at 60 ct. per dozen, for 40, 10, and $7\frac{1}{2}$% off: what did I pay for them?

7. A retail dealer buys a case of slates containing 10 dozen for $50 list, and gets off 50, 10, and 10%; paying for them in the usual time, he gets an additional 2%: what did he pay per dozen for the slates?

PROFIT AND LOSS.

174. 1. The **cost** is the price paid for goods.

2. The **selling price** is the price received for goods.

REM.—The cost to the consumer is the selling price of the merchant; and the cost to the retail dealer is the selling price of the wholesale dealer.

3. Goods are usually sold *at a profit* or *at a loss.*

4. The **profit** is what the goods sell for more than they cost.

5. The **loss** is what the goods sell for less than they cost.

6. The cost is the *base;* the profit or the loss is the *percentage;* and the selling price is the *sum or the difference of the base and percentage.*

EXAMPLES.

1. A merchant's profit on a piece of cloth which cost \$40 is 10%: for how much does he sell it?

2. Prints that cost 6 ct. a yard are sold for 5 ct. a yard: what is the per cent of loss?

3. A grocer, by retailing coffee at 27 cents per pound, gains 12½%: what did it cost per pound?

4. Selling a lot of goods at a loss of 4%, the loss on the entire lot was \$15.30: what did the goods cost?

5. To make a profit of 37½%, at what price must a dry-goods merchant sell shawls that cost \$8?

6. A bookseller sells a grammar for 90 ct. which cost 75 ct.: what is his gain per cent?

7. What is the cost of tea, which, when sold at 6¼% profit yields a profit of 5 ct. per pound?

8. A grocer sells apples at $4.75 per barrel, making a profit of $18\frac{3}{4}\%$: what was the cost?

9. Sold silk at $1.35 per yard, and lost 10%: at what price per yard would I have sold it to make a profit of $16\frac{2}{3}\%$?

10. A peddler bought a stock of goods for $874, and disposed of them at a profit of 25%: how much money did he make?

11. If a bookseller makes 25 ct. on an atlas, which he sells for $1.75: what is his per cent of profit?

12. A dealer sold two horses for $150 each; on one he gained 25%, and on the other he lost 25%: how much did he lose by the transaction?

13. A merchant reduced the price of a certain piece of cloth 5 ct. per yard, and thereby reduced his profit on the cloth from 10% to 8%: what was the cost of the cloth per yard?

14. A speculator bought 10000 bushels of corn, at 60 ct. per bushel; in a few days, corn advancing in price, he sold 7000 bushels, at 65 ct. per bushel; corn then falling in price, he disposed of the remainder at 55 ct. per bushel: what per cent profit did he get out of the transaction?

15. A speculator in real estate sold a house and lot for $12000, which sale afforded him a profit of $33\frac{1}{3}\%$ on the cost; he then invested the $12000 in city lots, which he was obliged to sell at a loss of $33\frac{1}{3}\%$: how much did he lose by the two transactions?

Miscellaneous Examples.

175. 1. A bookseller purchases books from the publisher at 20% off the list price; if he retail them at the list price, what will be his per cent of profit?

2. A grocer bought 5 half chests of tea of 74 lb. each, at 45 ct. per lb., at 2% off for cash: if he retail it at $12\frac{1}{3}$% advance, what will be his profit?

3. Bought 5 assorted cases of men's boots, containing 12 pairs each, for \$45 per case, 5% off for cash; I retail them at \$4.25 a pair: what is my profit?

4. Sold a case of hats containing 3 dozen, on which I had received a discount of 10% and made a profit of $12\frac{1}{2}$% or $37\frac{1}{2}$ ct. on each hat: what was the wholesale merchant's price per case?

5. A merchant bought 100 packs of pins, of 12 papers each, for \$1.00 per pack, 60, 5 and 5% off; if he retail them so as to make a profit of \$23.90, for how much a paper will he sell them?

6. I sent a car-load of flour, 100 bbl., to a commission merchant in New York; he disposed of the flour at \$9.50 per barrel, his commission was $2\frac{1}{2}$% with charges of \$17.25: if the flour cost me \$7.50 per barrel, how much did I make?

7. A contractor bought 80 horses for government, at \$125 apiece; the freight was \$200, and the agent's commission was such that the horses cost the government \$10450: what per cent was the commission?

8. A commission merchant sells a consignment of 50 hhd. of sugar, 1500 lb. each net, at $10\frac{1}{2}$ ct. per pound; his commission is 2% and charges \$22.50; the consignor clears 14% by the transaction: what did he pay per pound for the sugar?

9. A dealer in notions buys 60 gross shoe-strings, at 70 ct. per gross, list, for 50, 10 and 5% off; if he sell them at 20, 10 and 5% off list, what will be his profit?

10. Bought 50 gross of rubber buttons for 25, 10 and 5% off; disposed of the lot for \$35.91, at a profit of 12%: what was the list price of the buttons per gross?

STOCK TRANSACTIONS.

DEFINITIONS.

176. 1. **Stock Transactions** relate to the purchase and sale of stocks, bonds, and gold.

2. **Stock** is capital in the form of transferable shares.

REM.—The capital of banks, of railroad, insurance, telegraph and other companies is held in this way.

3. The **Stockholders** are the owners of the stock.

4. A share is usually $100.

REM.—A share is sometimes $50 or some other number. Stocks are quoted, in the New York market, invariably as $100 to the share.

5. A **bond** is a written promise, under seal, to pay a certain sum of money at a specified time.

REM. 1.—Bonds are the notes of the Government and of the various corporate bodies which are allowed to issue them; usually they bear a given rate of interest and are payable within a specified time.

REM. 2.—In quoting United States bonds, the different issues are distinguished, 1st. By the rate of interest; as 6's, 5's, $4\frac{1}{2}$'s, 4's; 2d. By the time at which they mature; as 5–20's, which are payable in 20 years, but may be paid after 5 years. The 5–20's are also distinguished by the date of their issue, as 5–20's of 1868. Bonds of the Funded Loan bear 5% interest, and later ones $4\frac{1}{2}$ and 4%.

REM. 3.—The bonds of local corporations take the name of the company which issues them; as, "Chicago and Northwestern," "Adams Express," "Western Union Telegraph," etc.

6. **Currency** is the money of the country in use.

REM.—It now consists of gold and silver coin, legal-tender notes, and National Bank notes.

7. The **par value** of stocks and bonds is the value given on the face of them.

REM.—The quotations for stocks, bonds, and gold at a premium are all based on the current dollar.

8. The chief Stock transactions involving an application of Percentage are (1) *Brokerage*, (2) *Assessments and Dividends*, (3) *Stock Values*, and (4) *Stock Investments*.

BROKERAGE.

177. 1. A **broker** is an agent who buys and sells stocks, bonds, gold, etc.

REM.—Persons who "operate" in stocks usually do so through brokers; the latter buy and sell stocks in kind and amount as they are authorized by the "operator."

2. **Brokerage** is the sum paid the broker for transacting the business, and is calculated on the *par value*.

3. The par value is the *base*, the brokerage the *percentage*.

EXAMPLES.

1. A broker bought for me 75 shares New York Central and Hudson River stock: required the brokerage at $\frac{1}{4}\%$.

2. The brokerage for buying 50 shares of Chicago and Rock Island stock was $6.25: what was the per cent?

3. At $\frac{1}{4}\%$ brokerage a broker received $10 for making an investment in bank stock: how many shares did he buy?

4. A broker buys 17 shares Milwaukee and St. Paul preferred stock: what is his brokerage, at $\frac{1}{4}\%$?

5. The brokerage on 95 shares of Vermont Central stock is \$11.87$\frac{1}{2}$: what is the per cent?

6. A broker received \$9.50, or a brokerage of $\frac{1}{4}\%$, for buying Union Pacific stock: how many shares did he purchase?

ASSESSMENTS AND DIVIDENDS.

178. 1. An **assessment** is a sum of money paid by the stockholders.

REM.—In the formation of a company for the transaction of any business, the stock subscribed is not usually all paid for at once; but *assessments* are made from time to time as the needs of the business require. The stock is then said to be paid for in *installments.*

2. A **dividend** is a sum of money paid to the stockholders.

REM.—The *gross earnings* of a company are its total receipts in the transaction of the business; the *net earnings* are what is left of the receipts after deducting all expenses. The dividends are paid out of the net earnings.

EXAMPLES.

1. I own 35 shares of bank stock; if the bank declare a dividend of 4%, what will I receive?

2. A man pays an assessment of $7\frac{1}{2}\%$, or \$300, on his insurance stock: how many shares does he own?

3. A mining company declares a dividend of 15%: what does Mr. Jones receive who owns 80 shares of stock?

4. A man owns 60 shares of railroad stock: if the company declare a dividend of 5% payable in stock, how much stock will he then own?

5. A gas company has a capital stock of $160000; its gross earnings are $15700, and its expenses $4500 annually: what per cent does it pay the stockholders?

STOCK VALUES.

179. 1. The **market value** of stocks, bonds, and gold is the price at which they sell.

REM.—Stock is *above par*, or *at a premium*, when it sells for more than the par value; stock is *below par*, or *at a discount*, when it sells for less than the par value.

2. The market value of stocks, bonds, and gold is estimated at a certain per cent of the par value.

Thus, "gold, $106\frac{7}{8}$," means that the gold dollar is worth $106\frac{7}{8}$ % of the currency dollar, or is at a premium of $6\frac{7}{8}$ %. "New York Central and Hudson River, $91\frac{1}{2}$," means that the stock of this railroad sells for $91\frac{1}{2}$ % of the par value, or is at a discount of $8\frac{1}{2}$ %.

3. The par value is the *base;* the premium or discount is the *percentage;* the market value, the *amount* or *difference.*

EXAMPLES.

1. What will be the cost of 150 shares ($50 each) of Harlem, at $139\frac{3}{4}$, brokerage $\frac{1}{4}$%?

2. Bought $8000 in gold at 110, brokerage $\frac{1}{8}$%: what did I pay for the gold in currency?

3. My broker sells 50 shares of Chicago and Northwestern, brokerage $\frac{1}{4}$%; he remits me $2475: at what per cent did the stock sell?

4. What will be the cost of 25 1000-dollar 5–20 U. S. Bonds of 1867, at $114\frac{1}{4}$, brokerage $\frac{1}{8}$%?

5. I paid $1560 for Milwaukee & St. Paul, at $19\frac{1}{4}$. brokerage $\frac{1}{4}$%: how many shares did I buy?

6. When gold is at 105, what is the value in gold of a dollar in currency?

7. When gold was at $112\frac{1}{2}$, what was the value of a dollar in currency?

8. In 1864, the "greenback" dollar was worth only $35\frac{5}{7}$ ct. in gold: what was the price of gold?

9. A merchant paid $8946.25 for gold, at 105, brokerage $\frac{1}{4}\%$: how much gold did he buy?

10. My broker sells a certain amount of gold, and remits me 25734.37\frac{1}{2}$? His brokerage, at $\frac{1}{16}\%$, was 15.62\frac{1}{2}$: what was the price of the gold?

STOCK INVESTMENTS.

180. Interest on bonds and **dividends** on stocks are computed on the par value as a base; but in reckoning the rate of income on an investment, the cost of the investment is the base.

EXAMPLES.

1. If I invest $39900 in 6% bonds, at par, what will be my income?

2. If I invest $39900 in 6% bonds, at 105, what will be my income?

3. If I invest $39900 in 6% bonds, at 95, what will be my income?

4. What is a man's income who owns 20 1000-dollar U. S. 6% bonds, when gold is 107?

5. What income in currency would a man receive by investing $5220 in U. S. 5–20 6% bonds, at 116, when gold is 105?

6. What per cent of income do U. S. $4\frac{1}{2}$ per cents, at 108, yield when gold is 105?

7. If I receive an annual dividend of 6% on Michigan Central stock, which cost me but $37\frac{1}{2}$, what per cent of income do I receive on my investment?

8. What sum invested in U. S. 5's of 1881, at 118, yielded an annual income of $1921 in currency, when gold was at 113?

9. How many shares of stock bought at $95\frac{1}{4}$, and sold at 105, brokerage $\frac{1}{4}$% on each transaction, will yield a profit of $925?

10. What must be paid for 6% bonds to realize an income of 8%?

11. When U. S. 4% bonds are quoted at 106, what yearly income will be received in gold from the bonds that can be bought for $4982?

12. If I pay $87\frac{1}{2}$ for railroad bonds that yield an annual income of 7%, what per cent do I get on my investment?

13. What could I afford to pay for bonds yielding an annual income of 7% to invest my money so as to realize 6%?

INTEREST.

DEFINITIONS.

181. 1. **Interest** is money paid for the use of money.

REM.—The interest is paid by the *borrower* to the *lender*.

2. The **principal** is the money for the use of which interest is paid.

3. The **amount** is the sum of the principal and interest.

4. A **promissory note** is a written promise to pay a certain sum of money at a specified time.

REM.—The borrower always gives the lender his note for the money. The following is a common form:

$500.00. DAYTON, O., *June* 16, 1877.

One year after date I promise to pay Charles Thomas, or order, five hundred dollars, with interest at 8%, for value received. JAMES Q. DEAN.

REM.—When a note is made to draw interest from date, the words "from date" are frequently inserted after the word "interest."

5. The **face** of the note is the principal.

6. **Legal interest** is interest at a per cent that is allowed by law.

REM.—The per cent of interest that is legal in the different States and Territories, is exhibited in the following

TABLE.

NAME OF STATE.	RATE.		NAME OF STATE.	RATE.	
Alabama	8%	....	Missouri	6%	10%
Arizona	10%	Any.	Montana	10%	Any.
Arkansas	6%	10%	Nebraska	10%	12%
California	10%	Any.	Nevada	10%	Any.
Colorado	10%	Any.	New Hampshire	6%	....
Connecticut	6%	....	New Jersey	6%	....
Dakotas	7%	12%	New Mexico	6%	12%
Delaware	6%	....	New York	6%	....
District Columbia.	6%	10%	North Carolina	6%	8%
Florida	8%	Any.	Ohio	6%	8%
Georgia	7%	Any.	Oregon	10%	12%
Idaho	10%	24%	Pennsylvania	6%	....
Illinois	6%	10%	Rhode Island	6%	Any.
Indiana	6%	8%	South Carolina	7%	Any.
Iowa	6%	10%	Tennessee	6%	....
Kansas	7%	12%	Texas	8%	12%
Kentucky	6%	10%	United States	6%	....
Louisiana	5%	8%	Utah	10%	Any.
Maine	6%	Any.	Vermont	6%	....
Maryland	6%	....	Virginia	6%	8%
Massachusetts	6%	....	Washington	10%	Any.
Michigan	7%	10%	West Virginia	6%	....
Minnesota	7%	10%	Wisconsin	7%	10%
Mississippi	6%	10%	Wyoming	12%	Any.

When the per cent of interest is not mentioned in the note or contract, the first column gives the per cent that may be collected by law. If stipulated in the note, a rate of interest as high as that in the second column may be collected.

7. **Usury is** charging interest **at a per cent** greater **than** that allowed **by** law.

REM.—It will be seen from the table above that usury is now practically abolished in nearly half the States and Territories.

8. The subject of Interest may be divided into (1) *Simple Interest*, (2) *Compound Interest*, (3) *Annual Interest*, (4) *Partial Payments.*

SIMPLE INTEREST.

182. 1. **Simple Interest** is interest on the principal only.

REM.—Simple interest is not due and can not be collected till the principal is due.

2. In Simple Interest four quantities are considered, (1) the *principal*, (2) the *per cent*, (3) the *time*, and (4) the *interest.*

3. Any *three* of these quantities being given, the fourth may be found. There are *five cases.*

CASE I.

183. Given the principal, the time, and the per cent, to find the interest.

1st. When the time is one year.

1. Find the interest of \$25 for 1 yr., at 6%.

SOLUTION.—6% is .06 (Art. **162**, 3). Then, since one year is the unit of time, the interest for 1 yr. is \$25 × .06 = \$1.50.

OPERATION.

25
.06
1.50

2. Find the interest of $18.75 for 1 yr., at $6\frac{2}{3}$%.

OPERATION.

```
15)18.75(1.25
   15
    37
    30
     75
     75
```

SOLUTION.—$6\frac{2}{3}$% is $\frac{1}{15}$ (Art. 162, Rem. 2). Then, the interest for 1 yr. is $18.75 ÷ 15 = $1.25.

3. Find the amount of $215 for 1 yr., at 6%.

OPERATION.

```
  $215
   .06
 12.90
 215
$227.90
```

SOLUTION.—The interest of $215 for 1 yr. at 6% is $12.90; then the amount is $215 + $12.90 = $227.90.

Rule.—*Multiply the principal by the rate.*

REM.—To find the amount add the principal and interest.

Find the interest

4. Of $200 for 1 yr., at 8%.
5. Of $150 for 1 yr., at 5%.
6. Of $85 for 1 yr., at 7%.
7. Of $7200 for 1 yr., at $6\frac{1}{4}$%.

Find the amount

8. Of $28.20 for 1 yr., at $8\frac{1}{3}$%.
9. Of $45.50 for 1 yr., at 10%.
10. Of $420 for 1 yr., at $5\frac{1}{3}$%.
11. Of $857 for 1 yr., at 9%.
12. Of $96 for 1 yr., at $8\frac{1}{2}$%.
13. Of $2000 for 1 yr., at $4\frac{1}{2}$%.
14. Of $164 for 1 yr., at $12\frac{1}{2}$%.

2d. *When the time is Two or More Years.*

1. Find the interest of $50 for 3 yr., at 7%.

SOLUTION.—The interest of $50 for 1 yr., at 7%, is $3.50; then, the interest for 3 yr. is $3.50 × 3 = $10.50.

OPERATION.

```
  $50
  .07
 3.50
    3
$10.50
```

REM.—It is sometimes more convenient first to multiply the per cent and time together. In the above example, the per cent for 3 yr. is 21.

2. Find the amount of $225.18 for 3 yr., at $4\frac{1}{2}$%.

SOLUTION.—The interest of $225.18 for 1 yr., at $4\frac{1}{2}$%, is $10.1331; then, the interest for 3 yr. is $10.1331 × 3 = $30.3993; and the amount is $30.3993 + $225.18 = $255.58.

OPERATION.

```
 $225.18
    .04½
   90072
   11259
 10.1331
       3
 30.3993
 225.18
$255.5793
```

REM.—In business, it is customary to take the final result to the nearest unit. Thus, in the example, 57 cents 9 mills and 3 tenths of a mill are nearest 58 cents.

Rule.—1. *Find the interest for one year. Multiply this by the given number of years.*

Find the interest

3. Of $65 for 4 yr., at 5%.
4. Of $300 for 2 yr., at 6%.
5. Of $275 for 3 yr., at 6%.
6. Of $187.50 for 4 yr., at 5%.
7. Of $233.80 for 10 yr., at 6%.

Find the amount

8. Of $45 for 2 yr., at 8%.
9. Of $80 for 4 yr., at 7%.

10. Of \$237.16 for 2 yr., at $3\frac{3}{4}\%$.
11. Of \$74.75 for 5 yr., at 4%.
12. Of \$85.45 for 4 yr., at 6%.
13. Of \$325 for 3 yr., at $5\frac{2}{5}\%$.
14. Of \$129.36 for 4 yr., at $4\frac{3}{8}\%$.
15. Of \$8745 for 2 yr., at 8%.

3d. When the Time is any Number of Months.

1. Find the interest of \$24 for 9 mo., at 6%.

Solution I.—9 mo. are $\frac{3}{4}$ of a year. The interest of \$24 for 1 yr., at 6%, is \$1.44; then, the interest for 9 mo. is $\frac{3}{4}$ of \$1.44, which is \$1.08.

OPERATION.

$$\begin{array}{r} 24 \\ .06 \\ 4\,)\,\overline{1.44} \\ \hline .36 \\ 3 \\ \hline 1.08 \end{array}$$

Solution II.—(Art. **130**) 6 mo. are $\frac{1}{2}$ of a year, and 3 mo. are $\frac{1}{2}$ of 6 mo. The interest of \$24 for 1 yr., at 6%, is \$1.44; then, the interest for 6 mo. is $\frac{1}{2}$ of \$1.44, which is 72 ct., and the interest for 3 mo. is $\frac{1}{2}$ of 72 ct., which is 36 ct. Then, the interest for 9 mo. is 72 ct. + 36 ct. = \$1.08.

OPERATION.

$$\begin{array}{r|r} & 24 \\ & .06 \\ \hline & 1.44 \\ 6 \text{ mo.} = \frac{1}{2} & .72 \\ 3 \text{ mo.} = \frac{1}{2} & .36 \\ \hline & 1.08 \end{array}$$

Rule.—1. *Find the interest for one year. Take such a part of this as the given number of months is part of a year.*

Find the interest

2. Of \$300 for 1 mo., at 6%.
3. Of \$240 for 2 mo., at 8%.
4. Of \$ 50 for 5 mo., at 6%.
5. Of \$ 86 for 3 mo., at 6%.
6. Of \$ 50 for 4 mo., at 8%.

Find the amount

7. Of \$150.25 for 6 mo., at 8%.
8. Of \$360 for 7 mo., at 5%.
9. Of \$204 for 11 mo., at 7%.
10. Of \$228 for 9 mo., at 6%.
11. Of \$137.50 for 8 mo., at 6%.
12. Of \$7596 for 10 mo., at 8%.

4th. When the Time is any Number of Days.

1. Find the interest of \$288 for 24 da., at 5%.

SOLUTION I.—24 da. are $\frac{4}{5}$ of a month. The interest of \$288 for 1 mo., at 5%, is \$1.20; then, the interest for 24 da. is $\frac{4}{5}$ of \$1.20, which is 96 ct.

OPERATION.

288
.05
12) 14.40
5) 1.20
.24
4
.96

SOLUTION II.—(Art. **130**) 15 da. are $\frac{1}{2}$ of a month, 6 da. are $\frac{1}{5}$ of a month, and 3 da. are $\frac{1}{2}$ of 6 da. The interest of \$288 for 1 mo. at 5%, is \$1.20; then, the interest for 15 da. is $\frac{1}{2}$ of \$1.20, which is 60 ct.; the interest for 6 da. is $\frac{1}{5}$ of \$1.20, which is 24 ct., and the interest for 3 da. is $\frac{1}{2}$ of 24 ct., which is 12 ct. Then, the interest for 24 da. is 60 ct. + 24 ct. + 12 ct. = 96 ct.

OPERATION.

	288
	.05
12)	14.40
	1.20
15 da. = $\frac{1}{2}$	60
6 da. = $\frac{1}{5}$	.24
3 da. = $\frac{1}{2}$	.12
	.96

Rule.—1. *Find the interest for one month. Take such a part of this as the given number of days is part of a month.*

REM.—In computing interest, it is customary to regard 30 days as 1 month.

Find the interest

2. Of \$360 for 20 da., at 6%.
3. Of \$726 for 10 da., at 6%.
4. Of \$1200 for 15 da., at 6%.
5. Of \$180 for 19 da., at 8%.
6. Of \$240 for 27 da., at 7%.
7. Of \$320 for 21 da., at 5%.
8. Of \$450 for 25 da., at 10%.

Find the amount

9. Of \$100.80 for 28 da., at 5%.
10. Of \$150 for 18 da., at 5%.
11. Of \$360 for 11 da., at 6%.
12. Of \$264 for 9 da., at 6%.
13. Of \$900 for 14 da., at 7%.
14. Of \$430 for 19 da., at $4\frac{1}{2}$%.

5th. *When the Time is Years, Months, and Days, or any Two of these Periods.*

First Method.

1. Find the interest of \$360 for 2 yr. 7 mo. 25 da., at 8%.

OPERATION.

\$360	12)28.80
.08	2.40
28.80	7
2	\$16.80
57.60	
16.80	6)2.40
2.00	.40
\$76.40	5
	\$2.00

SOLUTION I.—The interest of \$360 for 1 yr., at 8%, is \$28.80; then, for 2 yr. the interest is \$57.60; for 7 mo., or $\frac{7}{12}$ of a year, the interest is \$16.80; and for 25 da., or $\frac{5}{6}$ of a month, the interest is \$2. Then, the interest for 2 yr. 7 mo. 25 da. is \$57.60 + \$16.80 + \$2 = \$76.40.

SOLUTION II.—(Art. **130**). The interest of \$360 for 1 yr., at 8%, is 28.80, and for 2 yr. it is \$57.60; for 6 mo., or half of a year, the interest is \$14.40, and for 1 mo., or $\frac{1}{6}$ of 6 mo., it is \$2.40; for 15 da., or $\frac{1}{2}$ of a month, the interest is \$1.20, and for 10 da., or $\frac{1}{3}$ of a month, it is 80 ct. Then, the interest for 2 yr. 7 mo. 25 da. is \$57.60 + \$14.40 + \$2.40 + \$1.20 + \$0.80 = \$76.40.

OPERATION.

	\$360
	.08
	28.80
	2
	57.60
6 mo. = $\frac{1}{2}$	14.40
1 mo. = $\frac{1}{6}$	2.40
15 da. = $\frac{1}{2}$	1.20
10 da. = $\frac{1}{3}$	.80
	\$76.40

Rule I.—1. *Find the interest for each period, and add the results.*

SECOND METHOD.

2. Find the interest of \$120 for 4 yr. 6 mo. 20 da., at 6%.

SOLUTION.—20 da. are $\frac{2}{3}$ of a mo.; $6\frac{2}{3}$ mo. are $\frac{5}{9}$ of a year. Then, the interest of \$120 for 4 yr. 6 mo. 20 da., at 6%, will be $\$120 \times .06 \times 4\frac{5}{9} =$ \$32.80.

OPERATION.

$$\frac{20}{30} = \frac{2}{3}$$

$$6\frac{2}{3} = \frac{20}{3}$$

$$\frac{20}{3} \times \frac{1}{12} = \frac{5}{9}$$

$$4\frac{5}{9} = \frac{41}{9}$$

$$\frac{120 \times .06 \times 41}{9} = 32.80$$

Rule II.—1. *Reduce the months and days to the fraction of a year.*

2. *Multiply the principal by the rate, and multiply the product by the time expressed in years.*

REM.—Indicate the operation as far as is practicable, and employ cancellation.

3. Find the interest of \$150 for 4 yr. 2 mo., at 6%.

Find the interest of

4. $375.40 for 1 yr. 8 mo., at 6%.
5. $ 92.75 for 3 yr. 5 mo., at 6%.
6. $500 for 1 yr. 1 mo. 18 da., at 6%.
7. $560 for 2 yr. 4 mo. 15 da., at 8%.
8. $750 for 4 yr. 3 mo. 6 da., at 6%.
9. $456 for 3 yr. 5 mo. 18 da., at 5%.
10. $216 for 5 yr. 7 mo. 27 da., at 10%.
11. $380 for 3 yr. 9 mo. 9 da., at 15%.

Find the amount of

12. $300 for 3 yr. 8 mo., at 6%.
13. $250 for 1 yr. 7 mo., at 6%.
14. $205.25 for 2 yr. 8 mo. 15 da., at 6%.
15. $150.62 for 3 yr. 5 mo. 12 da., at 5%.
16. $210.25 for 2 yr. 7 mo. 20 da., at 7%.
17. $ 57.85 for 2 yr. 3 mo. 23 da., at 5%.

18. Find the interest of $150, from January 9, 1847, to April 19, 1849, at 6%.

REM.—To find the time between two dates, see Art. **77.**

19. The interest of $240, from February 15, 1848, to April 27, 1849, at 8%.

20. The interest of $180, from May 14, 1843, to August 28, 1845, at 7%.

21. The interest of $137.50, from July 3, to November 27, at 9%.

22. The amount of $125.40, from March 1, to August 28, at $8\frac{1}{2}$%.

23. The amount of $234.60, from August 2, 1847, to March 9, 1848, at $5\frac{1}{4}$%.

24. The amount of $153.80, from October 25, 1846, to July 24, 1847, at 5%.

184. The twelve per cent method of finding interest.

1st. To find the interest of $1 for any time, at 12%.

EXPLANATION.—The interest of $1 for 1 mo., at 12%, is $0.01, or 1 ct.; for 2 mo., it is 2 ct.; for 3 mo., it is 3 ct., etc. Hence,

The interest of $1 for any number of months, at 12%, is as many cents as there are months.

The interest of $1 for 3 da., at 12%, is $0.001, or 1 mill; for 6 da., it is 2 mills; for 9 da., it is 3 mills, etc. Hence,

The interest of $1 for any number of days, at 12%, is ⅓ as many mills as there are days.

Rule.—*Call the months cents, and one-third of the days mills.*

REM.—Reduce years to months.

Find the interest of $1, at 12%,

1. For 9 mo. 12 da.
2. For 4 mo. 18 da.
3. For 7 mo. 12 da.
4. For 9 mo. 3 da.
5. For 1 yr. 4 mo.
6. For 1 yr. 5 mo. 27 da.
7. For 2 yr. 3 mo. 21 da.
8. For 3 yr. 7 mo. 12 da.
9. For 4 yr. 2 mo. 15 da.
10. For 2 mo. 1 da.
11. For 5 mo. 17 da.
12. For 10 mo. 13 da.
13. For 1 yr. 2 mo. 4 da.
14. For 2 yr. 9 mo. 20 da.
15. For 3 yr. 5 mo. 29 da.

2d. To find the interest of $1, for any time at any per cent.

1. Find the interest of $1, for 2 yr. 5 mo. 18 da., at 6%.

SOLUTION.—6% is $\frac{1}{2}$ of 12%. The interest of $1 for 2 yr. 5 mo. 18 da., at 12%, is $0.296; then, the interest, at 6%, will be $\frac{1}{2}$ of $0.296, which is $0.148.

OPERATION.

$$\begin{array}{r} 2\overline{).296} \\ \hline .148 \end{array}$$

2. Find the interest of $1, for 3 yr. 7 mo. 20 da., at 8%.

SOLUTION.—8% is $\frac{2}{3}$ of 12%. The interest of $1 for 3 yr. 7 mo. 20 da., at 12%, is 0.436\frac{2}{3}$; then, the interest, at 8%, will be $\frac{2}{3}$ of 0.436\frac{2}{3}$, which is 0.291\frac{1}{9}$.

OPERATION.

$$\begin{array}{r} 3\overline{).436\frac{2}{3}} \\ \hline .145\frac{5}{9} \\ 2 \\ \hline .291\frac{1}{9} \end{array}$$

Rule.—1. *Find the interest, at 12%, and take such a part of this as the given per cent is of 12%.*

Find the interest of $1,

3. For 7 mo. 24 da., at 6%.
4. For 10 mo. 15 da., at 5%.
5. For 11 mo. 18 da., at 9%.
6. For 1 yr. 2 mo. 9 da., at 6%.
7. For 2 yr. 5 mo. 12 da., at 8%.
8. For 3 yr. 10 mo. 17 da., at 10%.
9. For 4 yr. 3 mo. 11 da., at 7%.
10. For 5 yr. 7 mo. 24 da., at 4%.

3d. To find the interest of any sum for any time, at any per cent.

1. Find the interest of $25, for 1 yr. 5 mo. 18 da., at 6%.

OPERATION.

```
2 ).176
   .088
     25
    440
   176
  $2.20
```

Solution.—The interest of $1 for 1 yr. 5 mo. 18 da., at 12%, is $0.176; then, at 6%, it is $0.088. Then, the interest of $25 will be $0.088 × 25 = $2.20.

2. Find the interest of $134.45, for 1 yr. 7 mo. 15 da., at 8%.

OPERATION.

```
3 ).195      $134.45
   .065          .13
      2       40335
   .130      13445
             $17.4785
```

Solution.—The interest of $1 for 1 yr. 7 mo. 15 da., at 12%, is $0.195; then, at 8%, it is $0.13. Then, the interest of $134.45 will be .13 × 134.45 = $17.48.

Rule.—1. *Find the interest of* $1, *and multiply this by the given sum.*

Rem.—Take either factor for the multiplier as is most convenient.

Find the interest

3. Of $40, for 6 mo. 21 da., at 6%.
4. Of $50, for 8 mo. 24 da., at 9%.
5. Of $120, for 10 mo. 12 da., at 7%.
6. Of $200, for 11 mo. 15 da., at 6%.
7. Of $500, for 1 yr. 3 mo. 6 da., at 3%.
8. Of $750, for 1 yr. 5 mo. 27 da., at 8%.
9. Of $48.75, for 1 yr. 9 mo. 3 da., at 6%.
10. Of $76.32, for 1 yr. 10 mo. 25 da., at 4%.

Find the amount

11. Of $600, for 2 yr. 1 mo. 9 da., at 5%.
12. Of $900, for 2 yr. 4 mo. 10 da., at 6%.

13. Of $86.25, for 2 yr. 7 mo. 17 da., at 9%.
14. Of $450, for 3 yr. 2 mo. 13 da., at 8%.
15. Of $534.78, for 3 yr. 5 mo. 22 da., at 4%.

16. Of $1200, for 3 yr. 11 mo. 15 da., at 10%.

CASE II.

185. Given the principal, the per cent, and the interest, to find the time.

1. The interest of $225 for a certain time, at 4%, was $66: what was the time?

SOLUTION.—The interest of $225 for 1 yr., at 4%, is $9; then, $66 will be the interest for as many years as 9 is contained times in 66, which is $7\frac{1}{3}$, or 7 yr. 4 mo.

OPERATION.

$$\begin{array}{r} \$225 \\ .04 \\ \hline \$9.00 \end{array} \qquad 9)\underline{66} \quad 7\tfrac{1}{3}$$

$7\frac{1}{3}$ yr. = 7 yr. 4 mo.

2. In what time, at 10%, will $500 amount to $800?

SOLUTION.—The interest will be $800 — $500 = $300. The interest of $500 for 1 yr., at 10%, is $50; then, $300 will be the interest for as many years as 50 is contained times in 300, which is 6.

OPERATION.

$$\begin{array}{r} 800 \\ 500 \\ \hline 300 \\ \hline 500 \\ .10 \\ \hline 50)\underline{300} \\ 6 \end{array}$$

3. In what time, at 8%, will any principal double itself?

SOLUTION.—A principal has doubled itself when the interest becomes 100%. Since the interest is 8% in 1 yr., it will be 100% in as many years as 8 is contained times in 100, which is $12\frac{1}{2}$, or 12 yr. 6 mo.

OPERATION.

$$8)\underline{100} \quad 12\tfrac{1}{2}$$

$12\frac{1}{2}$ yr. = 12 yr. 6 mo.

Rule.—1. *Divide the given interest by the interest of the principal for one year.*

Rem. 1.—If the principal and amount are given, subtract the principal from the amount to find the interest.

Rem. 2.—If there be a fractional part of a year in the result, reduce it to months and days.

4. I lent \$200, at 6%, and received \$36 interest: how long was the money lent?

5. In what time, at 5%, will \$60 amount to \$72?

6. In what time, at 6%, will any principal be doubled?

7. A man lent \$375, at 8%, and received \$90 interest: how long was it lent?

8. In what time, at 9%, will \$600 amount to \$798?

9. In what time, at 10%, will any principal double itself?

10. How long will it take \$250, at 6%, to yield \$34.50 interest?

11. How long will it take \$60, at 6%, to amount to \$73.77?

12. How long will it take any principal to treble itself, at 6%?

13. The interest on \$400, at 7%, was \$68.60: how long was it loaned?

14. In what time, at 9%, will \$700 amount to \$924.70?

15. How long will it take any principal to increase one-half, at 8%?

16. In what time, at 10%, will \$1200 amount to \$1675?

CASE III.

186. Given the principal, the time, and the interest, to find the per cent.

1. A merchant paid \$30 interest for the use of \$300, for 1 yr. 8 mo.: what was the per cent?

OPERATION.

1 yr. 8 mo. $= \frac{5}{3}$ yr.

$\frac{30}{1} \times \frac{3}{5} = 18$

$\frac{18}{300} = \frac{3}{50}$

$\frac{3}{50} = 6\%$.

SOLUTION.—1 yr 8 mo. are $1\frac{2}{3}$, or $\frac{5}{3}$ yr. Since the interest for $\frac{5}{3}$ yr. is \$30, the interest for 1 yr. is \$18. \$18 is $\frac{3}{50}$ of \$300; $\frac{3}{50}$ are 6% (Art. **162**).

2. At what per cent will any principal double itself in 20 yr?

OPERATION.

$100 \div 20 = 5$

SOLUTION.—A principal has doubled itself when the interest has become 100%. Since the interest for 20 yr. is 100%, the interest for 1 yr. is $\frac{1}{20}$ of $100\% = 5\%$.

Rule.—1. *Find the interest for one year, and find what per cent this is of the principal.*

3. I borrowed \$600 for 2 years and paid \$48 interest: what per cent did I pay?

4. A broker paid \$200 interest for the use of \$1000 for 2 yr. 6 mo.: what was the per cent?

5. The amount of \$250 for 2 yr. 4 mo. 24 da. was \$310: what was the per cent?

6. \$23.40 interest was paid for the use of \$260 for 2 yr.: what was the per cent?

7. At what per cent will any principal double itself in 12 yr. 6 mo.?

8. The amount of \$175 for 3 yr. 7 mo. was \$250.25. what was the per cent?

9. The interest of \$450 for 1 yr. 8 mo. 12 da. is \$61.20: what is the per cent?

10. At what per cent will any principal double itself in 11 yr. 1 mo. 10 da.?

11. The amount of \$650 for 2 yr. 5 mo. 18 da. is \$746.20: what is the per cent?

12. The interest of \$640 for 6 yr. was \$110.40: what was the per cent?

CASE IV.

187. Given the time, per cent, and interest, to find the principal.

1. The interest for 2 yr., at 6%, is \$27: what is the principal?

SOLUTION.—6% is $\frac{3}{50}$ (Art. **162**, 3). Since the interest for 1 yr. is $\frac{3}{50}$ of the principal, for 2 yr. it is $\frac{3}{25}$ of the principal. Then, $\frac{3}{25}$ of the principal are \$27, $\frac{1}{25}$ of the principal is \$9, and the principal is \$225.

OPERATION.

$6\% = \frac{3}{50}$

$\frac{3}{50} \times \frac{2}{1} = \frac{3}{25}$

$\frac{\overset{9}{\cancel{27}}}{1} \times \frac{25}{\cancel{3}} = 225$

2. The interest for 3 yr., at 9%, is \$21.60: what is the principal?

SOLUTION.—9% is .09. Since the interest for 1 yr. is .09, the principal, for 3 yr. it is .27, the principal. Then, the principal, multiplied by .27, is \$21.60, and the principal is \$21.60 ÷ .27 = \$80.

OPERATION.

$9\% = .09$

$.09 \times 3 = .27$

$\$21.60 \div .27 = 80$

Rule.—*Multiply the rate by the time, and divide the interest by the product.*

3. The interest for 3 yr., at 5%, is \$8.25: what is the principal?

4. The interest for 3 yr., at 5%, is $341.25: what is the principal?

5. The interest for 1 yr. 4 mo., at 6%, is $2.26: what is the principal?

6. What principal, at 5%, will produce a yearly interest of $1023.75?

7. What principal, at 8%, will produce $30.24 interest in 1 yr. 6 mo. 27 da.?

8. What principal, at 9%, will produce $525.40 interest in 12 yr. 3 mo. 20 da.?

9. The interest for 2 yr. 7 mo. 11 da., at 4%, is $9.41: what is the principal?

10. The interest for 5 yr. 8 mo. 24 da., at 6%, is $28.38: what is the principal?

CASE V.

188. Given the time, per cent, and amount, to find the principal.

1. What principal in 5 yr., at 6%, will amount to $650?

SOLUTION.—6% is $\frac{3}{50}$. Since the interest for 1 yr. is $\frac{3}{50}$ of the principal, for 5 yr. it is $\frac{3}{10}$ of the principal, and the amount is $\frac{13}{10}$ of the principal. Then, $\frac{13}{10}$ of the principal are $650, $\frac{1}{10}$ of the principal is $50, and the principal is $500.

OPERATION.

$$6\% = \frac{3}{50}$$
$$\frac{3}{50} \times \frac{5}{1} = \frac{3}{10}$$
$$\frac{10}{10} + \frac{3}{10} = \frac{13}{10}$$
$$\frac{\overset{50}{\cancel{650}}}{1} \times \frac{10}{\cancel{13}} = 500$$

Rule.—*Multiply the rate by the time, and divide the amount by 1 + the product.*

2. What principal in 9 yr., at 5%, will amount to $435?

3. The amount for 4 yr., at 5%, is \$571.20: what is the interest?

4. The amount for 6 yr., at 7%, is \$532.50: what is the interest?

5. The amount for 2 yr. 9 mo., at 8%, is \$285.48: what is the principal?

6. The amount for 2 yr. 6 mo., at 6%, is \$690: what is the interest?

7. The amount for 3 yr. 4 mo. 24 da., at 7%, is \$643.76: what is the principal?

8. The amount for 4 yr. 3 mo. 27 da., at 4%, is \$914.94: what is the interest?

189. Formulas for the five cases of Interest.

Let b represent the principal, t the time, r the rate, and i the interest. Then,

Case I. $b \times r \times t = i.$

Case II. $i \div (b \times r) = t.$

Case III. $(i \div t) \div b = r.$

Case IV. $i \div (r \times t) = b.$

Case V. $\dfrac{b + i}{1 + (r \times t)} = b.$

COMPOUND INTEREST.

190. In **Compound Interest** the principal is increased yearly by the addition of the interest.

REM. 1.—Sometimes the interest is added semi-annually, or quarterly.

REM. 2.—The way in which interest is legally compounded is, at the end of each year, to take up the old note and give a new one with a face equal to both the principal and interest of the former note.

1. Find the compound interest of $300 for 3 yr., at 6%.

SOLUTION.—The interest of $300 for 1 yr., at 6%, is $18; the amount is $18 + $300 = $318. The interest of $318 for 1 yr., at 6%, is $19.08; the amount is $19.08 + $318 = $337.08. The interest of $337.08 for 1 yr., at 6%, is $20.2248; the amount is $20.2248 + $337.08 = $357.3048. Then, the compound interest is $357.3048 − $300 = $57.30.

OPERATION.

```
  $300            $337.08
    .06               .06
  -----          --------
  18.00           20.2248
 300             337.08
 ----            --------
 318.            357.3048
    .06          300
 -----           --------
 19.08           $57.3048
318
------
337.08
```

Rule.—1. *Find the amount of the given principal for the first year, and make it the principal for the second year.*

2. *Find the amount of this principal for the second year, make it the principal for the third year, and so on for the given number of years.*

3. *From the last amount subtract the given principal; the remainder will be the compound interest.*

REM. 1.—When the interest is payable half-yearly, or quarterly, find the interest for a half, or a quarter year, and proceed in other respects as when the interest is payable yearly.

REM. 2.—When the time is years, months, and days, find the amount for the years, then compute the interest on this for the months and days, and add it to the last amount.

Find the amount, at 6%, compound interest,

2. Of $500, for 3 years.
3. Of $800, for 4 years.

Find the compound interest

4. Of $250, for 3 yr., at 6%.
5. Of $300, for 4 yr., at 5%.
6. Of $200, for 2 yr., at 6%, payable semi-annually.

7. Find the amount of $500, for 2 yr., at 20% compound interest, payable quarterly.

8. What is the compound interest of $300, for 2 yr. 6 mo., at 6%?

9. What is the compound interest of $1000, for 2 yr. 8 mo. 15 da., at 6%?

10. What is the amount of $620 at compound interest semi-annually, for 3 yr. 6 mo., at 6%?

11. What is the difference between simple interest and compound interest on $500, for 4 yr. 8 mo., at 6%?

ANNUAL INTEREST.

191. Annual Interest is interest on the principal, and on each annual interest after it is due.

REM. 1.—This interest is sometimes semi-annual or quarterly.

REM. 2.—Annual interest may be collected when the note or bond, reads "with interest payable annually."

REM. 3.—The annual interest is sometimes represented by *interest notes;* these are given at the same time as the note for the principal, and draw interest if not paid when due.

REM. 4.—The annual interest on bonds is sometimes represented by interest notes, called *coupons;* these are detached from the bond and presented for payment when the interest is due.

1. No interest having been paid, find the amount due in 4 yr. 8 mo. 24 da., on a note for $400, with interest at 6%, payable annually.

SOLUTION.—The interest of $400 for 4 yr. 8 mo. 24 da., at 6%, is $113.60. One annual interest of $400, at 6%, is $24. The first annual interest remains unpaid 3 yr. 8 mo. 24 da.; the second, 2 yr. 8 mo. 24 da.; the third, 1 yr. 8 mo. 24 da., and the fourth, 8 mo. 24 da.; hence, interest must be reckoned on $24 for 8 yr. 11 mo. 6 da.; this is $12.864. The amount, then, is $12.864 + $113.60 + $400 = $526.46.

OPERATION.

```
2).568                      400
   .284                      .06
    400                    24.00
113.600
                       2)1.072
yr. mo. da.               .536
 3   8  24                  24
 2   8  24                2144
 1   8  24               1072
     8  24               12.864
 8  11   6              113.60
                        400.
                       $526.464
```

Rule.—1. *Find the interest of the principal for the time during which no annual interest is paid.*

2. *Find the interest of one annual interest for the sum of the times each annual interest remains unpaid.*

3. *The sum of the two interests will be the interest due, and this, added to the principal, will be the amount due.*

2. No interest having been paid, find the amount due in 3 yr. on a note for $800, with interest at 8%, payable annually.

3. The interest having been paid for 2 yr., find the amount due in 5 yr. on a note for $750, with interest at 10%, payable annually.

4. No interest having been paid for 4 yr., find the interest due on a bond for $10000, with interest at 5%, payable annually.

5. No interest having been paid, find the amount due Sept. 1, 1877, on a note for $500, dated June 1, 1875, with interest at 6%, payable semi-annually.

6. [$1200.] MILWAUKEE, WIS., *May* 12, 1873.

For value received, on demand, I promise to pay John G. Morgan, or order, twelve hundred dollars, with interest at 6%, payable annually. H. W. SLOCUM.

No interest having been paid, what was the amount due on this note, September 20, 1877?

7. [$1500.] NEW ORLEANS, LA., *October* 10, 1872.

On the first day of May, 1877, for value received, I promise to pay Andrew Jackson, or order, fifteen hundred dollars, with interest, payable annually, at 5%.

GEORGE QUITMAN.

No interest having been paid, what amount was due at maturity?

8. What is the difference between simple and annual interest on $1000 for 5 yr., at 6%?

9. What will be due on six 500-dollar city bonds running 3 yr., with interest at 6%, payable semi-annually, if the interest should not be paid?

10. The interest on U. S. 4 per cent bonds is payable quarterly in gold; granting that the income from them might be immediately invested, at 6 %, payable in gold, what would the income on 20 1000-dollar bonds amount to n 5 yr., with gold at 105?

PARTIAL PAYMENTS.

192. 1. A **partial payment** is a sum of money, less than the face, paid on a note.

2. The receipt of a partial payment is acknowledged by **indorsing** it on the back of the note.

3. The **indorsement** consists of the date and amount of the payment.

4. The rule announced by Chancellor Kent with reference to Partial Payments, is as follows:

"*When partial payments have been made, apply the payment, in the first place, to the discharge of the interest then due.*

"*If the payment exceeds the interest, the surplus goes toward discharging the principal, and the subsequent interest is to be computed on the balance of principal remaining due.*

"*If the payment be less than the interest, the surplus of interest must not be taken to augment the principal, but interest continues on the former principal, until the period when the payments, taken together, exceed the interest due, and then the surplus is to be applied toward discharging the principal; and interest is to be computed on the balance, as aforesaid.*"—KENT.

REM.—This rule is founded on the principle that neither interest nor payment shall draw interest.

1. [$1000.] BOSTON, MASS., *May* 1, 1875.

For value received, on demand, I promise to pay to Alonzo Warren, or order, one thousand dollars, with interest at 6%. WILLIAM MURDOCK.

On this note partial payments were indorsed as follows:

November 25, 1875, $134; March 7, 1876, $315.30; August 13, 1876, $15.60; June 1, 1877, $25; April 25, 1878, $236.20. What was the amount due on settlement, September 10, 1878?

SOLUTION.—The time from May 1, 1875, to November 25, 1875, is 6 mo. 24 da.; the interest of $1000 for this time is $34; the payment, $134, *exceeds* the interest; the amount is $1034; $1034 — $134 = $900, *the second principal.*

The time from November 25, 1875, to March 7, 1876, is 3 mo. 12 da.; the interest of $900 for this time is $15.30; the payment, $315.30, *exceeds* the interest; the amount is $915.30; $915.30—$315.30 = $600, *the third principal.*

The time from March 7, 1876, to August 13, 1876, is 5 mo. 6 da.; the interest of $600 for this time is $15.60; the payment, $15.60, *equals* the interest; the amount is $615.60; $615.60—$15.60 = $600, *the fourth principal.*

The time from August 13, 1876, to June 1, 1877, is 9 mo. 18 da.; the interest of $600 for this time is $28.80; the payment, $25, *is less* than the interest; continue to find the interest on $600, *the fourth principal.*

OPERATION.

1875	11	25	$134	1000
1875	5	1		.034
	6	24		34
	2).068			1000
	.034			1034
				134
1876	3	7	$315.30	900
1875	11	25		.017
	3	12		15.30
	2).034			900
	.017			915.30
				315.30
				600
1876	8	13	$15.60	.026
1876	3	7		15.60
	5	6		600
	2).052			615.60
	.026			15.60
				600
1877	6	1	$25	.048
1876	8	13		28.80
	9	18		
	2).096			
	.048			600
				.054
1878	4	25	$236.20	32.40
1877	6	1	261.20	28.80
	10	24		61.20
	2).108			600.
	.054			661.20
				261.20
1878	9	10		400
1878	4	25		.0225
	4	15		9
	2).045			400
	.0225			409

The time from June 1, 1877, to April 25, 1878, is 10 mo. 24 da.; the interest of $600 for this time is $32.40; the sum of the payments, $261.20, *exceeds* the sum of the interests, $61.20; the amount is $661.20; $661.20 — $261.20 = $400, *the fifth principal.*

The time from April 25, 1878, to September 10, 1878, is 4 mo. 15 da.; the interest of $400 for this time is $9; the amount due on settlement is $409.

RULE.

I. When each payment equals or exceeds the interest.

1. *Find the time from the date of the note to the date of the first payment.*
2. *Find the amount of the given principal for this time.*
3. *From this amount subtract the payment; the remainder is the second principal.*
4. *Find the time from the date of the first payment to the date of the second payment.*
5. *Then proceed with the second principal as with the first, and so on to the date of settlement.*

II. When one or more payments are less than the interest.

1. *Continue to find the interest on the same principal until a date is reached, when the sum of the payments equals or exceeds the sum of the interests.*
2. *Then subtract the sum of the payments from the amount; the remainder is the next principal.*

REM.—Sometimes it may be determined, by inspection, that the payment is less than the interest; when this can be done, it is not necessary to find the intermediate time and interest, but interest may at once be found to the date when it is apparent that the sum of the payments exceeds the interest.

2. [$350.] Boston, Mass., *July* 1, 1875.

For value received, I promise to pay Edward Sargent, or order, on demand, three hundred and fifty dollars, with interest at 6%. James Gordon.

Indorsements: March 1, 1876, $44; October 1, 1876, $10; January 1, 1877, $26; December 1, 1877, $15. What was the amount due on settlement, March 16, 1878?

3. A note of $200 is dated January 1, 1875. Indorsement: January 1, 1876, $70. What was the amount due January 1, 1877, interest at 6%?

4. A note of $300 is dated July 1, 1873. Indorsements: January 1, 1874, $109; July 1, 1874, $100. What was the amount due January 1, 1875, interest at 6%?

5. A note of $150 is dated May 10, 1870. Indorsements: September 10, 1871, $32; September 10, 1872, $6.80. What was the amount due November 10, 1872, interest at 6%?

6. A note of $200 is dated March 5, 1871. Indorsements: June 5, 1872, $20; December 5, 1872, $50.50. What was the amount due June 5, 1874, interest at 10%?

7. A note of $250 is dated January 1, 1875. Indorsements: June 1, 1875, $6; January 1, 1876, $21.50. What was the amount due July 1, 1876, interest at 7%?

8. A note of $180 is dated August 1, 1874. Indorsements: February 1, 1875, $25.40; August 1, 1875, $4.30; January 1, 1876, $30. What was the amount due July 1, 1876, interest at 6%?

9. A note of $400 is dated March 1, 1875. Indorsements: September 1, 1875, $10; January 1, 1876, $30;

July 1, 1876, $11; September 1, 1876, $80. What was the amount due March 1, 1877, interest at 6%?

10. A note of $450 is dated April 16, 1876. Indorsements: January 1, 1877, $20; April 1, 1877, $14; July 16, 1877, $31; December 25, 1877, $10; July 4, 1878, $18. What was the amount due June 1, 1879, interest at 8%?

11. A note of $1000 is dated January 1, 1870. Indorsements: May 1, 1870, $18; September 4, 1870, $20; December 16, 1870, $15; April 10, 1871, $21; July 13, 1871, $118; December 23, 1871, $324. What was the amount due October 1, 1873, interest at 6%?

193. When partial payments are made on notes and accounts running a year or less, the amount due is commonly found by the

MERCANTILE RULE.

1. *Find the amount of the principal from the date of the note to the date of settlement.*

2. *Find the amount of each payment from its date to the date of settlement.*

3. *From the amount of the principal subtract the sum of the amounts of the payments.*

1. A note of $320 is dated Jan. 1, 1876. Indorsements: May 1, 1876, $50; Nov. 16, 1876, $100. What was the amount due Jan. 1, 1877, interest at 6%?

2. An account of $540 was due March 1, 1877. Credits: May 1, 1877, $90; July 1, 1877, $100; Aug. 1, 1877, $150; Oct. 11, 1877, $180. What was the amount due on settlement Jan. 1, 1878, interest at 8%?

DISCOUNT.

DEFINITIONS.

194. 1. **Discount** is interest paid in advance.

2. There are two kinds of discount, *Bank Discount* and *True Discount*.

BANK DISCOUNT.

195. 1. Banks lend money on two sorts of notes. (1) *accommodation* notes, and (2) *business* notes.

REM.—These notes are frequently termed accommodation *paper*, and business *paper*.

2. An **accommodation** note is made payable to the bank which lends the money.

REM.—The following is a common form of an accommodation note:

$500. CHICAGO, ILL., *October* 20, 1877.

Ninety days after date, we, or either of us, promise to pay to the Second National Bank of Chicago, Ill., five hundred dollars, for value received.

O. S. WEST.

W. B SHARP.

Due January $^{18}/_{21}$, 1878.

3. A **business** note is payable to an individual.

4. A business note may be *negotiable* or *not negotiable.*

5. A **negotiable** note is one that can be bought and sold.

REM.—The following are common forms of business notes:

1st. Not negotiable.

$200. BUFFALO, N. Y., *March* 21, 1877.

On demand, I promise to pay Charles H. Peck, two hundred dollars, for value received.

G. W. CLINTON.

This note is payable only to Charles H. Peck; it is due at once, and bears interest from date.

2d. Negotiable.

$1000. ST. LOUIS, MO., *May* 1, 1877.

One year after date, I promise to pay to David King, or order, one thousand dollars, for value received.

ELMER B. ARCHER.

The words "or order" make this note negotiable. If David King transfers it, he must indorse it—that is, write his name across the back of it. This note bears no interest till after it is due.

3d. Negotiable.

$150. WASHINGTON, D. C., *August* 10, 1877.

On or before the first day of May, 1878, I promise to pay Amos Durand, or bearer, one hundred and fifty dollars, with interest at 10% from date, for value received.

JOHN SHERWOOD.

The words "or bearer" make this note negotiable without indorsement. This note bears interest from date, it being so specified.

6. A note is **payable**, or *nominally due*, at the end of the time specified in the note.

7. A note **matures**, or is *legally due*, in most states, three days after the specified time.

8. The three days after the specified time are called *days of grace*.

REM. 1.—Alas., Cal., Colo., Conn., Del., D. C., Fla., Ida., Ill., Me., Md., Mass., Mont., N. H., N. J., N. Y., N. D., O., Ore., Pa., R. I., Tenn., Utah, Vt., Va., Wash., W. Va. and Wis. have abolished days of grace.

REM. 2.—Banks lend money only on short time; rarely beyond 3 months.

To find when a note matures:

1st. When the time is expressed in days:

Rule.—*Count the days from the date of the note and add three days, where grace is allowed.*

2d. When the time is expressed in months:

Rule.—*Count the months from the date and add three days, where grace is allowed.*

REM. 3.—In Del., Md., Pa., Mo., and the D. C., *the day of discount* is the first day of the time.

REM. 4.—When a note in bank is not paid at maturity, it *goes to protest*—that is, a written notice of this fact, made out in legal form, by a notary public, is served on the indorsers, or security.

9. The **bank discount** is simple interest taken in advance.

10. The **proceeds** is the money received on the note.

11. In Bank Discount four quantities are considered: (1) The *face of the note*, (2) the *per cent*, (3) the *time*, and (4) the *discount*.

12. Any *three* of these quantities being given, the fourth may be found. We will consider *two cases*.

CASE I.

196. Given the face of the note, the per cent, and the time, to find the discount and the proceeds.

1st. When the note does not bear interest.

1. Find the date when due, bank discount, and proceeds of the following accommodation note, discounted at 6%:

$700. MOBILE, ALA., *June* 25, 1877.

Sixty days after date we, or either of us, promise to pay to the First National Bank, of Mobile, Ala., seven hundred dollars for value received.

CHARLES WALKER.
WALTER SMITH.

SOLUTION.—The note is due August $^{24}/_{27}$, 1877 (Art. **78**). The interest of $1 for 63 days, at 6%, is $0.0105, and the interest of $700 is $0.0105 × 700 = $7.35; this is the discount; then, $700 — $7.35 = $692.65, the proceeds.

OPERATION.

$$\begin{array}{r} 2\,)\,.021 \\ \hline .0105 \\ 700 \\ \hline 7.3500 \\ \hline\hline 700.00 \\ 7.35 \\ \hline 692.65 \end{array}$$

Rule.—1. *Find the interest on the face of the note for the given time; this is the bank discount.*

2. *From the face of the note subtract the discount; the remainder is the proceeds.*

Find the date when due, bank discount, and proceeds of:

2. A note of $100, dated June 20, payable in 60 days, and discounted at 6%.

3. A note of $120, dated October 12, payable in 30 days, and discounted at 8%.

4. A note of $140, dated January 15, payable in 4 months and discounted at 6%.

5. A note of $180, dated April 10, payable in 6 months, and discounted at 4%.

6. A note of $250, dated December 1, payable in 5 months, and discounted at 8%.

7. A note of $375, dated August 4, payable in 30 days, and discounted at 6%.

8. A note of $600, dated February 12, 1876, payable in 60 days, and discounted at 9%.

9. A note of $1200, dated February 20, 1877, payable in 90 days, and discounted at 10%.

10. A note of $1780, dated January 11, 1872, payable in 90 days, and discounted at 6%.

Find the date when due, time of discount, bank dis count, and proceeds of the following business notes:

11. [$600.] MOBILE, ALA., *Sept.* 15, 1876.
One year after date, I promise to pay to the order of Abel E. Worth, at the First National Bank of San Francisco, Cal., six hundred dollars, for value received.
GEORGE M. BURGESS.

Discounted May 21, 1877, at 10%.

12. [$1000.] KEOKUK, IA., *May* 8, 1877.
Ninety days after date, I promise to pay Albert E. Kirk, or order, one thousand dollars, for value received.
JACOB SIMMONS.

Discounted June 22, 1877, at 6%.

13. [$1500.] ST. JOSEPH, MO., *July* 10, 1877.
Six months after date, I promise to pay Alex. M. Guthrie, or bearer, fifteen hundred dollars, for value received. ORLANDO WATSON.

Discounted October 25, 1877, at 6%.

2d. When the note bears interest.

1. Find the date when due, time of discount, bank discount, and proceeds of the following business note:

$800. DETROIT, MICH., *January* 5, 1877.
Six months after date, I promise to pay to the order of Charles Stuart, at the Dayton National Bank, of Dayton, O., eight hundred dollars, with interest at 6%, for value received. FRANCIS MURPHY.

Discounted April 15, 1877, at 8%.

SOLUTION.—The note is due July $^{5}/_{8}$, 1877. The time of discount, from April 15 to July 8, is 84 days. The amount of $800 for 6 mo. 3 da., at 6%, is $824.40. The bank discount of $824.40 for 84 days, at 8%, is $15.39. The proceeds are $809.01.

OPERATION.

2).061	800
.0305	.0305
	24.4000
3) 84	800
3).028	824.40
.009$\frac{1}{3}$	.018$\frac{2}{3}$
2	54960
.018$\frac{2}{3}$	659520
	82440
824.40	15.38880
15.39	
$809.01	

Rule.—1. *Find the amount of the note for the given time.* 2. *Find the bank discount and proceeds of this amount.*

REM.—In the following examples, remember that in leap years February has 29 days.

Find the date when due, time of discount, bank discount, and proceeds of·

2. A note of $150, dated May 20, 1875, payable in 6 months, with interest at 6%, and discounted September 9, 1875, at 8%.

3. A note of $300, dated August 5, 1876, payable in 1 year, with interest at 8%, and discounted April 16, 1877, at 6%.

4. A note of $450, dated March 4, 1877, due January 1, 1878, with interest at 6%, and discounted August 13, 1877, at 10%.

5. A note of $650, dated May 16, 1876, due Sept. 1, 1878, with interest at 9%, and discounted April 25, 1878, at 6%.

6. A note of $840, dated September 1, 1875, payable in 6 months, with interest at 10%, and discounted December 20, 1875, at 8%.

7. A note of $1400, dated July 19, 1875, due May 1, 1876, with interest at 6%, and discounted Jan. 17, 1876, at 10%.

8. A note of $2400, dated Oct. 16, 1876, due Jan. 1, 1878, with interest at 8%, and discounted July 26, 1877, at 10%.

9. [$3500.] MACON, ALA., *October*, 15, 1877.

One year after date, I promise to pay Adam Moore, or order, thirty-five hundred dollars, with interest at 6%, for value received. JOSEPH STEPHENS.

Discounted May 15, 1878, at 9%.

10. [$6000.] FRANKFORT, KY., *May* 10, 1875.

One year after date, I promise to pay Henry Warren, or order, six thousand dollars, with interest at 8%, for value received. AMOS E. BURTON.

Discounted November 21, 1875, at 10%.

CASE II.

197. Given the per cent, the time, and the proceeds, to find the face of the note.

1. For what sum due 90 days hence, must I give a note to a bank, that, when discounted at 6%, the proceeds will be $177.21?

OPERATION.

```
  3 ) 9 3             1.0 0 0 0
2 ) .0 3 1              .0 1 5 5
    .0 1 5 5            .9 8 4 5

.9 8 4 5 ) 1 7 7.2 1 ( 1 8 0
           9 8 4 5
           7 8 7 6 0
           7 8 7 6 0
```

SOLUTION.—The bank discount of $1 for 93 days, at 6%, is $0.0155, and the proceeds $1 — $0.0155 = $0.9845. Then, $177.21 is the proceeds of 177.21 ÷ .9845 = $180.

Rule.—1. *Find the proceeds of* $1 *for the given time at the given per cent.*

2. *By this divide the given proceeds.*

2. The proceeds of a note discounted at a bank for 60 days, at 6%, were $197.90: what was the face of the note?

3. For what sum must a note be made, so that when discounted at a bank, for 90 days, at 6%, the proceeds will be $393.80?

4. What must be the face of a note, that when discounted at a bank for 5 months, at 8%, the proceeds may be $217.35?

5. The proceeds of a note are $352.62, the time 4 months, and the discount at 6%: what is the face?

6. I wish to borrow $400 from a bank for 30 days: what must be the face of my note, that, when discounted at 6%, I may receive this amount?

7. I wish to obtain from a bank $500 for 60 days: for what sum must I give my note, at 8% discount?

8. I wish to use $1500 for 6 months; if I can obtain money from a bank, at a discount of 10%, for what sum must I give my note to realize this amount?

9. A note dated February 19, 1876, payable January 1, 1877, and bearing 8% interest, was discounted October 12, 1876, at 6%; the proceeds were $1055.02: what was the face of the note?

TRUE DISCOUNT.

198. 1. The **present worth** of a note is a sum of money, which, being on interest for the given time at a given per cent, will amount to the same as the note.

2. The **true discount** is the difference between the present worth and the amount of the note.

REM. 1.—Notes, debts, and running accounts are discounted by True Discount.

REM. 2.—Banks sometimes discount by the method of True Discount.

199. Given the face of the note, the time, and the per cent, to find the present worth and discount.

1. Find the present worth and discount, at 6%, of a note of $430.50, due in 2 yr. 5 mo. 18 da.

OPERATION.

```
   2 ).296
      .148
     1.00
     1.148

1.148)430.50(375
      3444
       8610
       8036
        5740
        5740

     430.50
     375
    $55.50
```

SOLUTION.—The amount of \$1 for 2 yr. 5 mo. 18 da., at 6%, is \$1.148. Then, the present worth of \$430.50 is 430.50 ÷ 1.148 = \$375; and the discount is \$430.50 — \$375 = \$55.50.

2. Find the present worth and discount, at 8%, of a note of \$500, due in 3 yr., and bearing interest at 6%.

OPERATION.

```
     500          .08
     .06            3
   30.00          .24
      3          1.00
     90          1.24
    500
    590

1.24)590(475.81
     496
      940
      868
       720
       620
       1000
        992
          80

590
475.81
114.19
```

SOLUTION.—The amount of \$500 for 3 yr., at 6%, is \$590. The amount of \$1 for 3 yr., at 8%, is \$1.24. Then, the present worth of \$590 is 590 ÷ 1.24 = \$475.81; and the discount is \$590 — \$475.81 = \$114.19.

Rule.—1. *Find the amount of $1 for the given time at the given per cent.*

2. *By this divide the amount of the note; this is the present worth.*

3. *From the amount of the note subtract the present worth; this is the discount.*

REM.—When the note does not bear interest, of course the amount is the same as the face of the note.

3. Find the present worth and discount, at 6%, of a note of $224, due in 2 yr.

4. Find the present worth and discount, at 6%, of a note of $300, due in 2 yr., and bearing interest at 8%.

5. Find the present worth and discount, at 6%, of a debt of $675, due in 5 yr. 10 mo.

6. Find the present worth and discount for 5 mo., at 10%, of an account of $368.75.

7. A note of $800, dated September 10, 1876, due January 1, 1878, and bearing interest at 6%, was disposed of for the present worth, at 10%, July 19, 1877: what was the present worth at this date and the discount?

8. A merchant bought a bill of goods amounting to $775, on 4 months' credit: if money is worth 10% to him, what might he pay for the goods in cash?

9. Bought a bill of goods, amounting to $260, on 8 months' credit: if money is worth 6%, what sum will pay the debt in cash?

10. A merchant buys a bill of goods amounting to $2480; he can have 4 months' credit, or 5% off, for cash: if money is worth only 10% to him, what is his gain if he pays cash?

11. Find the present worth, at 5%, of a debt of $956.34, one-third to be paid in 1 yr., one-third in 2 yr., and one-third in 3 yr.

12. Omitting the three days of grace, what is the difference between the true discount and the bank discount of $535, for 1 yr., at 7%?

13. A man bought goods amounting to $750, the bill payable in 3 months, or 4% allowed for cash. If money is worth 8% to him, how much will he gain by paying cash?

14. A man offers to sell his farm for $8000 in cash, or for $10296, payable in three equal installments at the end of 1, 2, and 3 years, without interest: considering money to be worth 10%, what will be the gain to the buyer by paying cash?

15. A note of $2000, dated July 4, 1876, due May 1, 1878, and bearing interest at 8%, was cancelled October 25, 1877, by payment of the present worth at 6%: what was the present worth, at this date, and the discount?

EXCHANGE.

200. 1. A **draft,** or **bill of exchange,** is a written order, from one person to another, for a certain amount of money.

REM. 1.—The person upon whom the bill is drawn is called the *drawee;* the person in whose favor it is drawn is called the *payee.*

REM. 2.—When the draft is to be paid upon presentation, it is called a *sight* draft; when it is to be paid at the end of a certain time, it is called a *time* draft.

2. **Exchange** is the method of making a payment by means of a draft, or bill of exchange.

3. There are two sorts of exchange: *domestic* or *inland,* and *foreign.*

4. **Domestic** exchange takes place between localities in the same country.

REM.—The following is a common form of an inland bill of exchange, which is commonly termed a *draft* or *check:*

$500. CINCINNATI, O., *May* 1, 1877.

At sight, pay to John Jones, or order, five hundred dollars, for value received, and charge to account of

SILAS THOMPSON.

To Charles Smith & Co., New York.

5. **Foreign** exchange takes place between localities in different countries.

REM.—The following is a common form of a foreign bill of exchange:

£500. CINCINNATI, O., *May* 1, 1877.

At sight of this first of exchange (second and third of the same tenor and date unpaid), pay to Amos Carroll, or order, five hundred pounds sterling, for value received, and charge to account of

STANLEY BINGHAM.

To James Smith & Co., London.

A foreign bill of exchange is usually drawn in duplicate or triplicate, called a *set of exchange;* the different copies, termed respectively the *first*, *second*, and *third* of exchange, are then sent by different mails, that miscarriage or delay may be avoided. When one is paid, the others are void.

6. The **acceptance** of a bill of exchange is the agreement by the drawee to pay it when due.

REM.—A bill is accepted by the drawee's writing the word "accepted," with his name, across the face of the bill; the bill is then an *acceptance*.

201. To find the cost or face of a domestic bill of exchange (Art. **170,** Rule).

REM.—Interest and premium are calculated on the face of the draft.

1. What is the cost of a sight draft on New York for $1400, at $\frac{1}{2}\%$ premium?

2. What is the cost of a sight draft on Boston, for $2580, at $\frac{1}{2}\%$ discount?

3. What is the face of a sight draft on Wheeling, which cost \$375.87, at $\frac{1}{8}\%$ premium?

4. What is the cost of a sight draft on Chicago, for \$2785, at $\frac{1}{4}\%$ discount?

5. What is the face of a sight draft, which cost \$1852.55, at $1\frac{1}{4}\%$ discount?

6. What is the cost of a draft on New Orleans for \$5680, payable in 60 days, exchange being at $\frac{1}{2}\%$ premium, and interest 6%?

7. What is the cost of a draft on Mobile for \$1575, payable in 30 days, exchange being at $\frac{3}{4}\%$ premium, and interest 6%?

8. The face of a draft, payable in 60 days, is \$2625; exchange being at $1\frac{1}{2}\%$ premium, and interest 6%, what is the cost of the draft?

FOREIGN EXCHANGE.

202. Foreign bills of exchange are drawn in the money of the country in which they are to be paid.

REM.—The foreign exchange of the United States is chiefly with Great Britain, France, Germany, and Canada.

ENGLISH MONEY.

The unit of English money is the pound sterling.

4 farthings	make	1 penny,	marked	d.
12 pence	"	1 shilling,	"	s.
20 shillings	"	1 pound,	"	£.

REM.—The usual coins are: *gold*, sovereign = 1 £, and half sovereign; *silver*, crown = 5 s., half crown, florin = 2 s., shilling, sixpenny, and three-penny; *copper*, the penny, half penny, and farthing.

FRENCH MONEY.

The unit of French money is the **franc**, marked **fr.**

10 centimes make 1 decime.
10 decimes " 1 franc.

REM.—The usual coins are: *gold* pieces for 100, 40, 20, 10, and 5 francs; *silver* pieces for 5, 2, 1, $\frac{1}{2}$, and $\frac{1}{4}$ francs; *bronze* pieces for 10, 5, 2, and 1 centimes.

GERMAN MONEY.

The unit of German money is the **mark, which is** divided into 100 pennies (pfennige).

REM.—The usual coins are: *gold* pieces for 20, 10, and 5 marks; *silver* pieces for 2, 1, and $\frac{1}{2}$ marks; *nickel* pieces for 10, 5, and 1 pennies.

Canadian money is in dollars and cents, corresponding with United States currency.

The **par of exchange** is the comparative value of the standard coins of two countries.

REM.—The commercial value of foreign exchange may be above or below the par value. Quotations are always in gold.

The par value of the pound is $4.8665. Its quoted commercial value varies from $4.83 to $4.90 gold.

The par value of the franc is $0.193. It is usually quoted at about 5 fr. 14$\frac{3}{8}$ centimes, equal to one dollar gold.

The par value of the mark is $0.238. The commercial quotations, always for four marks, vary from $0.95 to $0.98.

To find the cost or face of a foreign bill of exchange:

1. What will a sight bill on London, for £500 10s., cost in New York, exchange being at \$4.87?

SOLUTION.—Since 20 s. = £1, 10 s. = £.5. If £1 is worth \$4.87, £500.5 are worth \$4.87 × 500.5 = \$2437.44.

OPERATION.

10 s. = £.5

```
    500.5
     4.87
   35035
  40040
 20020
$2437.435
```

2. How large a bill on London can be bought for \$1808.04, exchange being at \$4.88?

SOLUTION.—Since £1 is worth \$4.88, as many pounds can be bought for \$1808.04 as \$4.88 is contained times in \$1808.04. It is contained 370 times, with a remainder. Reduce the remainder to shillings by multiplying by 20. 4.88 is contained in the product 10 times. The bill will be for £370 10s.

OPERATION.

```
4.88)1808.04(370
     1464
      3440
      3416
        244
         20
4.88)4880(10 s.
     488
       0
```

3. What will a bill on London for £890 8s. cost, exchange being at \$4.86?

4. How large a bill on London can be bought for \$2130.12, exchange being at \$4.88?

5. What will a bill on Paris cost for 1290 francs, exchange being 5 fr. 15 centimes to \$1?

6. How large a bill on Paris can be bought for \$1657.60, exchange being at 5 fr. 16 centimes?

7. What will a bill on Berlin cost for 12680 reichsmarks, exchange being \$.97 per 4 reichsmarks?

8. How large a bill on Frankfort can be bought for \$1470, exchange being at \$.98?

INSURANCE

DEFINITIONS.

203. 1. **Insurance Companies** agree, for specified sums of money, to pay a certain amount to the person insured on the occurrence of a certain event.

2. The **policy** is the written contract given by the company.

REM.—The persons insured are called the policy holders. The companies are sometimes styled the underwriters.

3. The **premium** is the sum paid to the company for insurance.

4. **Fire Insurance** is indemnity for a certain amount in case of loss by fire.

5. **Marine Insurance** is indemnity for a certain amount in case of loss by the dangers of navigation.

6. **Life Insurance** is an agreement to pay a specified sum at the death, or at a certain time in the life, of the insured.

FIRE AND MARINE INSURANCE.

204. The **premium** in fire and marine insurance is a certain percentage of the amount insured (Art. **170**, Rule).

Rem.—Insurance companies will seldom insure property at its full value. The insurance is commonly upon $\frac{2}{3}$ or $\frac{3}{4}$ of the value.

1. What is the cost of insuring a house worth \$3375, at $\frac{2}{3}$ of its value, the premium being $1\frac{1}{2}\%$ and the policy costing \$1?

OPERATION.

3) 3375	2250
1125	.01½
2	2250
2250	1125
	33.75
	1.00
	34.75

Solution.—$\frac{2}{3}$ of the value of the house is \$2250. The premium is $1\frac{1}{2}\%$ of \$2250, which is \$33.75; adding \$1, the cost of the policy, the sum is \$34.75; the cost of insurance.

2. What is the cost of insuring a house worth \$5000, at $\frac{3}{4}$ of its value, the premium being $\frac{1}{2}\%$, and the policy costing \$1.50?

3. A store is valued at \$12600, and the goods at \$14400; $\frac{2}{3}$ of the value of the store is insured at $\frac{3}{4}\%$ and $\frac{1}{2}$ the value of the goods at 2%; the cost of the two policies is \$1.25 apiece: what was the total cost of insurance?

4. A man owns a manufactory valued at \$21000, and a dwelling-house worth \$7200: what will it cost to insure the manufactory, at $\frac{4}{7}$ of its value, at $1\frac{1}{2}\%$, and the house, at its full value, at $\frac{3}{4}\%$, the two policies costing \$1.25 each?

5. A man's dwelling, valued at \$5600, was burned; it had been insured, in a certain company, 20 years, for $\frac{3}{4}$ of its value, at $1\frac{1}{2}\%$: how much did he receive from the company more than the sum total of the annual premiums?

6. A man secures a policy of insurance, on his house, for \$3600, furniture for \$1600, and library \$800; the

premium is $\frac{7}{8}\%$, and cost of policy \$1.25: what is the cost of the insurance?

7. A hotel is insured, for $\frac{2}{3}$ of its value, at $1\frac{1}{2}\%$; the policy costs \$1.25 and the total cost of insurance is \$151.25: at what sum is the hotel valued?

8. The cost of insuring a house worth \$4500, for $\frac{4}{5}$ of its value, was \$32.75; the cost of the policy was \$1.25: what was the per cent of insurance?

9. A farmer, with an insurance of \$1000 on his house, and \$1500 on his barn, in the Vermont Mutual, pays an annual assessment of \$3.50: what is the per cent of the premium?

LIFE INSURANCE.

205. 1. **Life Insurance** policies are of two principal kinds (1) *life* policies, (2) *endowment* policies.

2. A **life** policy is payable at the death of the person insured.

3. An **endowment** policy is payable at a specified time, or at death if it occurs within this time.

REM.—In life insurance the premium is commonly a regular annual payment, dependent, in amount, upon the age of the individual when he effects his insurance. The tables of a company show the annual premium, at any age, for \$1000 of insurance.

1. A man at the age of 40 insures his life for \$5000; the company's annual premium on \$1000, for a life policy at this age, is \$31.30; if he dies at the age of 70, how much money will he have paid the company?

OPERATION.

$$\begin{array}{r} \$31.30 \\ 5 \\ \hline 156.50 \\ 30 \\ \hline \$4695.00 \end{array}$$

SOLUTION.—Since the annual premium on \$1000 is \$31.30, on \$5000 it is \$31.30 × 5 = \$156.50; then, the amount paid, in 30 yr., will be \$156.50 × 30 = \$4695.

2. Mr. Harris, aged 35, takes out an endowment policy in a life insurance company for \$10000, payable in 10 years; the cost of the annual premium on \$1000, at his age, is \$105.53: if he lives to receive the endowment, what will be the cost of the paid-up policy, without interest?

3. At the age of 50, the cost of a life policy, payable annually, is \$47.18 on \$1000; the cost of an endowment policy, payable in 20 years, is \$60.45 on \$1000; at the end of 20 years, how much more will have been paid on a policy of \$8000 by the endowment plan than by the life plan?

4. At the age of 44, a man insures his life to the amount of \$12000 in favor of his wife; the company's annual premium at this age, for a life policy, is \$36.46 on \$1000: if the man die after the payment of 5 premiums, how much more than he paid out, will his widow receive?

5. At the age of 21, a young man takes out a life policy for \$5000, upon which the annual premium is \$19.89 on \$1000: if he lives to the age of 75, how much will it cost him to keep up his insurance?

6. At the age of 30, to secure an endowment policy for \$1000, payable in 10 years, costs an annual premium of \$104.58; what will be the amount of the ten payments at the end of the time, allowing interest at 6%?

7. At the age of 38, a gentleman took out a policy for \$6000, on the life plan, paying annually \$29.15 on \$1000. After keeping up his premiums for 15 years, he suffered his policy to lapse: how much money had he paid out, allowing interest at 6%?

TAXES.

DEFINITIONS.

206. 1. A **tax** is money paid by the citizens of a country for the support of government or for other public purposes.

2. A tax is either *direct* or *indirect.*

3. A **direct** tax is one which is levied upon the person or property of the citizens.

4. A tax upon the person is called a *poll tax;* upon property, a *property tax.*

5. An **indirect** tax is one which, in some way, is levied upon the business of the citizens.

6. The taxes of the United States, considered in reference to their nature and purpose, are of two classes, (1) *State and Local Taxes;* (2) *United States Revenue.*

STATE AND LOCAL TAXES.

207. 1. The money for State and local purposes arises chiefly from direct taxation.

REM.—Some revenue accrues to the State from the rent of school lands, from licenses, fines, etc.

2. For the purposes of taxation, property is classed as *Real Estate* and *Personal Property.*

3. **Real Estate** is property which is fixed, as lands, houses, etc.

4. **Personal Property** is that which is movable, as furniture, merchandise, etc.

5. The **valuation** is the estimated worth of the property.

REM.—The valuation is generally the basis upon which to estimate the tax. In some states, however, the specific tax upon the polls must first be subtracted; in Massachusetts, a sixth part of the tax is assessed upon the polls, provided it does not exceed $2 for each individual; in Vermont, the basis is what is called the Grand List, which is ascertained by dividing the valuation by 100 and adding $2 for each poll.

6. The valuation is made by an officer called an *assessor.*

REM.—This official makes out a list called an *assessment roll;* it contains the names of the persons to be taxed, along with the valuation of their property.

208. To find the rate of taxation.

The rate of taxation is expressed as so many mills on each dollar of taxable property, or as such a per cent of it.

1. The property of a certain town is valued at $1049905; there are 483 persons subject to poll-tax. In a certain year the total taxes of the town are $13323.36; the poll-tax being $1.50 for each person, what is the rate of taxation upon the property?

SOLUTION.—The poll-tax is $1.50×483=$724.50; then, the property tax is $13323.36—$724.50 = $12598.86. Then, since the tax on $1049905 is $12598.86, the tax on $1 is $12598.86 ÷ 1049905 = $0.012, 12 mills, or $1\frac{1}{5}$%.

OPERATION.

```
                483
               1.50
              24150
              483
              724.50
           13323.36
             724.50
1049905)12598.86(.012
          1049905
          2099810
          2099810
```

Rule.—1. *Multiply the tax on each poll by the number of polls; the product is the poll-tax.*

2. *From the total amount of tax subtract the poll-tax; the remainder is the property tax.*

3. *Divide the property tax by the valuation; the quotient is the rate of taxation.*

REM.—Of course, where there is no specific poll-tax, the total amount of the tax is to be divided immediately by the valuation.

2. A tax of $2500 is assessed upon a certain district to build a school-house. The property of the district is valued at $618000, and there are 28 persons subject to poll-tax: if the poll-tax is $1, what will be the rate of taxation?

3. Upon a valuation of $2876475 the tax is $18409.44: there being no poll-tax, what is the rate?

4. The total valuation of property in the State of Wisconsin, for 1874, was $421285359; the tax levied upon this valuation was $656491.61: what was the rate to the hundredth of a mill?

209. To apportion the tax among the tax-payers.

I. A tax of $1373.64 is assessed upon a village, the property of which is valued at $748500; 57 persons pay a poll-tax of $1.25 each; find the rate of taxation, and construct a tax table to $9000.

TAX TABLE.

Rate, 1.74 mills on $1.

PROP.	TAX.	PROP.	TAX.	PROP.	TAX.	PROP.	TAX.
$1	$0.002	$10	$0.017	$100	$0.174	$1000	$ 1.74
2	.003	20	.035	200	.348	2000	3.48
3	.005	30	.052	300	.522	3000	5.22
4	.007	40	.070	400	.696	4000	6.96
5	.009	50	.087	500	.870	5000	8.70
6	.010	60	.104	600	1.044	6000	10.44
7	.012	70	.122	700	1.218	7000	12.18
8	.014	80	.139	800	1.392	8000	13.92
9	.016	90	.157	900	1.566	9000	15.66

REM.—In order to facilitate the calculation of each person's tax, it is customary to construct such a table. It is not necessary to carry it out in any column farther than the nearest mill.

1. James Turner's property is valued at $7851, and he pays poll-tax for 2 persons: what is his tax?

OPERATION.

$ 7851
12.180
1.392
.087
.002
13.66
2.50
16.16

SOLUTION.—By the table, the tax on $7000 is $12.18; on $800, $1.392; on $50, $0.087; and on $1, $0.002; then, the tax on $7851 is $12.18 + $1.392 + $0.087 + $0.002 = $13.66; this is his property tax. The poll-tax is $1.25 × 2 = $2.50. Then, James Turner's tax is $13.66 + $2.50 = $16.16.

EXPLANATION.—It is evident that the operation is equivalent to multiplying $7851 by the rate, 1.74, and adding the poll-tax.

2. John Brown's property is valued at $2576, and he pays poll-tax for 1 person: what is his tax?

3. Henry Adams' property is valued at $9265, and he pays poll-tax for 3 persons: what is his tax?

4. Amos Clarke's property is valued at $4759, and he pays poll-tax for 1 person: what is his tax?

5. Emily Wood's property is valued at $8367: what is her tax?

II. The tax to be raised in a city is $64375; its taxable property is valued at $16869758; find the rate of taxation to thousandths of a mill, and construct a tax table to $90000. Rate 3.816 mills on $1.

1. William Mill's property is valued at $56875: what is his tax?

2. Samuel Young's property is valued at $27543: what is his tax?

3. Charles O'Neil's property is valued at $83612: what is his tax?

4. Adolph Meyer's property is valued at $72968: what is his tax?

5. Louis Ganot's property is valued at $69547: what is his tax?

UNITED STATES REVENUE.

210. 1. The **United States Revenue** arises wholly from indirect taxation; it consists of *Internal Revenue* and the revenue from *Duties* or *Customs.*

2. The **Internal Revenue** arises from the sale of public lands, from a tax upon certain manufactures, from the sale of postage stamps, etc.

3. **Duties** or **Customs** are taxes on goods imported from foreign countries.

INTERNAL REVENUE.

211. 1. The public lands are disposed of at $1.25 per acre: what will the government receive for a township containing 36 sq. miles?

2. Letter postage is 2 ct. for each ounce, or fraction thereof; what is the necessary postage on a letter weighing $1\frac{1}{4}$ oz.?

3. The postage on books is 1 ct. for each 2 oz., or fraction thereof: what is the postage on a book weighing 1 lb. 5 oz.?

4. The tax on proof spirits is 70 ct. per gallon: what is the tax on a barrel of 40 gallons?

5. The tax on cigars per 1000 is $5: how much does this enhance the price of a single cigar?

6. The tax on beer is $1 per barrel of 31 gal. Each wholesale dealer in malt liquors pays a special tax of $50, and each retail dealer a special tax of $20; in a certain city there are 12 wholesale dealers, 250 retail dealers, and the annual manufacture of beer is 30000 bbl.: what is the revenue to government?

DUTIES OR CUSTOMS.

212. 1. Duties are of two kinds, *specific* and *ad valorem.*

2. A **specific** duty is levied upon the quantity of the goods.

REM.—In levying specific duties, allowance is made (1) for waste called *draft,* (2) for the weight of the box, cask, etc., containing the goods, called *tare.* The waste of liquors, imported in casks or barrels, is called *leakage;* that of liquors imported in bottles, *breakage. Gross weight* is the weight before deducting draft and tare; *net weight* is the weight after deducting draft and tare.

3. An **ad valorem** duty is levied upon the cost of the goods.

REM.—The cost of the goods is shown by the foreign invoice, or it is determined by appraisement at the custom-house.

4. Duties must be paid in coin.

REM.—The duty is computed on the net weight and on the total cost of the article in the foreign country. The *dutiable value* upon which the duty is estimated is always the nearest exact number of dollars, pounds, etc. If the total cost is $85.49 the dutiable value is $85; if it is $85.50 or $85.51, etc., the dutiable value is $86.00.

1. The gross weight of a hogshead of imported sugar is 1760 lb.; allowing $12\frac{1}{2}\%$ tare, what is the duty at $1\frac{3}{4}$ ct. per pound?

2. A manufacturer imported from Spain 40 bales of wool, of 400 lb. each, tare 5%; the cost was 45 ct. per pound: what was the duty, at 9 ct. per pound and 10% ad valorem?

3. A merchant imported a case of glassware; the cost of the ware in France was 365.15 francs, the case and charges were 57.15 francs, and the commission 5%: what was the duty at 40% in U. S. money, reckoning the franc at $19\frac{3}{10}$ ct.?

4. A book-seller imports a case of books; their cost in Germany was 1317.04 marks, case and charges 34.36 marks, and commission 6%: what was the duty at 25% in U. S. money, the mark being estimated at 23.8 ct.?

5. A merchant imports six cases of woolen cloth, net weight 1500 lb.; the cost in England was £500, cases and charges £8 4s. 6d., commission $2\frac{1}{2}\%$: what was the duty, at 50 ct. per lb. and 35% ad valorem in U. S. money, estimating the pound at $4.8665?

RATIO.

DEFINITIONS.

213. 1. **Ratio** is the relation of two numbers expressed by their quotient.

Thus, the ratio of 6 to 2 is $6 \div 2 = 3$; that is, 6 is 3 times 2

REM.—The established custom in several departments of mathematics makes it advisable to change the treatment of ratio as given in former editions of Ray's Arithmetics.

2. The ratio of two numbers is indicated by writing the sign (:) between them.

Thus, 2 : 6 is read the ratio of 2 to 6.

3. The two numbers are styled the **terms** of the ratio.

4. The first term is called the **antecedent**, and the second term the **consequent**.

5. 6 : 2 is 3, a ratio between two abstract numbers. \$6 : \$2 is 3, a ratio between two concrete numbers of the same denomination. To find 2 yd. : 2 ft., reduce the 2 yd. to ft.; 6 ft. : 2 ft. is 3.

A ratio can not exist between 2 ft. and \$6, because

they can not be reduced to the same denomination. Hence,

1st. *The terms of the ratio may be either abstract or concrete.*

2d. *When the terms are concrete, both must be of the same denomination.*

3d. *The ratio is always an abstract number.*

6. Ratios are either *simple* or *compound.*

7. A **simple** ratio is a single ratio.

Thus, 2 : 6 is a simple ratio.

8. A **compound** ratio consists of two or more simple ratios.

Thus, $\left.\begin{matrix} 2 : 6 \\ 3 : 9 \end{matrix}\right\}$ is a compound ratio.

9. In Ratio three quantities are considered: (1) *the antecedent*, (2) *the consequent*, and (3) *the ratio.* Any two of these being given, the third may be found.

214. Given the terms, to find the ratio.

1. What is the ratio of 6 to 3?

OPERATION.

$6 : 3$

$6 \div 3 = 2$

SOLUTION. The ratio of 6 to 3 is 6 divided by 3, equal to 2.

2. What is the ratio of $\frac{2}{3}$ to $\frac{3}{4}$?

OPERATION.

$\frac{2}{3} : \frac{3}{4}$

$\frac{2}{3} \div \frac{3}{4}$

$\frac{2}{3} \times \frac{4}{3} = \frac{8}{9}$

SOLUTION.—The ratio of $\frac{2}{3}$ to $\frac{3}{4}$ is $\frac{2}{3}$ divided by $\frac{3}{4}$, or $\frac{2}{3}$ multiplied by $\frac{4}{3}$, equal to $\frac{8}{9}$.

Rule.—*Divide the antecedent by the consequent.*

REM.—When the terms are of different denominations, they must be reduced to the same denomination.

What is the ratio of

3. 12 to 3?	13. 36 to 28?
4. 30 to 5?	14. 49 to 35?
5. 35 to 7?	15. $\frac{1}{2}$ to $\frac{2}{3}$?
6. 56 to 8?	16. $\frac{1}{3}$ to $\frac{3}{4}$?
7. 5 to 10?	17. $\frac{1}{3}$ to $\frac{1}{2}$?
8. 7 to 21?	18. $\frac{1}{5}$ to $\frac{1}{3}$?
9. 12 to 18?	19. $1\frac{1}{2}$ to $\frac{3}{4}$?
10. 15 to 20?	20. $3\frac{1}{2}$ to $2\frac{1}{4}$?
11. 15 to 25?	21. $5\frac{5}{6}$ to $2\frac{1}{3}$?
12. 25 to 15?	22. $6\frac{9}{10}$ to $4\frac{3}{5}$?

What is the ratio of

23. $18 to $6?
24. 54 days to 9 days?
25. 96 men to 12 men?
26. 221 bu. to 17 bu.?
27. 1 ft. 9 in. to 3 in.?
28. 5 yd. 1 ft. to 5 ft. 4 in.?

215. Given the ratio and the consequent, to find the antecedent.

1. 7 is the ratio of what number to 4?

OPERATION.
$4 \times 7 = 28$

SOLUTION.—The number is 4 multiplied by 7, equal to 28.

Rule.—*Multiply the consequent by the ratio.*

2. 4 is the ratio of what number to 13?
3. $\frac{5}{9}$ is the ratio of what number to 27?
4. $\frac{7}{13}$ is the ratio of what number to 52?
5. $2\frac{5}{8}$ is the ratio of what number to 24?
6. $4\frac{2}{5}$ is the ratio of what number to $1\frac{2}{3}$?

7. 3 is the ratio of what to 75 ct.?
8. $\frac{7}{8}$ is the ratio of what to 4 lb. 8 oz.?
9. 2.6 is the ratio of what to $4.

216. Given the ratio and the antecedent, to find the consequent.

1. 5 is the ratio of 45 to what number?

OPERATION.

$45 \div 5 = 9$

SOLUTION.—The number is 45 divided by 5, equal to 9.

Rule.—*Divide the antecedent by the ratio.*

2. 4 is the ratio of 56 to what number?
3. $\frac{7}{10}$ is the ratio of 42 to what number?
4. $2\frac{3}{4}$ is the ratio of $23\frac{3}{8}$ to what number?
5. $7\frac{5}{9}$ is the ratio of $27.20 to what?

217. To find the value of a compound ratio.

1 Find the value of the compound ratio $\left.\begin{matrix} 6 : 2 \\ 9 : 3 \end{matrix}\right\}$

OPERATION.

$6 \times 9 = 54$
$2 \times 3 = 6$
$54 \div 6 = 9$

SOLUTION.—The product of the antecedents 6 and 9 is 54, the product of the consequents 2 and 3 is 6; then, the value of the compound ratio is 54 divided by 6, equal to 9.

Rule.—*Divide the product of the antecedents by the product of the consequents.*

REM.—Multiplying the antecedents together and the consequents together, evidently reduces the compound ratio to a simple one; thus, in the above example the compound ratio $\left.\begin{matrix} 6 : 2 \\ 9 : 3 \end{matrix}\right\}$ is equivalent to the simple ratio 54 : 6.

Find the value

2. Of the compound ratio $\left.\begin{matrix} 10 : 5 \\ 9 : 6 \end{matrix}\right\}$

3. Of the compound ratio $\left.\begin{matrix} 12\frac{1}{2} : 6\frac{1}{4} \\ 33\frac{1}{3} : 8\frac{1}{3} \end{matrix}\right\}$

4. Of the compound ratio $\left.\begin{matrix} \frac{2}{3} : \frac{1}{2} \\ \frac{3}{4} : 1\frac{1}{4} \end{matrix}\right\}$

5. Of the compound ratio $\left.\begin{matrix} \text{8 men} : \text{2 men.} \\ \text{12 da.} : \text{24 da.} \end{matrix}\right\}$

6. Of the compound ratio $\left.\begin{matrix} \$6.75 : \$2.25 \\ \text{6 bu.} : \text{3 bu.} \end{matrix}\right\}$

7. Of the compound ratio $\left.\begin{matrix} 5 : 2 \\ 7 : 3 \\ 9 : 5 \end{matrix}\right\}$

218. The terms of a ratio correspond to the terms of a fraction, the antecedent to the numerator, the consequent to the denominator.

Thus, in 2 : 3 the ratio is $\frac{2}{3}$, in which the antecedent 2 is the numerator and the consequent 3 the denominator. Hence (Art. 101) we have the following

Principles.

I. A ratio is multiplied

1*st. By multiplying the antecedent.*
2*d. By dividing the consequent.*

II. A ratio is divided

1*st. By dividing the antecedent.*
2*d. By multiplying the consequent.*

III. A ratio is not changed

1*st. By multiplying both terms by the same number*
2*d. By dividing both terms by the same number.*

219. To reduce a ratio to its lowest terms.

1. Reduce 16 : 24 to its lowest terms.

OPERATION.

$$8\,)\,\underline{16:24}$$
$$2:\ 3$$

SOLUTION.—The G. C. D. of 16 and 24 is 8; dividing both terms of 16 : 24 by 8, it becomes 2 : 3 (Art. **218**, III, 2d).

Rule.—*Divide both terms of the ratio by their greatest common divisor.*

2. Reduce 20 : 25 to its lowest terms.
3. Reduce 10 : 30 to its lowest terms.
4. Reduce 34 : 51 to its lowest terms.
5. Reduce 95 : 133 to its lowest terms.
6. Reduce 75 : 125 to its lowest terms.
7. Reduce 217 : 279 to its lowest terms.

220. To clear a ratio of fractions.

1. Clear $1\frac{1}{2} : 2\frac{1}{3}$ of fractions.

OPERATION

$$1\tfrac{1}{2} : 2\tfrac{1}{3}$$
$$\underline{\qquad 6}$$
$$9 : 14$$

SOLUTION.—The L. C. M. of the denominators 2 and 3 is 6; multiplying both terms of $1\frac{1}{2} : 2\frac{1}{3}$ by 6, it becomes 9 : 14 (Art. **218**, III, 1st).

Rule.—*Multiply both terms of the ratio by the least common multiple of the denominators of the fractions.*

2. Clear $3\frac{3}{4} : 4\frac{2}{5}$ of fractions.
3. Clear $7\frac{1}{2} : 10\frac{2}{3}$ of fractions.
4. Clear $\frac{5}{6} : \frac{7}{9}$ of fractions.
5. Clear $6\frac{3}{10} : 9\frac{7}{15}$ of fractions.

PROPORTION.

DEFINITIONS.

221. 1. **Proportion** is an expression for the equality of two ratios.

Thus, 2 : 4 and 3 : 6 may form a proportion, for the ratio of each is $\frac{1}{2}$.

2. The proportion is indicated by writing : : between the ratios.

Thus, 2 : 4 : : 3 : 6 is read 2 is to 4 as 3 is to 6.

3. A proportion is either *simple* or *compound*.

4. In a **simple** proportion both the ratios are simple.

Thus, 2 : 4 : : 3 : 6 is a simple proportion.

5. In a **compound** proportion one or both the ratios are compound.

Thus, $\left.\begin{array}{c}2:3\\3:4\end{array}\right\} :: \left.\begin{array}{c}4:5\\5:8\end{array}\right\}$ is a compound proportion.

6. Every proportion consists of four *terms*.

7. The first and fourth terms of a proportion are called the *extremes*.

8. The second and third terms of a proportion are called the *means*.

9. The last term is said to be a *fourth proportional* to the other three taken in order.

Thus, in the proportion 2 : 4 : : 3 : 6, the extremes are 2 and 6; the means are 4 and 3; and 6 is a fourth proportional to 2, 4, and 3.

10. When three numbers form a proportion, the second number is said to be a *mean proportional* between the other two.

Thus, in the proportion 2 : 4 : : 4 : 8, 4 is a mean proportional between 2 and 8.

222. The operations of proportion depend upon the following.

PRINCIPLE.—*In every proportion the product of the extremes is equal to the product of the means.*

Thus, in the proportion 2 : 4 : : 3 : 6, $2 \times 6 = 4 \times 3$; in the proportion $\left.\begin{matrix} 2 : 3 \\ 3 : 4 \end{matrix}\right\} : : \left.\begin{matrix} 4 : 5 \\ 5 : 8 \end{matrix}\right\}$ $2 \times 3 \times 5 \times 8 = 3 \times 4 \times 4 \times 5$; and the same may be shown for any other proportion. Hence (**36**, 4),

1st. *If the product of the means be divided by one of the extremes, the quotient will be the other extreme.*

2d. *If the product of the extremes be divided by one of the means, the quotient will be the other mean.*

223. Given three terms of a proportion, to find the fourth.

1. What : 6 : : 4 : 8?

SOLUTION.—The product of the means 6 and 4, is 24; then, 24 divided by 8, one of the extremes, equals 3, the other extreme (**222**, 1st).

OPERATION.

$$6 \times 4 = 24$$
$$24 \div 8 = 3$$

2. $4 : \text{what} :: \left.\begin{matrix} 3 : 5 \\ 10 : 12 \end{matrix}\right\} ?$

SOLUTION.—The product of the extremes, $4 \times 5 \times 12$, divided by 3×10, one of the means equals 8, the other mean (**222**, 2d).

OPERATION.

$$\frac{\overset{2}{\cancel{4}} \times \cancel{5} \times \overset{4}{\cancel{12}}}{\cancel{3} \times \underset{2}{\cancel{10}}} = 8$$

Rule.—*Divide the product of the terms of the same name by the other given term.*

REM.—Indicate the operation and cancel whenever it is practicable (**91**).

3. 2 : 8 : : 6 : what?
4. 5 : 7 : : 10 : what?
5. What : 8 : : 6 : 16?
6. 5 : what : : 6 : 12?
7. 3 : 7 : : what : 14?
8. 7 : 14 : : 9 : what?
9. $\left.\begin{matrix} 2 : 4 \\ 8 : 9 \end{matrix}\right\} :: \text{what} : 45?$
10. $\left.\begin{matrix} 5 : 8 \\ 4 : 10 \end{matrix}\right\} :: \left.\begin{matrix} 3 : 4 \\ 7 : \text{what} \end{matrix}\right\} ?$
11. $\left.\begin{matrix} 10 : \text{what} \\ 14 : 21 \end{matrix}\right\} :: \left.\begin{matrix} 22 : 33 \\ 26 : 39 \end{matrix}\right\} ?$
12. $\frac{2}{3} : \frac{3}{4} :: \frac{4}{5} : \text{what?}$
13. $\frac{3}{5} : \text{what} :: \frac{9}{10} : 1\frac{1}{4}?$
14. $\text{What} : 4\frac{2}{3} :: 7\frac{1}{2} : 10\frac{1}{2}?$
15. 4 : 6 : : 6 : what?

224. Proportion, when applied to the solution of concrete problems, has been styled "*The Rule of Three,*" because three terms are given to find the fourth. The use of Proportion was formerly so extensive that it was often called "*The Golden Rule.*"

The solution of a problem by proportion consists of two parts:

1st. *The statement;* that is, the proper arrangement of the numbers into a proportion.

2d. *The operation* of finding the required term.

REM.—In arranging the numbers in a proportion, it is customary, though not necessary, to make the number or quantity required *a fourth proportional* to the other three; then, the first three terms of the proportion always are given to find the fourth.

I. SIMPLE PROPORTION.

1. If 2 yd. of cloth cost $4, what will 6 yd. cost?

OPERATION.

$$2 : 6 :: 4 : \text{what?}$$

$$\frac{\overset{3}{\not{6}} \times 4}{\not{2}} = 12$$

SOLUTION.—Since the number required, or fourth term of the proportion, is dollars, the third term is $4. Since the cost of 6 yd. will be greater than the cost of 2 yd., 6 yd. is the second term of the proportion, and 2 yd. the first term. Dividing the product of 6 and 4 by 2 (Art. **223,** Rule), the required term is $12.

REM.—In this example, the number of dollars is in a *direct ratio* to the number of yards; that is, the *greater* the number of yards, the *greater* the number of dollars they will cost.

2. If 3 men can dig a cellar in 10 days, in how many days can 5 men dig it?

OPERATION.

$$5 : 3 :: 10 : \text{what?}$$

$$\frac{3 \times \overset{2}{\cancel{10}}}{\cancel{5}} = 6$$

SOLUTION.—Since the number required, or fourth term of the proportion, is days, the third term is 10 da. Since 5 men will dig the cellar in a less number of days than 3 men, 3 men is the second term of the proportion and 5 men the first term. Dividing the product of 3 and 10 by 5 (Art. **223,** Rule), the required term is 6 da.

REM.—In this example, the number of days is in an *inverse ratio* to the number of men; that is, the *greater* the number of men, the *less* the number of days in which they will dig the cellar.

Rule.—1. *For the third term, write that number which is of the same denomination as the number required.*

2. *For the second term, write the* GREATER *of the two remaining numbers, when the fourth term is to be greater than the third; and the* LESS, *when the fourth term is to be less than the third.*

3. *Divide the product of the second and third terms by the first; the quotient will be the fourth term, or number required.*

3. If 3 men can dig a cellar in 12 days, how many men will dig it in 6 days?

4. If 3 yd. cloth cost $8, what cost 6 yd.?

5. If 5 bl. flour cost $30, what cost 3 bl.?

6. If 3 lb. 12 oz. tea cost $3.50, what cost 11 lb. 4 oz.?

7. If 2 lb. 8 oz. of tea cost $2, what quantity can you buy for $5?

8. If 4 hats cost $14, what cost 10 hats?

9. If 3 caps cost 69 cents, what cost 11 caps?

10. If 4 yd. cloth cost \$7, what cost 9 yd.?

11. If 8 yd. cloth cost \$32, what cost 12 yd.?

12. If 12 yd. cloth cost \$48, what cost 8 yd.?

13. If \$32 purchase 8 yd. of cloth, how many yards will \$48 buy?

14. If \$48 purchase 12 yd. of cloth, how many yards can be bought for \$32?

15. A man receives \$152 for 19 months' work: how much should he have for 4 months' work?

16. If 8 men perform a piece of work in 24 days, in what time can 12 men perform it?

17. If 60 men perform a piece of work in 8 da., how many men will perform it in 2 days?

18. If 15 oz. of pepper cost 25 ct., what cost 6 lb.?

19. If 6 gal. of molasses cost \$2.70, what cost 26 gal.?

20. If 5 cwt. 85 lb. of sugar cost \$42.12, what will 35 cwt. 25 lb. cost?

21. If $1\frac{1}{2}$ yd. of cloth cost \$2.50, what will be the cost of $1\frac{1}{8}$ yd.?

22. If 90 bu. of oats supply 40 horses 6 da., how long will 450 bu. supply them?

23. If 6 men build a wall in 15 da., how many men can build it in 5 da.?

24. If 15 bu. of corn pay for 30 bu. of potatoes, how much corn can be had for 140 bu. potatoes?

25. If 3 cwt. 25 lb. of sugar cost \$22.60, what will be the cost of 16 cwt. 25 lb.?

26. If a perpendicular staff, 3 ft. long, cast a shadow 4 ft. 6 in., what is the height of a steeple whose shadow measures 180 ft.?

27. If a man perform a journey in 60 da., traveling 9

hr. each day, in how many days can he perform it by traveling 12 hr. a day?

28. A merchant, failing, paid 60 ct. on each dollar of his debts. He owed A \$2200, and B \$1800: what did each receive?

29. A merchant, having failed, owes A \$800.30; B \$250; C \$375.10; D \$500; F \$115; his property, worth \$612.12, goes to his creditors: how much will this pay on the dollar?

30. If the 4-cent loaf weigh 9 oz. when flour is \$8 a bl., what will it weigh when flour is \$6 a bl.?

31. I borrowed \$250 for 6 mo.: how long should I lend \$300 to compensate the favor?

32. A starts on a journey, and travels 27 mi. a day; 7 da. after, B starts and travels the same road 36 mi. a day: in how many days will B overtake A?

33. If William's services are worth $\$15\frac{2}{3}$ a mo., when he labors 9 hr. a day, what ought he to receive for $4\frac{2}{5}$ mo., when he labors 12 hr. a day?

34. If 5 lb. of butter cost $\$\frac{5}{8}$, what cost $\frac{3}{4}$ lb.?

35. If 6 yd. cloth cost $\$5\frac{3}{5}$, what cost $7\frac{3}{8}$ yd.?

36. If $\frac{1}{3}$ bu. wheat cost $\$\frac{3}{8}$, what cost $\frac{1}{2}$ bu.?

37. If $1\frac{3}{4}$ yd. cloth cost $\$\frac{7}{24}$, what cost 2 yd.?

38. If $\$29\frac{3}{4}$ buy $59\frac{1}{2}$ yd. of cloth, how much will $\$31\frac{1}{4}$ buy?

39. If .85 of a gallon of milk cost \$1.36, what will be the cost of .25 of a gallon?

40. If 61.3 lb. of tea cost \$44.9942, what will be the cost of 1.08 lb.?

41. If $\frac{5}{7}$ of a yard of cloth cost $\$\frac{3}{5}$, what will $\frac{9}{11}$ of a yard cost?

42. If $\frac{3}{7}$ of a yard of velvet cost $\$4\frac{2}{5}$, what cost $17\frac{3}{8}$ yd.?

43. A wheel has 35 cogs; a smaller wheel working in

it, 26 cogs: in how many revolutions of the larger wheel will the smaller gain 10 revolutions?

44. If a grocer, instead of a true gallon, use a measure deficient by 1 gill, what will be the *true* measure of 100 of these *false* gallons?

45. If the velocity of sound be 1142 feet per sec., and the number of pulsations in a person 70 per min., what is the distance of a cloud, if 20 pulsations are counted between the time of seeing a flash of lightning and hearing the thunder?

46. The length of a wall, by a measuring line, was 643 ft. 8 in., but the line was found to be 25 ft. 5.25 in. long, instead of 25 feet, its supposed length: what was the true length of the wall?

II. COMPOUND PROPORTION.

225. 1. If 2 men earn \$20 in 5 da., what sum can 6 men earn in 10 da.?

OPERATION.

$$\left.\begin{matrix} 2 : 6 \\ 5 : 10 \end{matrix}\right\} :: 20 : \text{what?}$$

$$\frac{\overset{3}{\not{6}} \times \overset{2}{\not{1}\not{0}} \times 20}{\not{2} \times \not{5}} = 120$$

SOLUTION.—Since the number required or fourth term of the proportion is dollars, the third term is \$20. Since 6 men can earn a greater number of dollars than 2 men, 6 men is in the second term of the proportion and 2 men in the first term; and since in 10 da. a greater number of dollars can be earned than in 5 da., 10 da. is in the second term of the proportion and 5 da. in the first term. Dividing the product of 6, 10, and 20 by the product of 2 and 5 (Art. **223,** Rule), the required term is \$120.

2. If 6 men, in 10 da., build a wall 20 ft. long, 3 ft. high, and 2 ft. thick, in how many days could 15 men build a wall 80 ft. long, 2 ft. high, and 3 ft. thick?

OPERATION.

$$\left.\begin{array}{r}15 : 6\\ 20 : 80\\ 3 : 2\\ 2 : 3\end{array}\right\} :: 10 : \text{what?}$$

$$\frac{\overset{2}{\not 6} \times \overset{4}{\not 8\not 0} \times \not 2 \times \not 3 \times \overset{2}{\not 1\not 0}}{\underset{\not 3}{\not 1\not 5} \times \not 2\not 0 \times \not 3 \times \not 2} = 16$$

SOLUTION.—Since the number required, or fourth term of the proportion, is days, the third term is 10 days. Since 15 men can build a wall in a less number of days than 6 men, 6 men is in the second term of the proportion, and 15 men in the first term; since to build a wall 80 ft. long will take a greater number of days than to build a wall 20 ft. long, 80 ft. is in the second term of the proportion and 20 ft. in the first term; since to build a wall 2 ft. high will take a less number of days than to build a wall 3 ft. high, 2 ft. is in the second term of the proportion and 3 ft. in the first term; and since to build a wall 3 ft. thick will take a greater number of days than to build a wall 2 ft. thick, 3 ft. is in the second term of the proportion and 2 ft. in the first term. Dividing the product of 6, 80, 2, 3, and 10 by the product of 15, 20, 3, and 2 (Art. **223**, Rule), the required term is 16 da.

Rule.—1. *For the third term, write that number which is of the same denomination as the number required.*

2. *Arrange each pair of the numbers forming the compound ratio as if, with the third term, they formed a simple proportion.*

3. *Divide the product of the numbers in the second and third terms by the product of the numbers in the first term; the quotient will be the fourth term or number required.*

3. If a man travel 24 mi. in 2 da., by walking 4 hr. a day: at the same rate, how far will he travel in 10 da., walking 8 hr. a day?

4. If 16 men build 18 rods of fence in 12 days, how many men can build 72 rd. in 8 da.?

5. If 6 men spend $150 in 8 mo., how much will 15 men spend in 20 mo.?

6. I travel 217 mi. in 7 days of 6 hr. each: how far can I travel in 9 days of 11 hr. each?

7. If $100 gain $6 in 12 mo., what sum will $75 gain in 9 mo.?

8. If 100 lb. be carried 20 mi. for 20 ct., how far will 10100 lb. be carried for $60.60?

9. To carry 12 cwt. 75 lb. 400 mi., costs $57.12: what will it cost to carry 10 tons 75 mi.?

10. If 18 men, in 15 da., build a wall 40 rd. long, 5 ft. high, 4 ft. thick, in what time could 20 men build a wall 87 rd. long, 8 ft. high, and 5 ft. thick?

11. If 180 men, in 6 days, of 10 hr. each, dig a trench 200 yd. long, 3 yd. wide, 2 yd. deep, in how many days can 100 men, working 8 hr. a day, dig a trench 180 yd. long, 4 yd. wide, and 3 yd. deep?

PARTNERSHIP.

226. 1. A **Partnership** is an association of persons for the transaction of business. Such an association is called a *firm*, or *house*, and each member, a *partner*.

2. The **capital, or stock,** is the amount of money or property contributed by the firm.

3. The **assets** are the amounts due a firm, together with the property of all kinds belonging to it.

4. The **liabilities** of a firm are its *debts*.

5. The **net capital** is the *difference* between the assets and liabilities.

1. A and B engaged in trade; A's capital was $200; B's, $300; they gained $100: find each partner's share.

Solution.—The whole capital is $200 + $300 = $500; of this A owns $\frac{200}{500} = \frac{2}{5}$, and B owns $\frac{300}{500} = \frac{3}{5}$ of the capital; hence, A's gain will be $\frac{2}{5}$ of $100 = $40, and B's gain will be $\frac{3}{5}$ of $100 = $60.

Or, SOLUTION.—The whole capital is $200 + $300 = $500; then,

$500 : $200 :: $100 : $40, A's share;
$500 : $300 :: $100 : $60, B's share.

Rule.—*Take such part of the whole gain or loss, as each partner's stock is part of the whole stock.*

Or, **Rule.**—*As the whole stock is to each partner's stock, so is the whole gain or loss to each partner's gain or loss.*

REM.—This rule is applicable when required to divide a sum into parts having a given ratio to each other; as in Bankruptcy, General Average, etc.

2. A and B form a partnership, with a capital of $800: A's part is $300; B's, $500; they gain $232: what is the share of each?

3. A's stock was $70; B's, $150; C's, $80; they gained $120: what was each man's share of it?

4. A, B, and C traded together: A put in $200; B, $400; C, $600: they gained $427.26: find each man's share.

5. Divide $90 among 3 persons, so that the parts shall be to each other as 1, 3, and 5.

6. Divide $735.93 among 4 men, in the ratio of 2, 3, 5, and 7.

7. A person left an estate of $22361 to be divided among 6 children, in the ratio of their ages, which are 3, 6, 9, 11, 13, and 17 yr.: what are the shares?

8. Divide $692.23 into 3 parts, that shall be to each other as $\frac{1}{3}$, $\frac{3}{5}$, and $\frac{7}{8}$.

BANKRUPTCY.

227. A **Bankrupt** is one who has failed to pay his debts when due.

REM.—The *assets* of a bankrupt are usually placed in the hands of an *assignee*, whose duty it is to convert them into cash, and divide the net proceeds among the creditors.

1. A man, failing, owes A $175; B, $500; C, $600; D, $210; E, $42.50; F, $20; G, $10; his property is worth $934.50: what will be each creditor's share?

2. A man owes A $234; B, $175; C, $326: his property is worth $492.45: what can he pay on $1; and what will each creditor get?

3. Mr. Smith failed in business, owing $37000. His assignee sold the stock for $25000, and charged $4650 for expenses: how much did he pay on the dollar?

GENERAL AVERAGE.

228. **General Average** is the method of apportioning among the owners of a ship and cargo, losses occasioned by casualties at sea.

1. A, B, and C freighted a ship with 108 tuns of wine. A owned 48, B 36, and C 24 tuns; they were obliged to cast 45 tuns overboard: how much of the loss must each sustain?

2. From a ship valued at \$10000, with a cargo valued at \$15000, there was thrown overboard goods valued at \$1125: what % was the general average, and what was the loss of A, whose goods were valued at \$2150?

PARTNERSHIP WITH TIME.

229. 1. A and B built a wall for \$82; A had 4 men at work 5 days, and B 3 men 7 days: how should they divide the money?

SOLUTION.—The work of 4 men 5 da. equals the work of 4×5, or 20 men 1 da.; and the work of 3 men 7 da., equals the work of 3×7, or 21 men 1 da.; it is then required to divide \$82 into two parts, having the same ratio to each other as 20 to 21; hence, A's part is $\frac{20}{41}$ of \$82 = \$40; B's part is $\frac{21}{41}$ of \$82 = \$42.

2. A put in trade \$50 for 4 mo.; B, \$60 for 5 mo.; they gained \$24: what was each man's share?

SOLUTION.—\$50 for 4 mo. equals $\$50 \times 4 = \$200$ for 1 mo.; and \$60 for 5 mo. equals $\$60 \times 5 = \$300$ for 1 mo. Hence, divide \$24 into two parts having the same ratio as 200 to 300, or 2 to 3. This gives A $\frac{2}{5}$ of \$24 = \$9.60, and B $\frac{3}{5}$ of \$24 = \$14.40.

Rule.—*Multiply each partner's stock by the time it was employed; then take such part of the gain or loss as each partner's product is part of the sum of all the products.*

3. A and B hire a pasture for \$54: A pastures 23 horses 27 da.; B, 21 horses 39 da.: what will each pay?

4. A put in \$300 for 5 mo.; B, \$400 for 8 mo.; C, \$500 for 3 mo.: they lost \$100; find each one's loss.

5. A, B, and C hire a pasture for \$18.12: A pastures 6 cows 30 da.; B, 5 cows 40 da.; C, 8 cows 28 da.: what shall each pay?

6. Two men formed a partnership for 16 mo.: A put in, at first, \$300, and, at the end of 8 mo., \$100 more; B put in, at first, \$600, but, at the end of 10 mo., drew out \$300; they gained \$442.20: find each man's share.

7. A and B are partners: A put in \$800 for 12 mo., and B, \$500. What sum must B put in at the end of 7 mo. to entitle him to half the year's profits?

EQUATION OF PAYMENTS.

230. Equation of payments is the method of finding the *mean* or *average* time of making two or more payments, due at different times.

1. A owes B \$2, due in 3 mo., and \$4, due in 6 mo.: at what period can both sums be paid so that neither party will be the loser?

SOLUTION.—The interest on \$2 for 3 mo. equals the interest on \$1 for $3 \times 2 = 6$ mo.; the interest on \$4 for 6 mo. equals the interest on \$1 for $6 \times 4 = 24$ mo.; then, the interest on $\$2 + \$4 = \$6$ equals the interest on \$1 for 6 mo. + 24 mo. = 30 mo.; hence, \$6 must be on interest $30 \div 6 = 5$ mo.

OPERATION.

$2 \times 3 = 6$

$4 \times 6 = 24$

$6 \;)\,30$

5

Rule.—1. *Multiply each payment by the time to elapse till it becomes due.*

2. *Divide the sum of the products by the sum of the payments; the quotient will be the equated time.*

REM.—When one of the payments is due on the day from which the equated time is reckoned, its product is 0; but, in finding the sum of the payment, this must be added with the others.

2. A owes B \$2, due in 4 mo., and \$6, due in 8 mo.: find the average time of paying both sums.

3. A owes B \$8, due in 5 mo., and \$4, due in 8 mo.: find the mean time of payment.

4. A buys \$1500 worth of goods; \$250 are to be paid in 2 mo., \$500 in 5 mo., \$750 in 8 mo.: find the mean time of payment.

5. A owes B \$300; 1 third due in 6 mo.; 1 fourth in 8 mo.; the remainder in 12 mo.: what is the average time of payment?

6. I buy \$200 worth of goods; 1 fifth to be paid now; 2 fifths in 5 mo.; the rest in 10 mo.: what is the average time of paying all?

231. In finding the *Average* or *Mean* time for the payment of several sums due at different times, any date may be taken from which to reckon the time.

1. A merchant buys goods as follows, on 60 days credit: May 1st, 1848, \$100; June 15th, \$200: what is the average time of payment? July 30th.

SOLUTION.—Counting from May 1, it is 60 days to the time of the first payment, and 105 days to that of the second; then, the equated time is 90 days from May 1st, that is, July 30th.

OPERATION.

$$\begin{array}{lr} \$100 \times\ \ 60 = & 6000 \\ \$200 \times 105 = & 21000 \\ \hline \$300 &)\,27000 \\ & \overline{90} \end{array}$$

2. I bought goods on 90 days credit, as follows: April 2d, 1853, \$200; June 1st, \$300: what is the average time of payment?

3. A merchant bought goods as follows: April 6, 1876, on 3 mo., \$1250; May 17, 1876, on 4 mo., \$4280; June 21, 1876, on 6 mo., \$675: what is the average time of payment?

AVERAGE.

232. Average is the method of finding the *mean* or *average* price of a mixture, when the ingredients composing it, and their prices, are known.

1. I mix 4 pounds of tea, worth 40 ct. a lb., with 6 lb., worth 50 ct. a lb.: what is 1 lb. of the mixture worth?

Solution.—4 lb. at 40 ct. per lb. are worth \$1.60, and 6 lb. at 50 ct. are worth \$3.00; then, $4 + 6 = 10$ lb. are worth \$4.60; hence, 1 lb. cost $\frac{1}{10}$ of \$4.60, or 46 ct.

OPERATION.

$$\begin{array}{r} 4 \times .40 = 1.60 \\ 6 \times .50 = 3.00 \\ \hline 10 \quad)\,4.60 \\ .46 \end{array}$$

Rule.—*Divide the whole cost by the whole number of ingredients; the quotient will be the average or mean price.*

2. Mix 6 lb. of sugar, at 3 ct. a lb., with 4 lb., at 8 ct. a lb., what will 1 lb. of the mixture be worth?

3. Mix 25 lb. sugar, at 12 ct. a lb., 25 lb., at 18 ct., and 40 lb., at 25 ct.: what is 1 lb. of the mixture worth?

4. A mixes 3 gal. water, with 12 gal. wine, at 50 ct. a gal.: what is 1 gal. of the mixture worth?

5. I have 30 sheep: 10 are worth \$3 each; 12, \$4 each; the rest, \$9 each: find the average value.

6. On a certain day the mercury in the thermometer stood as follows: from 6 till 10 A. M., at 63°; from 10 A. M. till 1 P. M., 70°; from 1 till 3 P. M., 75°; from 3 till 7 P. M., 73°; from 7 P. M. till 6 A. M. of the next day, 55°: what was the mean temperature of the day, from sunrise to sunrise?

INVOLUTION.

DEFINITIONS.

233. 1. **Involution** is the multiplication of a number into itself one or more times.

2. A **power** is the product obtained by involution.

3. The **first power** is the number itself.

4. The **second power,** or **square,** is the product obtained by taking the number twice as a factor.

Thus, $2 \times 2 = 4$, is the second power or square of 2.

5. The **third power,** or **cube,** is the product obtained by taking the number three times as a factor.

Thus, $2 \times 2 \times 2 = 8$ is the third power or cube of 2.

REM.—The second power is called the square, because the area of a square is the product of two equal factors (Art. 68). The third power is called the cube, because the solid contents of a cube is the product of three equal factors (Art. 70).

6. The higher powers of a number are denominated respectively the *fourth power*, *fifth power*, *sixth power*, etc.

Thus, $2 \times 2 \times 2 \times 2 = 16$, is the fourth power of 2; $2 \times 2 \times 2 \times 2 \times 2 = 32$, is the fifth power of 2; $2 \times 2 \times 2 \times 2 \times 2 \times 2 = 64$, is the sixth power of 2, etc.

7. The **exponent** is a number denoting the power to which the given number is to be raised.

Thus, in 3^2, read 3 *square*, the 2 denotes the square of 3; hence, $3^2 = 9$. In 5^3, read 5 *cube*, the 3 denotes the cube of 5; hence, $5^3 = 125$. 7^4 is read 7 *fourth power;* 9^5, 9 *fifth power*, etc.

234. To raise a number to any power.

1. Find the cube of 75.

SOLUTION.—75 multiplied by 75 is 5625; this is the square of 75. 5625 multiplied by 75 is 421875; this is the cube of 75.

OPERATION.

75	5625
75	75
375	28125
525	39375
5625	421875

Rule.—*Obtain a product in which the number is taken as a factor as many times as there are units in the exponent of the power.*

2. Find the square of 65.
3. Find the cube of 25.
4. Find the fourth power of 12.
5. Find the fifth power of 10.
6. Find the sixth power of 9.
7. Find the eighth power of 2.
8. Find the square of $\frac{2}{3}$.
9. Find the cube of $\frac{3}{4}$.
10. Find the fourth power of $\frac{4}{5}$.
11. Find the fifth power of $\frac{2}{3}$.
12. Find the square of $16\frac{1}{2}$.
13. Find the cube of $12\frac{1}{2}$.
14. Find the fourth power of .25
15. $14^3 =$ what?
16. $19^4 =$ what?
17. $(2\frac{1}{3})^5 =$ what?

EVOLUTION.

DEFINITIONS.

235. 1. **Evolution** is the process of resolving a number into two or more equal factors.

2. A **root** of a number is one of the two or more equal factors.

3. The **square root** of a number is one of two equal factors.

Thus, 3 is the square root of 9; for $9 = 3 \times 3$.

4. The **cube root** of a number is one of three equal factors.

Thus, 3 is the cube root of 27; for $27 = 3 \times 3 \times 3$.

5. The higher roots of a number are denominated respectively the *fourth root*, *fifth root*, etc.

Thus, 3 is the fourth root of 81; for $81 = 3 \times 3 \times 3 \times 3$. 3 is the fifth root of 243; for $243 = 3 \times 3 \times 3 \times 3 \times 3$.

6. The **radical sign** $\sqrt{}$ placed before a number shows that its root is to be extracted.

7. The **index** is a number placed above the radical sign to show the number of the root.

Rem.—It is customary, however, to omit 2, the index of the square root.

Thus, $\sqrt{25}$ is read the square root of 25; hence, $\sqrt{25}=5$. $\sqrt[3]{27}$ is read the cube root of 27; hence, $\sqrt[3]{27}=3$. $\sqrt[4]{16}$ is read the fourth root of 16; hence, $\sqrt[4]{16}=2$.

8. A **perfect power** is one whose root can be obtained exactly.

Thus, 25 and $\frac{16}{25}$ are perfect squares; 27 and $\frac{8}{27}$ are perfect cubes; 16 and $\frac{1}{16}$ are perfect fourth powers.

9. The squares and cubes of the first ten numbers are exhibited in the following

TABLE.

Numbers.	1	2	3	4	5	6	7	8	9	10
Squares.	1	4	9	16	25	36	49	64	81	100
Cubes.	1	8	27	64	125	216	343	512	729	1000

Rem.—The numbers in the first line are the square roots of the corresponding numbers in the second line, and the cube roots of those in the third line.

10. An **imperfect power** is one whose root can be obtained only approximately.

Thus, $\sqrt{2}=1.41421+$.

SQUARE ROOT.

236. To find the number of figures in the square root.

1. The square root of 1 is 1, and the square root of 100 is 10 (Art. **235,** 9, Table); between 1 and 100 are all numbers consisting of one or two figures, and between 1 and 10 are all numbers consisting of one figure; therefore,

When a number consists of one or two figures, its square root consists of one figure.

2. The square root of 100 is 10, and the square root of 10000 is 100; between 100 and 10000 are all numbers consisting of three or four figures, and between 10 and 100 are all numbers consisting of two figures; therefore,

When a number consists of three or four figures, its square root consists of two figures.

3. In like manner it may be shown that,

When a number consists of five or six figures, its square root consists of three figures.

And so on; therefore,

1st. *If a number be pointed off into periods of two figures each, the number of periods will be the same as the number of figures in the square root.*

2d. *The square of the units will be found in the first period, the square of the tens in the second period, the square of the hundreds in the third period, etc.*

237. To point off a number into periods of two figures each.

1. Point off 368425.
2. Point off 6.843256.
3. Point off 83751.42963.

Rule.—*Place a point over the order units, and then over every second order from units to the left and to the right.*

Rem. 1.—The first period on the left of the integral part of the number will often contain but a single figure.

Rem. 2.—When the first period on the right of the decimal part contains but a single figure, a cipher must be annexed to complete the period.

4. Point off 864326; 4.758462; 7584.3769.
5. Point off 97285.46138; 75300; .046827; .0625; .625.

238. To extract the square root of a number.

1. Extract the square root of 256.

OPERATION.

$$\begin{array}{r|l} & \dot{2}5\dot{6}\,(16 \\ & 1 \\ 26 & 156 \\ & 156 \end{array}$$

Solution.—Point off 256 into periods of two figures each by placing a point over 6 and 2 (Art. **237**, Rule).

The largest square in 2 (Art. **235**, 9, Table) is 1; its root is 1; place the root 1 on the right and subtract the square 1 from 2; the remainder is 1, to which bring down the next period 56.

Double the root 1 and place the result 2 on the left of 156 for a trial divisor. Find how many times 2 is contained in 15 (making allowance for subsequent increase of the trial divisor); the result is 6; place 6 in the root on the right of 1 and also on the right of 2, the trial divisor; then 26 is the complete divisor. Multiply 26 by 6 and subtract the product 156 from 156; the remainder is 0. Therefore, 256 is a perfect square, and its square root is 16.

GEOMETRICAL EXPLANATION.

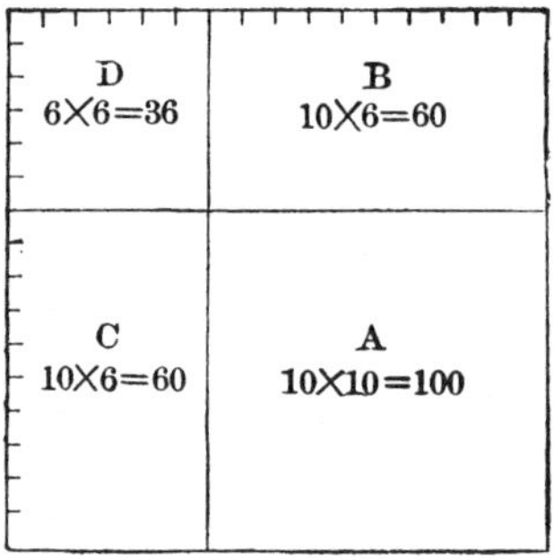

After finding that the sq. root of the given number will contain two places of figures (tens and units), and that the figure in tens' place is 1 (ten), form a square figure (A) 10 in. on each side, which contains (Art. **67**) 100 sq. in.; taking this sum from the whole number of squares, 156 sq. in. remain, which correspond to the number, 156, left after subtracting above.

It is obvious that to increase the figure A, and at the same time preserve it a square, both length and breadth must be *increased equally;* and, since each side is 10 in. long, it will take *twice* 10, that is, 20 in., to encompass two sides of the square A. For this reason, 10 is doubled in the numerical operation.

Now determine the breadth of the addition to be made to each side of the square A. After increasing each side equally, it will require a small square (D) of the *same breadth* as each of the figures B and C, to complete the entire square; hence, the superficial contents of B, C, and D, must be equal to the remainder, 156. Now their contents are obtained by multiplying their length by their breadth.

Then the figure in the units' place—that is, the breadth of B and C—must be found by *trial*, and it will be somewhat less than the number of times the length of B and C (20) is contained in the remainder (156). 20 is contained in 156 more than 7 times; let us try 7: 7 added to 20 makes 27 for the whole length of B, C, and D, and this, multiplied by 7, gives 189 for their superficial contents; this being more than 156, the breadth (7) was taken too great. Next, try 6 for the length and breadth of D; adding 6 to 20 gives 26 for the length of B, C, and D; multiplying 26 by the breadth (6) gives 156 for the superficial contents of B, C, and D.

Hence, the square root of 256 is 16; or, when 256 sq. in. are arranged in the form of a square, each side is 16 inches.

2. Extract the square root of 758.436.

Solution.—Point off 758.436 into periods of two figures each by placing a point over 8 and then over 7 to the left, and 3 and 0 to the right (Art. **237**, Rule). Then find the figures of the root as in Ex. 1. The last remainder is 5351. Therefore, 758.436 is an imperfect square, and its square root is 27.53 +.

OPERATION.

```
          7 58.43 60 ( 27.53 +
          4
    47 ) 358
         329
   545 ) 2943
         2725
  5503 ) 21860
         16509
          5351
```

Rem.—By bringing down one or more periods of decimal ciphers, the operation might be continued to any required number of decimal places in the root.

3. Extract the square root of $\frac{256}{625}$.

Solution.—The square root of the numerator 256 is 16, and the square root of the denominator 625 is 25 (Ex. 1); then, the square root of $\frac{256}{625}$ is $\frac{16}{25}$.

4. Extract the square root of $\frac{3}{8}$.

Solution.—$\frac{3}{8}$ reduced to a decimal is .375. The square root of .375, to five decimal places, is .61237 (Ex. 2); then, the square root of $\frac{3}{8}$ is .61237 +.

Rule.—1. *Point off the given number into periods of two figures each.*

2. *Find the greatest square in the first period on the left; place its root on the right, like a quotient in division; subtract the square from the period, and to the remainder bring down the next period for a dividend.*

3. *Double the root found, and place it on the left of the dividend for a trial divisor. Find how many times the trial divisor is contained in the dividend, exclusive of the right hand figure; place the quotient in the root, and also on the right of the trial divisor.*

4. *Multiply the complete divisor by the last figure of the root; subtract the product from the dividend, and to the remainder bring down the next period for a new dividend.*

5. *Double the whole root found, for a new trial divisor, and continue the operation in the same manner until all the periods are brought down.*

REM. 1.—When the number is an imperfect square, the operation may be continued to any required number of decimal places in the root by bringing down periods of decimal ciphers (Ex. 2).

REM. 2.—To extract the square root of a common fraction: (1) when both terms are perfect squares, extract the square root of the numerator and then of the denominator (Ex. 3); (2) when both terms are not perfect squares, reduce the fraction to a decimal and extract the square root of the decimal (Ex. 4).

Extract the square root of

5. 529.
6. 625.
7. 6561.
8. 56644.
9. 390625.
10. 1679616.
11. 5764801.
12. 43046721.
13. 987656329.
14. 289442169.
15. 234.09.
16. 145.2025.
17. 915.0625.
18. .0196.
19. 1.008016.
20. .00822649.
21. $\frac{25}{729}$.
22. $\frac{847}{1183}$.
23. $30\frac{1}{4}$.
24. 10.
25. 2.
26. $\frac{2}{3}$.
27. $6\frac{2}{5}$.
28. $384\frac{4}{7}$.

239. To extract the square root of a perfect square by factoring.

1. Extract the square root of 441.

SOLUTION. — $441 = 3 \times 3 \times 7 \times 7$; hence, $\sqrt{441} = 3 \times 7 = 21$.

Rule.—*Resolve the number into its prime factors, and find the product of one of each two equal factors.*

Extract the square root of

2. 16.	6. 400.
3. 36.	7. 1764.
4. 100.	8. 5184.
5. 225.	9. 3025.

240. Given two of the sides of a right angled triangle to find the third side.

1. A **triangle** is a plane figure bounded by three straight lines, called its *sides*.

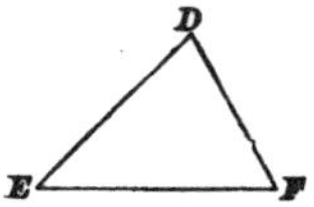

Thus, D E F is a triangle; its sides are D E, E F, and D F.

2. When one of the sides is perpendicular to another, they form a right-angle, and the triangle is called a **right-angled** triangle.

Thus, in the triangle A B C, the side A C being perpendicular to the side B C, they form a right-angle at C; hence, A B C is a right-angled triangle.

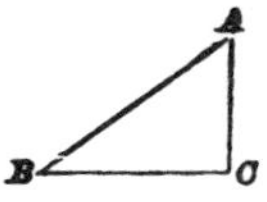

3. The side opposite the right-angle is called **the hypotenuse**; the other two sides, the **base** and the **perpendicular.**

Thus, in A B C, A B is the hypotenuse, B C the base, and A C the perpendicular.

4. **Proposition.**—*The square described on the hypotenuse of a right-angled triangle is equal to the sum of the squares described on the other two sides.*

Draw a right-angled triangle, A B C, with the side B C 4 in., and the side A C 3 in.; then, the side A B will be 5 in. Describe a square on each side of the triangle, and divide each square into smaller squares of 1 in. to the side. Then, the square described on A B will contain 25 square inches, and the two squares described on B C and A C will contain $16 + 9 = 25$ square inches.

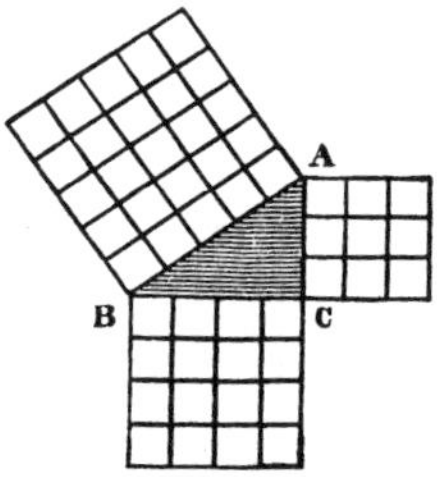

5. From this proposition we deduce the following

Rules.—1st. To find the hypotenuse; *To the square of the base add the square of the perpendicular, and extract the square root of the sum.*

2d. To find the base or the perpendicular; *From the square of the hypotenuse subtract the square of the other given side, and extract the square root of the difference.*

1. The base and perpendicular of a right-angled triangle are 30 and 40: what is the hypotenuse?

2. The hypotenuse of a right-angled triangle is 100, and the base 60: what is the perpendicular?

3. A castle 45 yd. high is surrounded by a ditch 60 yd. wide: what length of rope will reach from the outside of the ditch to the top of the castle?

4. A ladder 60 ft. long reaches a window 37 ft. from the ground on one side of the street, and, without moving it at the foot, will reach one 23 ft. high on the other side: find the width of the street.

5. A tree 140 ft. high is in the center of a circular island 100 ft. in diameter; a line 600 ft. long reaches from the top of the tree to the further shore: what is the breadth of the stream, the land on each side being of the same level?

6. A room is 20 ft. long, 16 ft. wide, and 12 ft. high: what is the distance from one of the lower corners to the opposite upper corner?

241. Given the area of a square to find its side (Art. **67**).

Rule.—*Extract the square root of the area.*

1. The area of a square field is 6241 sq. rd.: what is the length of one side?

2. The surface of a square table contains 8 sq. ft. 4 sq. in.: what is the length of one side?

3. The area of a circle is 4096 sq. yd.: what is the side of a square of equal area?

4. A square field measures 4 rd. on each side: what is the length of the side of a square field which contains 9 times as many square rods?

5. What is the length of one side of a square lot containing 1 acre?

CUBE ROOT.

242. To find the number of figures in the cube root.

1. The cube root of 1 is 1, and the cube root of 1000 is 10 (Art. **235,** 9, Table); between 1 and 1000 are all numbers consisting of one, two, or three figures, and between 1 and 10 are all numbers consisting of one figure; therefore,

When a number consists of one, two, or three figures, its cube root consists of one figure.

2. The cube root of 1000 is 10, and the cube root of 1000000 is 100; between 1000 and 1000000 are all numbers consisting of four, five, or six figures, and between 10 and 100 are all numbers consisting of two figures; therefore,

When a number consists of four, five, or six figures, its cube root consists of two figures.

3. In like manner it may be shown that,

When a number consists of seven, eight, or nine figures, its cube root consists of three figures.

And so on; therefore,

1st. *If a number be pointed off into periods of three figures each, the number of periods will be the same as the number of figures in the cube root.*

2d. *The cube of the units will be found in the first period, the cube of the tens in the second period, the cube of the hundreds in the third period, etc.*

243. To point off a number into periods of three figures each.

1. Point off 876453921.
2. Point off 7.356849227.
3. Point off 37683.5624.

Rule.—*Place a point over the order units, and then over every third order from units to the left and to the right.*

Rem. 1.—The first period on the left of the integral part of the number will often contain but one or two figures.

Rem. 2.—When the first period on the right of the decimal part contains but one or two figures, ciphers must be annexed to complete the period.

4. Point off 138975462; 3.561325482; 684536.256403.

5. Point off 2756.56843; 98451.3276; .856375; .0064.

244. To extract the cube root of a number.

1. Extract the cube root of 13824.

OPERATION.

$$\begin{array}{rr|l} & & 13\dot{8}24(24 \\ & & 8 \\ \hline 2\times2\times300= & 1200 & 5824 \\ 2\times4\times\ \ 30= & 240 & \\ 4\times4\qquad\ \ = & 16 & \\ \hline & 1456 & 5824 \\ \hline \end{array}$$

SOLUTION.—Point off 13824 into periods of three figures each by placing a point over 4 and 3 (Art. **243**, Rule).

The largest cube in 13 (Art. **235**, 9, Table) is 8; its root is 2; place the root 2 on the right, and subtract the cube 8 from 13; the remainder is 5, to which bring down the next period 824.

Square the root 2 and multiply it by 300; the result, 1200, is the trial divisor. Find how many times 1200 is contained in 5824; the result is 4; place 4 in the root on the right of 2.

Multiply 2 by 4 and by 30, and square 4; add the products 240 and 16 to 1200; the sum 1456 is the complete divisor. Multiply 1456 by 4, and subtract the product 5824 from 5824; the remainder is 0. Therefore, 13824 is a perfect cube, and its cube root is 24.

GEOMETRICAL EXPLANATION.

After finding that the cube root of the given number will contain two places of figures (tens and units), and that the figure in the tens' place is 2, form a cube, A, Fig. 1, 20 (2 tens) inches long, 20 in. wide, and 20 in. high; this cube will contain, (Art. **70**,) $20 \times 20 \times 20 = 8000$ cu. in.; take this sum from the whole number of cubes, and 5824 cu. in. are left, which correspond to the number 5824 in the numerical operation.

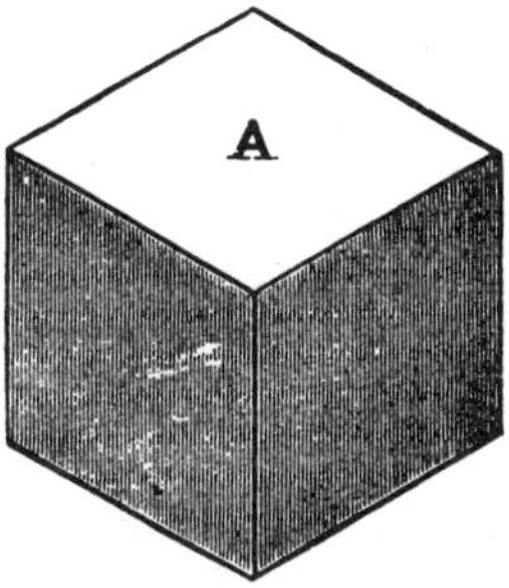

Fig. 1.

It is obvious that to increase the figure A, and at the same time preserve it a cube, the length, breadth, and height must each receive an equal addition. Then, since each side is 20 in. long, square 20, which gives $20 \times 20 = 400$, for the number of square inches in each face of the cube; and since an addition is to be made to three sides, multiply the 400 by 3, which gives 1200 for the number of square inches in the 3 sides. This 1200 is called the **trial divisor;** because, by means of it, the *thickness* of the additions is determined.

By examining Fig. 2 it will be seen that, after increasing each of the three sides equally, there will be required 3 oblong solids, C, C, C, of the same length as each of the sides, and whose thickness and height are each the same as the additional thickness; and also a cube, D, whose length, breadth, and height are each the same as the additional thickness. Hence, the solid contents of the first three rectangular solids, the three oblong solids, and the small cube, must together be equal to the remainder (5824).

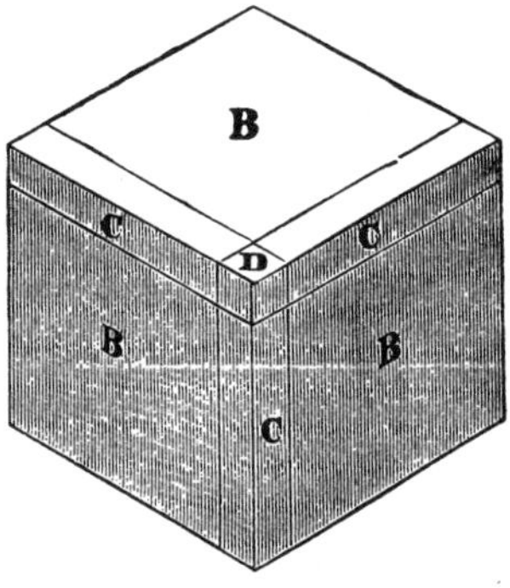

Fig. 2.

Now find the thickness of the additions. It will always be something less than the number of times the *trial divisor* (1200) is contained in the dividend (5824). By trial, we find 1200 is contained 4 times in 5824; proceed to find the contents of the different solids. The solid contents of the first three additions, B, B, B, are found by multiplying the number of sq. in. in the face by the thickness (Art. **70**); there are 400 sq. in. in the face of each, and $400 \times 3 = 1200$ sq. in. in one face of the three; then, multiplying by 4 (the thickness) gives 4800 cu. in. for their contents. The solid contents of the three oblong solids, C, C, C, are found by multiplying the number of sq. in. in the face by the thickness; now there are $20 \times 4 = 80$ sq. in. in one face of each, and $80 \times 3 = 240$ sq. in. in one face of the three; then multiplying by 4 (the thickness), gives 960 cu. in. for their contents. Lastly, find the contents of the small cube, D, by multiplying together its length, breadth, and thickness; this gives $4 \times 4 \times 4 = 64$ cu. in.

If the solid contents of the several additions be added together, as in the margin, their sum, 5824 cu. in. will be the number of small cubes remaining after forming the first cube, A. Hence, when 13824 cu. in. are arranged in the form of a cube, each side is 24 in.; that is, the cube root of 13824 is 24.

ADDITIONS.

B B B =	4800	cu.	in.
C C C =	960	"	"
D =	64	"	"
Sum,	5824		

REM.—It is obvious that the ADDITIONS in the margin may readily be arranged in the same way as in the operation of the example.

2. Extract the cube root of 413.5147.

OPERATION.

		$41\dot{3}.51\dot{4}70\dot{0}$ (7.45 +
		343
7 × 7 × 300 =	14700	70514
7 × 4 × 30 =	840	
4 × 4 =	16	
	15556	62224
74 × 74 × 300 =	1642800	8290700
74 × 5 × 30 =	11100	
5 × 5	25	
	1653925	8269625
		21075

SOLUTION.—Point off 413.5147 into periods of three figures each by placing a point over 3, and then over 4 and 0 to the right (Art. **243**, Rule). Then find the figures of the root as in Ex. 1. The last remainder is 21075. Therefore, 413.5147 is an imperfect cube, and its cube root is 7.45 +.

REM.—By bringing down one or more periods of decimal ciphers the operation might be continued to any required number of decimal places in the root.

3. Extract the cube root of $\frac{2197}{13824}$.

SOLUTION.—The cube root of the numerator 2197 is 13 and the cube root of the denominator 13824 is 24; (Ex. 1); then, the cube root of $\frac{2197}{13824}$ is $\frac{13}{24}$.

4. Extract the cube root of $\frac{4}{5}$.

SOLUTION.—$\frac{4}{5}$ reduced to a decimal is .8. The cube root of .8 to three decimal places is .928; (Ex. 2); then, the cube root of $\frac{4}{5}$ is .928 +.

Rule.—1. *Point off the given number into periods of three figures each.*

2. *Find the greatest cube in the first period on the left; place its root on the right, like a quotient in division; subtract the cube from the period, and to the remainder bring down the next period for a dividend.*

3. *Square the root found, and multiply it by* 300 *for a trial divisor. Find how many times the trial divisor is contained in the dividend, and place the quotient in the root.*

4. *Multiply the preceding figure, or figures, of the root by the last and by* 30, *and square the last figure; add the products to the trial divisor; the sum is the complete divisor.*

5. *Multiply the complete divisor by the last figure of the root; subtract the product from the dividend, and to the remainder bring down the next period for a new dividend.*

6. *Find a new trial divisor as before, and continue the operation in the same manner until all the periods are brought down.*

REM. 1.—When the number is an imperfect cube, the operation may be continued to any required number of decimal places in the root by bringing down periods of decimal ciphers. (Ex. 2).

REM. 2.—To extract the cube root of a common fraction: (1) when both terms are perfect cubes, extract the cube root of the numerator and then of the denominator; (Ex. 3); when both terms are not perfect cubes, reduce the fraction to a decimal and extract the cube root of the decimal. (Ex. 4).

Extract the cube root of

5. 91125.
6. 195112.
7. 912673.
8. 1225043.
9. 13312053.
10. 102503232.
11. 529475129.
12. 958585256.
13. 14760213677.
14. 128100283921.
15. 53.157376.
16. .199176704.
17. $\frac{216}{343}$.
18. $\frac{2744}{6859}$.
19. $\frac{48778}{118638}$.
20. $5\frac{104}{125}$.
21. 2.
22. 9.
23. 200.
24. $9\frac{1}{6}$.

245. Given the solid contents of a cube to find its side (Art. 70).

Rule.—*Extract the cube root of the solid contents.*

1. The contents of a cubical cellar are 1953.125 cu. ft.: find the length of one side.

2. Sixty-four 3-inch cubes are piled in the form of a cube: what is the length of each side?

3. A cubical box contains 512 half-inch cubes: what are the dimensions of the box inside?

4. A cubical excavation contains 450 cu. yd. 17 cu. ft.: what are its dimensions?

5. Find the side of a cube equal to a mass 288 ft. long, 216 ft. broad, and 48 ft. high.

6. The side of a cubical vessel is 1 foot: find the side of another cubical vessel that shall contain 3 times as much.

MENSURATION.

I. MEASUREMENT OF SURFACES.

DEFINITIONS.

246. 1. A **line** has length without breadth or thickness.

2. Lines are either *straight* or *curved*.

3. When two lines meet, they form an *angle*.

REM.—The point at which the lines meet is called the vertex of the angle.

4. Angles are either *acute*, *obtuse*, or *right* angles.

5. When two straight lines are perpendicular to each other, they form a **right** angle.

6. An **acute** angle is less than a right angle.

7. An **obtuse** angle is greater than a right angle.

8. When two straight lines are everywhere equally distant they are *parallel*.

9. A **surface** has length and breadth without thickness.

10. Surfaces are either *plane* or *curved.*

Thus, the surface of a table or floor is plane; that of a ball or globe is curved.

11. A **plane figure** is a portion of a plane surface bounded by one or more lines.

12. A **polygon** is a plane figure bounded by straight lines.

REM.—The straight lines are called the *sides* of the polygon; the *perimeter* of a polygon is the sum of all its sides.

13. A **triangle** is a plane figure bounded by three straight lines.

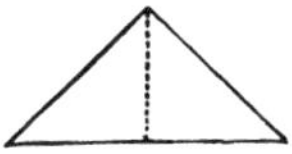

REM.—If one side be taken for the base, the perpendicular let fall upon the base from the opposite angle is called the altitude of the triangle.

14. A **quadrilateral** is a plane figure bounded by four straight lines.

15. There are three kinds of quadrilaterals: the *trapezium*, the *trapezoid*, and the *parallelogram.*

16. A **trapezium** is a quadrilateral with no two sides parallel.

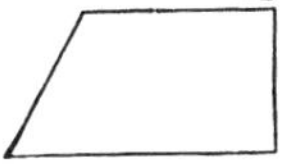

17. A **trapezoid** is a quadrilateral with only two sides parallel.

18. A **parallelogram** is a quadrilateral with its opposite sides equal and parallel.

REM.—If one side be taken as the base, the perpendicular let fall upon the base from the opposite side is called the altitude of the parallelogram.

19. A **rhombus** is a parallelogram with all its sides equal, and its angles not right angles.

20. A **rectangle** is a parallelogram with all its angles right angles.

21. A **square** is a rectangle with all its sides equal.

22. A polygon of five sides is called a **pentagon**; of six, a **hexagon**; of eight, an **octagon,** etc.

23. A **diagonal** is a line joining two angles not adjacent.

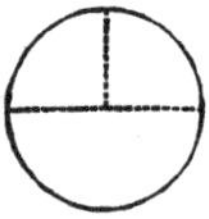

24. A **circle** is a plane figure bounded by a curved line, every point of which is equally distant from a point within called the *center.*

25. The **circumference** of a circle is the curved line which bounds the figure.

26. The **diameter** of a circle is a straight line passing through the center, and terminated, both ways, by the circumference.

27. The **radius** of a circle is a straight line drawn from the center to the circumference; it is half the diameter.

247. To find the area of a parallelogram (Art. **246,** 18, 19, 20, 21).

Rule.—*Multiply the base by the altitude.*

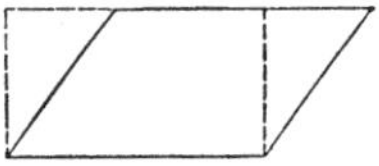

EXPLANATION.—The area of a parallelogram is equal to the area of a rectangle, having an equal base and the same altitude; but the area of the rectangle is equal to its length multiplied by its breadth; (Art. **68**); hence, the area of a parallelogram is equal to its base multiplied by its altitude.

1. How many square feet in a floor 17 ft. long and 15 ft. wide?

2. How many acres of land in a parallelogram, the length of which is 120 rd., and the perpendicular breadth 84 rd.?

3. How many acres in a square field, each side of which is 65 rd.?

4. How many acres in a field in the form of a rhombus, each side measuring 35 rd., and the perpendicular distance between two sides being 16 rd.?

5. Find the difference in area between a floor 30 ft. square, and two others each 15 ft. square.

6. A table is 3 ft. 4 in. long, and 2 ft. 10 in. wide: how many sq. ft. in its surface?

SOLUTION.—3 ft. 4 in. $= 3\frac{1}{3}$ or $\frac{10}{3}$ ft.; 2 ft. 10 in. $= 2\frac{5}{6}$ or $\frac{17}{6}$ ft.; then, the surface of the table is $\frac{10}{3} \times \frac{17}{6} = 9\frac{4}{9}$ sq. ft. Or

SOLUTION.—3 ft. 4 in. $= 40$ in.; 2 ft. 10 in. $= 34$ in.; then the surface of the table is $40 \times 34 = 1360$ sq. in.; $1360 \div 144 = 9$ sq. ft. 64 sq. in., or $9\frac{4}{9}$ sq. ft.

7. How many square feet in a marble slab 5 ft. 6 in. long and 1 ft. 8 in. wide?

8. How many square yards in a ceiling 25 ft. 9 in. long, and 21 ft. 3 in. wide?

9. A room is 10 ft. long: how wide must it be to contain 80 sq. ft.?

10. How many yards of carpet, $1\frac{1}{2}$ yd. wide, will cover a floor 18 ft. long and 15 ft. wide?

11. How many yards of flannel, $\frac{3}{4}$ yd. wide, will it take to line 3 yd. of cloth, $1\frac{1}{2}$ yd. wide?

12. How many yards of carpet, $1\frac{1}{4}$ yd. wide, will it take to cover a floor 21 ft. 3 in. long and 13 ft. 6 in. wide?

13. A rectangular field is 15 rd. long: what must be its width to contain 1 A.?

248. To find the area of a trapezoid (Art. **246, 17**).

Rule.—*Multiply half the sum of the parallel sides by the altitude.*

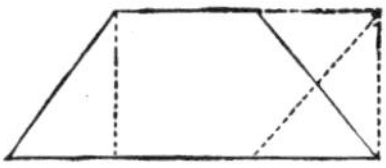

EXPLANATION.—The base of a parallelogram having the same altitude and equal area is one-half the sum of the parallel sides of the trapezoid.

1. The parallel sides of a trapezoid are 2 ft. 2 in. and 2 ft. 11 in.; its altitude is 11 in.: what is its area?

2. A field is in the form of a trapezoid; one of the parallel sides is 25 rd., and the other 19 rd.; the width is 32 rd.: how many acres in the field?

3. How many square yards in a piece of roof 10 ft. 8 in. wide on the lower side, and 6 ft. 2 in. wide on the upper side, the length being 12 ft.?

249. To find the area of a triangle.

1st. When the base and altitude are given.

Rule.—*Multiply the base by the altitude, and take half the product.*

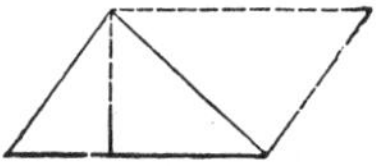

EXPLANATION.—The area of a triangle is one-half the area of a parallelogram having the same base and altitude.

2d. When the three sides are given.

Rule.—1. *From half the sum of the three sides take each side separately.*

2. *Multiply the half-sum and the three remainders together, and extract the square root of the product.*

1. The base of a triangle is 15 ft. and its altitude 12 ft.: what is its area?

2. One side of a triangular lot is 44 rd., and the perpendicular distance from the angle opposite to this side is 18 rd.: how many acres in the lot?

3. What is the area of a triangle, of which the base is 12 ft. 6 in. and the altitude 16 ft. 9 in.?

4. Find the area of a triangle whose sides are 13, 14, and 15 ft.

5. The sides of a triangle are 30, 40, and 50 ft.: what is the area?

250. To find the area of a trapezium (Art. **246,** 16) or other irregular figure.

Rule.—1. *Divide the figure into triangles by diagonals.*

2. *Find the areas of the triangles, and add them together.*

1. Find the area of a field in the form of a trapezium, of which a diagonal is 50 rd. and the perpendiculars to the diagonal from the opposite angles 30 rd. and 20 rd.

251. 1. To find the circumference of a circle when the diameter is given.

Rule.—*Multiply the diameter by* **3.1416.**

2. Conversely: to find the diameter of a circle when the circumference is given.

Rule.—*Divide the circumference by* 3.1416.

1. The diameter of a circle is 48 ft.: what is the circumference?
2. The circumference of a circle is 15 ft.: what is the diameter?
3. The diameter of a wheel is 4 ft.: what is its circumference?
4. If the girth of a tree is 12 ft. 5 in., what is its diameter?
5. What is the circumference of the earth, the diameter being 7912 mi.?

252. 1. To find the area of a circle, when the radius is given.

Rule.—*Multiply the square of the radius by* 3.1416.

2. Conversely: to find the radius of a circle when the area is given.

Rule.—*Divide the area by* 3.1416, *and extract the square root of the quotient.*

1. Find the area of a circle whose radius is 21 ft.

2. The area of a circle is 6 sq. ft. 98.115 sq. in.: what are its diameter and circumference?

3. How long a rope will it take to fasten a horse to a post so that he may graze over 1 A. of grass, and no more?

4. Two circles, 10 and 16 ft. in diameter, have the same center: what is the area of the ring between their circumferences?

5. The area of a circle is 1 square foot, what is its diameter?

II. MEASUREMENT OF SOLIDS.

DEFINITIONS.

253. 1. A **solid,** or **body,** has length, breadth, and thickness.

2. A **prism** is a solid with two parallel bases, which are polygons, and with its faces parallelograms.

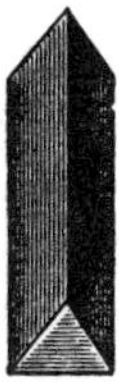

REM.—A prism is triangular, quadrangular, etc., according to the shape of the base.

3. A **right prism** has its faces rectangles.

4. The **altitude** of a prism is the perpendicular let fall from one base upon the other.

5. The **convex surface** of a prism is the sum of the areas of its faces.

6. A **parallelopipedon** is a prism with its bases parallelograms.

7. A **right parallelopipedon** is a solid with six rectangular faces (Art. 70).

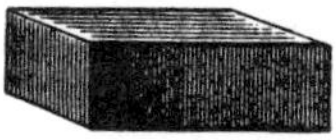

8. A **cube** is a solid with six equal square faces.

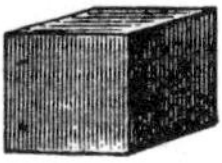

9. A **pyramid** is a solid with one base, which is a polygon, and with its faces triangles.

10. A **right pyramid** has all its faces equal.

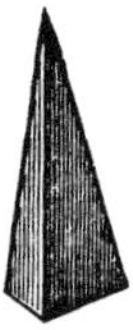

11. The **slant height** of a right pyramid is the distance from the vertex to the middle of each side of the base.

12. The three round bodies are the *cylinder*, the *cone*, and the *sphere.*

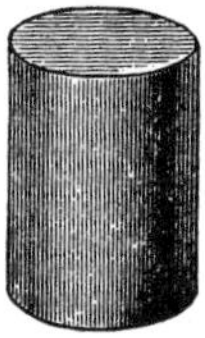

13. A **cylinder** is a solid with two parallel bases, which are circles, and with a curved surface.

14. The **axis** of a cylinder is a line joining the centers of the two bases.

15. The **convex surface** of a cylinder is the area of its curved surface.

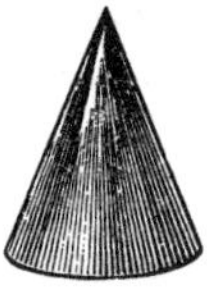

16. A **cone** is a solid with one base, which is a circle, and with a curved surface terminating in an apex.

17. A **sphere** is a solid with a curved surface, every point of which is equally distant from a point within called the *center.*

18. The **volume** of a body is its solid contents.

254. 1. To find the convex surface of a right prism.

Rule.—*Multiply the perimeter of the base by the altitude.*

2. To find the convex surface of a cylinder.

Rule.—*Multiply the circumference of the base by the altitude.*

3. To find the entire surface of a prism, or of a cylinder.

Rule.—*To the convex surface add the areas of the two bases.*

1. Find the surface of a cube, each side being 37 in.

2. Find the surface of a right prism, with a triangular base, each side of which is 4 ft.; the altitude of the prism is 5 ft.

3. Find the surface of a box which is 3 ft. 6 in. long, 2 ft. 9 in. wide, and 1 ft. 10 in. high.

4. Find the surface of a cylinder, its altitude being 5 ft. and the radius of the base, 2 ft.

255. To find the volume of a prism or of a cylinder.

Rule.—*Multiply the area of the base by the altitude.*

REM.—The rule for finding the volume of a right parallelopipedon is given in Art. **70**.

1. Find the volume of a right parallelopipedon, of which the length is 12 ft., the width 3 ft. 3 in., and the height 4 ft. 4 in. 169 cu. ft.

SOLUTION.—3 ft. 3 in. $= 3\frac{1}{4}$ or $\frac{13}{4}$ ft.; 4 ft. 4 in. $= 4\frac{1}{3}$ or $\frac{13}{3}$ ft.; then, the volume of the parallelopipedon is $12 \times \frac{13}{4} \times \frac{13}{3} = 169$ cu. ft.

2. How many cubic yards in a room 24 ft. long, 18 ft. 6 in. wide, and 10 ft. 7 in. high?

3. Each side of the base of a triangular prism is 2 ft.; its altitude is 14 ft.: what is the volume of the prism?

4. Find the volume of a cylinder whose altitude is 12 ft. and the radius of the base 2 ft.

5. How many cubic inches in a peck measure, the diameter of the bottom being $9\frac{1}{4}$ in. and the depth 8 in.?

256. 1. To find the convex surface of a right pyramid.

Rule.—*Multiply the perimeter of the base by the slant height, and take half the product.*

2. To find the convex surface of a cone.

Rule.—*Multiply the circumference of the base by the slant height, and take half the product.*

3. To find the entire surface of a pyramid or of a cone.

Rule.—*To the convex surface add the area of the base.*

1. Find the entire surface of a right pyramid, with a triangular base, each side of which is 5 ft. 4 in.; the slant height of the pyramid is 7 ft. 6 in.
2. What is the convex surface of a cone of which the slant height is 25 ft. and the diameter of the base 8 ft. 6 in.?
3. Find the entire surface of a cone, of which the slant height is 4 ft. 7 in. and the diameter of the base 2 ft. 11 in.

257. To find the volume of a pyramid or of a cone.

Rule.—*Multiply the area of the base by the altitude, and take one-third of the product.*

1. Find the volume of a square pyramid, of which each side of the base is 5 ft. and the altitude 21 ft.

2. Find the volume of a cone, of which the altitude is 15 ft. and the radius of the base 5 ft.

3. A square pyramid is 477 ft. high; each side of its base is 720 ft.: how many cubic yards in the pyramid?

4. The diameter of the base of a conical glass house, is 37 ft. 8 in., and its altitude 79 ft. 9 in.: what is the space inclosed?

258. To find the surface of a sphere.

Rule.—*Multiply the square of the diameter by* 3.1416.

1. What is the surface of a sphere, of which the diameter is 1 ft.?

2. What is the surface of a sphere, of which the diameter is 4 ft. 6 in.?

3. What is the area of the earth's surface, on the supposition that it be a perfect sphere 7912 miles in diameter?

259. To find the volume of a sphere.

Rule.—*Multiply the cube of the diameter by one-sixth of* 3.1416, *or* .5236.

1. Find the volume of a sphere 13 ft. in diameter.

2. Find the volume of a sphere 2 ft. 6 in. in diameter.

3. The volume of a sphere is 1 cu. ft.: what is its diameter?

III. APPLICATIONS OF MENSURATION.

260. 1. Plastering, house-painting, paving, paper-hanging, etc., are measured by the *square foot* or *square yard.*

2. Glazing is measured by the *square foot* or by the *pane.*

3. Stone cutting is measured by the *square foot.*

4. Flooring, roofing, etc., are measured by the *square yard* or by the *square* of 100 sq. ft.

1. A room is 20 ft. 6 in. long, 16 ft. 3 in. broad, 10 ft. 1 in. high: how many yards of plastering in it, deducting a fire-place 6 ft. 3 in. by 4 ft. 2 in.; a door 7 ft. by 4 ft. 2 in., and two windows, each 6 ft. by 3 ft. 3 in.?

2. A room is 20 ft. long, 14 ft. 6 in. broad, and 10 ft. 4 in. high: what will the papering of the walls cost, at 27 ct. per square yard, deducting a fire-place 4 ft. by 4 ft. 4 in., and two windows, each 6 ft. by 3 ft. 2 in.?

3. What will it cost to pave a rectangular court, 21 yd. long and 15 yd. broad, in which a foot-path, 5 ft. wide, runs the whole length: the path paved with flags, at 36 ct. per square yard, and the rest with bricks, at 24 ct. per square yard ?

4. At 10 ct. a square yard, what will it cost to paint both sides of a partition 15 ft. 6 in. long, 12 ft. 6 in. high?

5. A house has three tiers of windows, seven in a tier: the height of the first tier is 6 ft. 11 in.; of the second, 5 ft. 4 in.; of the third, 4 ft. 3 in.; each window is 3 ft. 6 in. wide: what will the glazing cost, at 16 ct. per square foot?

6. A floor is 36 ft. 3 in. long, 16 ft. 6 in. wide: what will it cost to lay it, at $3 a square?

7. At $3.50 per square, what will be the cost of a roof 40 ft. long, the rafters on each side 18 ft. 6 in. long?

BOARD MEASURE.

261. 1. **Board Measure** is used in measuring all lumber which is sawed into boards, planks, etc.

2. A **foot,** board measure, is 1 foot long, 1 foot wide, and 1 inch thick.

3. Hence, to find the number of feet in a board, we have the following

Rule.—1. *Find the surface of the board in square feet.*

2. *Multiply the surface by the thickness in inches.*

1. How many feet in an inch board 16 ft. long and 1 ft. 3 in. wide?

2. How many feet in a two-inch plank 12 ft. 6 in. long and 2 ft. 3 in. wide?

3. How many feet in a piece of scantling 15 ft. long, 4 in. wide, and 3 in. thick?

4. How many feet of inch boards will a stick of timber 12 ft. long and 2 ft. square make?

5. How many feet in an inch board, 12 ft. 6 in. long 1 ft. 3 in. wide, at one end, and 11 in. wide at the other end?

MASONS' AND BRICKLAYERS' WORK.

262. 1. Stone masonry is usually measured by the *perch*, which is $24\frac{3}{4}$ or 24.75 cu. ft. (Art. **70**).

2. Bricklaying is commonly measured by the 1000 bricks.

1. How many perches in a stone wall 97 ft. 5 in. long, 18 ft. 3 in. high, 2 ft. 3 in. thick?

2. What is the cost of a stone wall 53 ft. 6 in. long, 12 ft. 6 in. high, 2 ft. thick, at $2.25 a perch?

3. How many bricks in a wall 48 ft. 4 in. long, 16 ft. 6 in. high, 1 ft. 6 in. thick, allowing 20 bricks to the cubic ft.?

4. How many bricks, each 8 in. long, 4 in. wide, 2.25 in. thick, will be required for a wall 120 ft. long, 8 ft. high, and 1 ft. 6 in. thick?

5. Find the cost of building a wall 240 ft. long, 6 ft. high, 3 ft. thick, at $3.25 per 1000, each brick being 9 in. long, 4 in. wide, and 2 in. thick.

MEASUREMENT BY BUSHELS OR GALLONS.

263. 1. To find the number of bushels (Art. **61**).

Rule.—*Find the volume in cubic inches, and divide by* 2150.4.

2. To find the number of gallons (Art. **64**).

Rule.—*Find the volume in cubic inches, and divide by* 231.

1. How many bushels in a bin 15 ft. long, 5 ft. wide, and 4 ft. deep?

2. How many gallons in a trough 10 ft. long, 5 ft. wide, and 4 ft. deep?

3. How many bushels in a cylindrical tub 6 ft. in diameter and 8 ft. deep?

4. How many barrels, of $31\frac{1}{2}$ gal. each, in a cistern, in the form of a cylinder, of which the diameter is 4 ft. and the depth 6 ft.?

PROGRESSIONS

I. ARITHMETICAL PROGRESSION.

264. 1. An **Arithmetical Progression** is a series of numbers which *increase* or *decrease* by a *common difference.*

2. If the series increase, it is called an *increasing* series; if it decrease, a *decreasing* series.

Thus,	1,	3,	5,	7,	9,	11,	etc., is an *increasing* series.
	20,	17,	14,	11,	8,	5,	etc., is a *decreasing* series.

3. The numbers forming the series are called *terms;* the first and last terms are the *extremes;* the other terms, the *means.*

4. In every arithmetical series, five things are considered: (1) the *first* term, (2) the *last* term, (3) the *common difference,* (4) the *number* of terms, and (5) the *sum of the terms.*

CASE I.

265. To find the last term, when the first term, the common difference, and the number of terms are given.

1. I bought 10 yd. of muslin, at 3 ct. for the first yard, 7 ct. for the second, 11 ct. for the third, and so on: what did the last yard cost?

SOLUTION.—To find the cost of the *second* yard, add 4 ct. *once* to the cost of the first; to find the cost of the *third*, add 4 ct. *twice* to the cost of the first; to find the cost of the *fourth*, add 4 ct. *three times* to the cost of the first, and so on; hence, to find the cost of the *tenth* yard, *add* 4 ct. *nine times* to the cost of the first; but 9 times 4 ct. are 36 ct., and 3 ct. +36 ct. = 39 ct., the cost of the last yard, or *last term* of the progression.

OPERATION.

$4 \times 9 = 36$
$3 + 36 = 39$

2. The first term of a decreasing series is 39, the common difference 4, and the number of terms 10: find the last term.

SOLUTION.—In this case, 4 must be *subtracte* 9 times from 39, which will give 3 for the last term.

OPERATION.

$4 \times 9 = 36$
$39 - 36 = 3$

Rule.—1. *Multiply the common difference by the number of terms less one.*

2. *If an increasing series, add the product to the first term; if a decreasing series, subtract the product from the first term.*

3. Find the last term of an increasing series in which the first term is 2, the common difference 3, and the number of terms 50.

4. What is the 54th term of a decreasing series in which the first term is 140, and common difference 2?

5. What is the 99th term of a decreasing series in which the first term is 329, and common difference $\frac{7}{8}$?

CASE II.

266. To find the common difference, when the extremes and the number of terms are given.

1. The first term of a series is 2, the last 20, and the number of terms 7: what is the common difference?

SOLUTION.—The difference of the extremes 20 and 2 is 18; 18 divided by 6, the number of terms less 1, is 3, the common difference.

OPERATION.

$20 - 2 = 18$

$18 \div 6 = 3$

Rule.—*Divide the difference of the extremes by the number of terms less one.*

2. The extremes are 3 and 300; the number of terms 10: find the common difference.

3. A travels from Boston to Bangor in 10 da.; he goes 5 mi. the first day, and increases the distance traveled each day by the same number of miles; on the last day he goes 50 mi.: find the daily increase.

CASE III.

267. To find the sum of all the terms of the series when the extremes and the number of terms are given.

1. Find the sum of 6 terms of the series whose first term is 1, and last term 11.

SOLUTION.—The series is . .	1,	3,	5,	7,	9,	11.
In inverted order it is . .	11,	9,	7,	5,	3,	1.
The sum of the two is . .	12,	12,	12,	12,	12,	12.

Since the two series are the same, their sum is *twice* the first series; but their sum is obviously as many times 12, the sum of the extremes, as there are terms; hence, the sum of the series is 6 times 12 = 72 divided by 2 = 36.

Rule.—*Multiply the sum of the extremes by the number of terms; and take half the product.*

2. The extremes are 2 and 50; the number of terms, 24: find the sum of the series.

3. How many strokes does the hammer of a clock strike in 12 hours?

4. Place 100 apples in a right line, 3 yd. from each other, the first, 3 yd. from a basket: what distance will a boy travel who gathers them singly and places them in the basket?

5. A body falling by its own weight, if not resisted by the air, would descend in the first second a space of 16 ft. 1 in.; the next second, 3 times that space; the third, 5 times that space; the fourth, 7 times, etc.: at that rate, through what space would it fall in 1 minute?

II. GEOMETRICAL PROGRESSION.

268. 1. A **Geometrical Progression,** is a series of numbers *increasing* by a common *multiplier*, or *decreasing* by a common *divisor.*

Thus, 1, 3, 9, 27, 81, is an increasing geometric series.
48, 24, 12, 6, 3, is a decreasing geometric series.

2. The common multiplier or common divisor, is called the *ratio.*

Thus, in the first of the above series, the ratio is 3; in the second, 2.

3. The numbers forming the series are the *terms;* the first and last terms are *extremes;* the others, *means.*

4. In every geometric series, five things are considered: (1) the *first* term; (2) the *last* term; (3) the *number* of terms; (4) the *ratio;* (5) the *sum* of the terms.

CASE I.

269. To find the last term, when the first term, the ratio, and the number of terms are given.